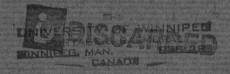

Shining Clarity: *God and Man in the works of*

Robinson Jeffers.

Whatever it is catches my heart in its hands, whatever it

is makes me shudder with love

And painful joy and the tears prickle...the Greeks were

not its inventors. The Greeks were not the inventors

Of shining clarity and jewel-sharp form and the beauty of

God. He was free with men before the Greeks came:

He is here naked on the shining water. Every eye that has

a man's nerves behind it has known him.

—''Hellenistics''
SUCH COUNSELS YOU GAVE TO ME AND OTHER POEMS, 1937
Robinson Jeffers

Shining Clarity

God and Man in the Works of Robinson Jeffers

by

Marlan Beilke

Illustrated by Kenneth Jack and Lumir Šindelář

Quintessence Publications

Quintessence Publications

356 Bunker Hill Mine Road
Amador City, California 95601
U.S.A.

92 Butler Avenue
Moonah, Tasmania 7009
Australia

Designed by Marlan and Irene Beilke

Library of Congress Catalogue Number: 77-70786
ISBN: 0-918466-00-8 (Trade Edition)
ISBN: 0-918466-01-6 (Separate Edition)
Wholly designed and set up in U.S.A.
Printed and bound in Hong Kong

For my wife, Irene

and our

Laura ,
Diane
and
Theodore

Look for foundations of sea-worn granite, my fingers had the art

To make stone love stone, you will find some remnant.

But if you should look in your idleness after ten thousand years:

It is the granite knoll on the granite

And lava tongue in the midst of the bay, by the mouth of the Carmel

River-valley, these four will remain

In the change of names. You will know it by the wild sea-fragrance of wind

Though the ocean may have climbed or retired a little;

You will know it by the valley inland that our sun and our moon were born from

Before the poles changed; and Orion in December

Evenings was strung in the throat of the valley like a lamp-lighted bridge.

—"Tor House"

Tor House 1969 Acrylic 11½ x 17½"

Artist—Kenneth Jack, Australia

If you should look for this place after a handful of lifetimes:

Perhaps of my planted forest a few

May stand yet, dark-leaved Australians or the coast cypress, haggard

With storm-drift; but fire and the axe are devils.

— **"Tor House"**

Robinson Jeffers, 1937

TABLE OF CONTENTS

❧

SHINING CLARITY: GOD AND MAN IN THE WORKS OF ROBINSON JEFFERS

CHAPTER ONE: THE HOLY SPIRIT BEAUTY

LIST OF ILLUSTRATIONS

LIST OF ILLUSTRATIONS — continued

PERMISSIONS

The author expresses his sincere appreciation to:

Horace Lyon ✦• for permission to present his photographs of Robinson Jeffers and of Tor House and for permission to reproduce his photograph and inscription from the Quercus Press 1939 edition of THE HOUSE-DOG'S GRAVE—HAIG'S GRAVE.

Karl Bissinger ✦• for permission to present his photograph of Robinson Jeffers.

Mrs. Theodore Max Lilienthal ✦• for permission to reproduce a facsimile of the 1939 Quercus Press edition of THE HOUSE-DOG'S GRAVE—HAIG'S GRAVE.

Hale Chatfield ✦• for permission to quote from his article "Robinson Jeffers: His Philosophy and His Major Themes" in "The Laurel Review", Fall 1966.

The Humanities Research Center, The University of Texas at Austin, ✦• for permission to print for the first time Robinson Jeffers' poem, "The Last Conservative".

ACKNOWLEDGEMENT

This book (and its bibliography) would be incomplete without recording my sincere debt of gratitude to the many people who gave generously of their time and personal knowledge of Robinson Jeffers. It is pleasant and humbling for me to recount their names as small token of my deep appreciation for the myriad ways they have enriched my understanding of Jeffers. To record their kindnesses would require another book.

Sydney S. Alberts, Irene Alexander, Mrs. Hans Barkan, Eric Barker, Donald Beilke, Melba Berry Bennett, Kamil and Emily Bednář, Karl Bissinger, Dr. Robert J. Brophy, Dr. Frederick Ives Carpenter, Herbert Cerwin, Hale Chatfield, Frederick Mortimer Clapp, Dr. Fraser Drew, Dr. Herbert M. Evans, Gerald Garbarini, Rudolph Gilbert, Edith and Maeve Greenan, Tyrus G. Harmsen, Dr. James D. Hart, Eva Hesse, Dr. Hamilton Jeffers, Donnan Jeffers, Gaye Kelly, Mina C. and H. Arthur Klein, Dr. Benjamin H. Lehman, Mr. and Mrs. Theodore Max Lilienthal, Horace and Edna Lyon, James McAuley, Robert F. Metzdorf, Tokuhiro Miura, Karel Oberthor, Mel Piestrup, Lawrence Clark Powell, Principessa Mary de Rachewiltz, Harry Ward Ritchie, Lumir Šindelář, Dr. James Radcliffe Squires, Dorothy Whitnah.

WITH SPECIAL THANKS TO

Bill Hotchkiss and The Blue Oak Press for the original idea to publish this book and for kind and persistent inspiration throughout.

Herbert C. Caplan of Argus Books, Sacramento, whose ideas, suggestions, and solid contributions transformed the book.

And this place, where I have planted trees and built a stone house,

Will be under sea. The poor trees will perish,

And little fish will flicker in and out the windows. I built it well,

Thick walls and Portland cement and gray granite,

The tower at least will hold against the sea's buffeting; it will become

Geological, fossil and permanent.

    —"Star-Swirls"

    — Robinson Jeffers

NOTE

God and Man in the Works of Robinson Jeffers grew out of my Master of Arts (British) thesis for The University of Tasmania, Australia, of 1972. In revision, I have attempted to offer a readable, internally documented text, one which an eager reader, perhaps new to Jeffers' verse, might find of merit should he also strike a commensurate interest in Jeffers' ideological values and seek further elucidation of them. Robinson Jeffers' basic convictions have been grossly misinterpreted. Too frequently critics have misunderstood the man, even refusing to comprehend the obvious from the poems.

My intent is modestly to provide (with a modicum of comment) an honest clarification of Jeffers' fundamental tenets of the human and the divine through chronological quotation from the short poems which most directly convey the poet's ideas. Footnotes have been eliminated to minimize distractions; instead, a second glance at the subject matter or reference to the bibliography or index should yield pertinent sources.

I have endeavored assiduously to present Jeffers' ideas as unassisted, unfiltered, and uninterpreted as possible. But opinion, like its parent the will, has subtle ways of asserting itself. Against this inevitability, I beg indulgence, and gratefully commend any gentle soul to the enduring beauty of the poems themselves, which, in the best analysis, interpret themselves.

Marlan Beilke
Sutter Creek, California
1976

PREFACE

Marlan Beilke has addressed himself to a subject centrally significant to the understanding of Robinson Jeffers' poetry. He has been a careful and thoughtful student of that poetry for a decade or more during which I have watched with pleasure his close critical concentration and his developing analysis. Out of studies at the University of California, Berkeley and later at the University of Tasmania has come this book which is a real contribution to the understanding of Jeffers.

Marlan Beilke knows what he thinks, and he has proper confidence in his interpretations. What he has found in a large and complex body of poetry he sets forth simply and clearly, period by period, and poem by poem. A long established intimacy with the canon of Jeffers' work allows Mr. Beilke to determine just which poem to cite and which to quote so as best to illustrate his full and thoughtful study. After long concern with the writings of Robinson Jeffers and close acquaintanceship with the commentators upon it, Marlan Beilke, though still a young man, now advances his own thesis and makes his own contribution to the understanding of that significant poetry.

Dr. James D. Hart, Director
The Bancroft Library
University of California, Berkeley

FOR ROBINSON JEFFERS
by Bill Hotchkiss

I:

You were the master spirit; you saw through to the terrible agony
Of God's self-immolation, the world-hawk that devours its own entrails
To give birth to itself in serene beauty.

You were the father: do your ashes sleep in the peace they desired?
The great waves still chew at the coast rocks, but human tenure is brief.
In the awful power of your lines, you pointed the way.

II:

I stare east toward the high, white peaks of the Sierra;
The tall wild plum is in full bloom, white, and white moths
Dance among the yellow mustard flowers. The sky
Is immense and blue, it leaps eastward from these greening foothills
And disappears beyond the far white rim. But here the wind
Flows on a soft steadiness from the south, bringing warmth.

III:

The dance of generation is patient and certain, it continues
All but imperceptible, fecund and lecherous. It knows the earth
Must be aroused, knows it is fearful. This wind will stroke the green thighs
And touch its tongue to the swelling buds, will not be satisfied
Until they all have flowered.

IV:

Yet now on the easy wind, two redtailed hawks have found a buoyant current:
They lie upon it, together, then apart, and once more together.
The sunlight burns their feathers into shining.

V:

I close my eyes to see a rain squall over the ocean, the vast glare of the sun
Sheening the blue-gray immensity of ocean westward from Pico Blanco, I hear the cries
Of the birds of the coast, shadows and brightness. I smell the good salt air.

VI:

This mild spring day, quite drunk with blossoming, obscures the long vision:
And yet there are storms to come, huge storms of human passion
And nerve-burning fire. The death-dance continues, the earth shifts slightly,
And the molten rock spews forth in red rivers; our promised land is before us
But the earth wrenches open, the granite splits.

VII:

You have peace. The daemon behind the screen of sea and rock
Has called you down—so now that angry spirit rich with patience
Threads earth where the big creek tumbles through orange-gray cliffs
To slip across the sand and join the sea: and now we seem to hear the hard old voice
In loving curses through the ever-restless waves.

VIII:

Far ages to come will pay you reverence: you saw to the mystery
And still loved it, you fleshed the bones of the swan.

THE LAST LIGHT

    If one drives the Coast Highway, north, from Morro Rock to the Bay of Monterey, a highway that is yet somewhat uncivilized and even treacherous if a bit of weather should blow in off the Pacific, then one may witness the panoramic unfolding of a land and seascape which remains one of the greatest natural beauties of Western America. It would be foolish for me to attempt, here, a description of this terrain—of the redwood canyons, of the cliffs breaking off to the Pacific surf, of the cascading streams, of the upward thrust of the Coast Range. In any case, it's scarcely enough to drive the highway; it would be far better to spend a few hours walking, away from the road, whether down to the jagged rocks of the hewn coast or up through a lush varanca to the domed ridges above. For as soon as one leaves the thin strip of highway, one immediately begins to experience something of the wildness of the place, and human perspectives dwindle even as natural perspectives increase. The fierce magic of the earth. The wildness. Jeffers country—for one always remembers that. Jeffers country.

But it is also true that as one approaches Carmel, even as the familiar Jeffers place names begin to appear on the road signs, so too the marks of modern technological sprawl begin to appear with ever greater frequency. North of Soberanes, one realizes that one has rejoined the twentieth century. Mal Paso Creek, where Jeffers vowed to shear the rhyme tassels from his verse, where Tamar enacted the ritual seduction of her brother, and where Arthur Barclay came to die, is no more than a small concrete bridge, a road sign, and a splay of expensive homes. And in Carmel itself, Tor House is lost among larger and more recent houses. Most of the trees that Jeffers planted have been cut down. Still, the house and the tower, built of stones cut from the tide-exposed boulders, remain. And inside the stone walls, in the courtyard, in the house, in the tower—almost tangible—the presence of the poet.

The Western Archetype. The violence and the death-wish at its heart. The long migration across the continent, ending here, against the Pacific Ocean. A recoil against this final barrier. Freedom through violation. The endemic violence of the region. And one man's discovery of "divinely superflous beauty" and "the transhuman magnificence."

He was our greatest poet.

And it makes little difference that so few within the Critical Establishment were able either to comprehend what he was saying or to perceive the artistic complexity or the stark beauty of his lines. For himself, it was sufficient to worship the beautiful, Inhuman God.

> *...there is not a maiden*
> *Burns and thirsts for love*
> *More than my blood for you, by the shore of seals while the wings*
> *Weave like a web in the air*
> *Divinely superfluous beauty.*

Over and again the poet assures us that we may find a portion of sanity, release from the trap of human illusion, by turning outward to the worship of beauty, the beauty of things—even beyond that to the Inhuman God which generates the beauty, which generates the magic of life itself. If humanity is the start of the race, then it must break out of the cage of its own human-centered awareness:

> *Integrity is wholeness, the greatest beauty is*
> *Organic wholeness, the wholeness of life and things, the divine beauty*
> > *of the universe. Love that, not man*
> *Apart from that, or else you will share man's pitiful confusions, or drown*
> > *in despair when his days darken.*

In *Archetype West,* William Everson ponders the relationship of Whitman and Jeffers:

> I say that by virtue of the law of apotheosis they define between them the positive and negative polarities of the American poetic achievement, as Shakespeare and Milton define the positive and negative polarities of English poetic achievement. ... Whitman is the sunrise in the East, but Jeffers is the sunset in the West. It is bloody and violent, but it is the last light given us. We deny it at our peril.

If the Critical Establishment did its best to bury the work of one of the three or four genuinely great American poets, there is now a new wind blowing on Parnassus. A number of Jeffers' works have been or are about to be republished. Hitherto unpublished work is now available. New volumes of criticism now appear with increasing regularity. The force of the New Critical aversion to Jeffers' ideational content has not only been weakened but now lies essentially in ruins. We shall come to an understanding directly.

I know, of course, that what I have written thus far may summarily be passed off as "mere appreciation." If it is true, as I have asserted, that Jeffers is a supremely great poet, then the best and most thorough critical treatment will not dislodge that elemental fact. Indeed, it is precisely such close critical and philosophical analysis which alone may allow us to draw our judgments toward a tentative finality. And Jeffers himself, I dare say, would not have had it otherwise. In an essay entitled "Poetry, Gongorism and a Thousand Years," the poet has proposed the following:

> ...great poetry is pointed at the future. Its author, whether consciously or not, intends to be understood a thousand years from now; therefore he chooses the more permanent aspects of things, and subjects that will remain valid. And therefore he would distrust the fashionable poetic dialect of his time: but the more so if it is studiously quaint and difficult; for if a poem has to be explained and diagramed even for the contemporary readers, what will the future make of it?.

A sustained study of Jeffers' short poems has long been needed; indeed, if we are ultimately to come to a reasoned comprehension of the underlying structure of ideas in this poet's work, it is to the short poems that we most properly turn. These short poems are "purer" than the narratives simply because they have no extended narrative burden to bear—and have, therefore, not the same need for distortion of philosophical, theological, social and psychological concepts. The speaker of most of the lyrics is a modified Jeffers figure, one who deals with conceptual constructs straight on. And it follows that the proper apprehension of the longer works requires, as a pre-existent condition, an accurate awareness of the cosmic whole which generates those longer works.

Lawrence Clark Powell, the first of the important Jeffers scholars, made the following observation:

> ...Jeffers' lyrics are apt to be ignored or passed over in favor of the more exciting tales: yet it is among the shorter poems that are to be found some of the most perfect examples of this poet's art. The best of Jeffers' lyrics are proportioned: passion is in them, but it is restrained and moulded by the intellect. Their phrasing is more tranquil than that of the narratives, their diction more sustained.

It is to the end of a critical comprehension of the underlying philosophical structure of these short poems that Marlan Beilke's *God and Man in the Works of Robinson Jeffers* directs itself. Beilke has chosen for analysis a sequence of Jeffers' lyrics which spans the poet's entire performance, from the very earliest work on through to those things upon which Jeffers was working until shortly before his death. The critic employs as defining devices those two most basic considerations: "What is the poet's concept of God?" and "What is the poet's concept of man?" In this study, we are able to witness the emergence of the poet's ideas, their elaboration through a subtlety of change, and at the same time their basic, if dynamic, consistency throughout a long career.

Beilke's is a keen, perceptive, and tenacious intellect. He takes us to the very generation of Jeffers' art and thought. He sticks clearly and constantly to the two-edged thesis with which he works. No serious student of the work of Robinson Jeffers will fail to profit immensely from the reading of this volume. As will become evident to the reader, and Beilke hammers the message home, all that Jeffers has required of us are a sufficient span of attention and a willingness to deal with ideas.

Jeffers, as well, hammers the message home—as in these lines from "Dē Rērum Naturā":

The Beauty of Things
Means virtue and value in them.
It is in the beholder's eye,
Not in the world? Certainly,
It is the human mind's
Translation of the transhuman
Intrinsic glory. It means
That the world is sound,
Whatever the sick microbe does.
But he too is part of it.

Bill Hotchkiss
October 6, 1976
Woodpecker Ravine
Nevada County, California

"LET THEM ALONE"

If God has been good enough to give you a poet
Then listen to him. But for God's sake let him alone until he is dead; no prizes, no ceremony,
They kill the man. A poet is one who listens
To nature and his own heart; and if the noise of the world grows up around him, and if he is
*   tough enough,*
He can shake off his enemies but not his friends.

    —Robinson Jeffers, "Let Them Alone"
     The Beginning and the End and Other Poems

It is the doom and the glory of Robinson Jeffers that he is destined to survive absolutely alone. You might say he *willed* it that way.

    —Brother Antoninus, "Not Without Wisdom"
     Fragments of an Older Fury

Shortly before his death Jeffers was asked if he wished to write anything further. His response was, "No, I have said it all."

    —Marlan Beilke, "The Final Years"
     Shining Clarity: God and Man in the Works of Robinson Jeffers

What are we doing here, presuming to raise the downed old hawksinger from his stony cold tower? He'd hardly notice, and if he should, he'd not come easy. Not only had he said it all — down to casting and voicing his own ghost — but, as Marlan Beilke so amply demonstrates in the present volume, he held and drummed the whole-God-center of it all over and over with such a rigorous singularity that it would seem the best his friends might do would be to echo the master, the worst his enemies do to ignore him altogether. Jeffers, by all legend, would undoubtedly have preferred the latter, detesting as he would the mass reduction of Echo no less than the abyssal duplication of Narcissus. His singularity, function of the "uncentered monism" which Beilke defines at length herein, would have no part of any following; the poetry stood, and stands, for itself. Thus when Bennett Cerf urged Jeffers to get himself into the critical fray upon publication of the Random House *Selected Poetry* in 1938 (at a point when Jeffers' poetical profile was still formidible, and controversial, and mysterious — all of which it surely remains, but to a rather diminished degree), his aloofness responded characteristically:

> A good friend of mine, who is also my publisher, wants me to turn this foreword to some account; he says that a number of people have written pro and con about my verses, and it is high time for the author himself to say something. Very likely. But I do not wish to commend or defend them, though sufficiently attacked; and it seems to me that their meaning is not obscure.

In truth, though, Jeffers *had* both commended and defended his verses, aesthetics, and philosophy — presumably to his private satisfaction: he chatted, in correspondences, as eagerly as any other poet about his new works, his sources, his goals; there exists in the Tor House collection a remarkable elucidative introduction he wrote for the *Tamar* book, but never published; and perhaps most notably, there is the letter he wrote to James Rorty defending *The Women at Point Sur* (1927) following publication of Mark Van Doren's friendly misinterpretation. But more distressing to savorers of the legendry of Jeffers' exalted reclusion — be they friend or foe — is the fact that scarcely three years after the above demurral, Jeffers actually had a Coming Out, an amazingly successful one for any American poet at any time, but especially for one whose career lay — again according to all legend — in critical disarray, and a genuine triumphal tour for a poet/prophet who stood, at the stormfront of America's Second World War involvement, distinctly against that involvement. The tour, Jeffers' one and only such public venture, was occasioned by his acceptance of an invitation to inaugurate a Poetry Series at the Library of Congress; his subject, "The Poet in Democracy." I'd like to quote one substantial paragraph from his address (published in part fifteen years later by The Book Club of California as *Themes in My Poems* — the complete text appeared in Melba Berry Bennett's *The Stone Mason of Tor House*) because it marks with prosaic precision a major theme which Marlan Beilke pursues impeccably through apposite short poems — a theme which gradually obsessed and very nearly consumed the lyric thrust of Jeffers' genius, causing him to violate *out of creative necessity* his own brave aesthetic: "Poetry must concern itself with (relatively) permanent things. These have poetic value; the ephemeral has only news value." The theme:

I say this as a duty. Europe will be physically and morally exhausted after this second world war; and perhaps it will be our destiny to carry this heritage of European culture, and what we have added to it, across a time of twilight to a new age; as Byzantium carried the culture of Greece and Rome across dark centuries, from that age to this one.

Therefore we must guard what we have, for it is precious; and if we feel ourselves forced to intervene in foreign conflicts, we must consult the interests of our people first; and our generosity second, — we have always been generous; and ideology last. But sentimentality, never. We can still afford the material risks of sentimentality, but not the disillusion that follows it.

So spoke the prophet and his say was true, and true to his duty as "the poet in democracy." He had already spoken far more bleakly in his poems, and as Beilke shows herein, he came finally to cease presuming to voice the mass of his people.

But, in the circular nature of the poet::prophet equation, Jeffers had also announced the perplex of contemporary American poetry, for no serious poet writing in and of this country since the fundamental national character changes of World War Two has had the honest leisure, or been ''off-duty'' enough to write solely of ''relatively permanent things.'' War, to be sure, is a rather permanent thing, but the modal vagaries of its political fixes are as ephemeral as a politician's word, the advertisements of power, and the smog of wasted energy. Jeffers' later lyric poems with all their painful suffering must be taken, aside from their peculiar merits and faults, paradigmatically for the ethical/aesthetical split in modern American poetics — this push-come-to-shove tension between political engagement and the proper, permanent concerns of the poets. Jeffers' isolated pacifism, his direct and determined ideological attacks on the Roosevelt war administration, and the subsequent ugly flab of postwar affluence, forespeak both in kind and quality the terribly wasted poetic energies drawn from the deepest creative wellsprings of this nation to douse the Viet Nam war — that awful symbol of what Gary Snyder calls our ''war against the earth.'' The visionary calling of our most absolutely conservative poet has devolved in actuality upon those of us burned — literally — out of the liberal tradition in American art.

So spoke the prophet. Americans have afforded many times over the ''material risks of sentimentality'' — if that means the unexamined and therefore erratic and manipulatable materialistic uses of emotion — and we have been disillusioned. But in the twilight banks of our drugged consciousness, we've lost none of our *delusions* of power, well-being, and final rectitude. We still daydream our poets in ivory towers instead of stone — while with the moon in our pocket, we might at least understand stone. We have not even understood the sentimentality of our flight to space.

> hard
> breaking out
> of stone hard
> breathing ice
> hard

> —Gary Elder, ''Now In My Land, Walt Whitman''
> *Making Touch*

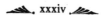

None of this is what I should like to be writing of Robinson Jeffers — of the austere wild landlored beauty of Jeffers Country with its maddening human complications of abysmal sexual brutality, and that perhaps ultimately American life-hate plunging over the Pacific deep-end of our continental tide in those strange jagged lines cut with swooping images and pounding, soughing rhythms — prosody of the Sur Coast itself; nor has it, I fear, very much to do with the vaster concerns of Marlan Beilke's honed work here.

But this question of Jeffers' unbending convervativism will not go away, and while it is not to be "resolved", it must be understood well before we can have the sustenance of his vision, and know his rightful stature as our second greatest poet. Second, that is, in time, in history; for if Walt Whitman is the great liberal-visioned beast of our dawn, Robinson Jeffers is the supernal conservative-sighted hawk of our sunset. And conservativism, to the contemporary American mind, is not the stuff of poetry. Our liberal arts idea would have its poets marching firmly to the left — all arrogantly out-of-step, to be sure, but in staunch camaraderie with the liberal academy and with effusions of humanism. Jeffers, standing wholly alone, his conservative ideology coupled with a bridled dionysian sensibility to a profoundly disturbing unhumanitarian theology, threatens all that. Who of the present generation could deny that his liberal education shielded him effectively from the dangerous substance of Jeffers' poetry?

As pertinent example, I recently asked that question of a group of friends among the younger gentry of the Monterey Peninsula, all highly educated, intellectually and spiritually active, and essentially liberal. Our consensus was a rather mellow impression of Jeffers as a sort of poetic noble, the reclusive nature poet of Tor House (and an admirable craftsman/prophet in that sense). Few had even read the poems, except as picturebook captions.

That won't do. And it's but an instance, a drastic one, of why such a book as Beilke's *Shining Clarity: God and Man in the Works of Robinson Jeffers* is desperately needed in this perishing republic. As the intellectual heartland of our upper middle-class turns more orientally inward in its genuine, and genuinely desperate, search for value — yea for salvation through transcendental meditation, Langian therapy, est, Rolfing, Japanese martial arts, "new tribalism," — even the most intelligently high-minded "New-Age-or-Doomsday"

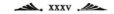

euphoria of Creative Initiative (Bless Man), we *must* have for fresh air, to keep from smothering in our own fetid love, the briskening unselfish power of Jeffers' frosty vision of man-*in*-God. We must for our own momentary health be given the terrible pause of the eternal beauty-of-things of Jeffers' God of starstoneseahawk music. Jeffers would smile at the idea of man as DNA's experiment.

William Everson (Brother Antoninus) has already written eloquently and elitely, in *Fragments of an Older Fury,* of the literary wars about Jeffers and of his lonely unwanted discipleship to the Master. But Everson's essays are so convoluted with his own Catholicism and the sophistries of his own theology, indeed his own eloquence, that anyone coming fresh to Jeffers through them might similarly come to Jesus through the epistles of St. Paul.

Beilke, on the other hand, has given us something more like a Biblical exegesis. He has performed the remarkably rational feat of simply stepping behind all the critical furies and contentions around Jeffers, exactly as if they *were* ephemeral, and looking directly at the poems; and his attention is laserlike. And I think I rather prefer this direct approach over any New Critical close-reading (that Trojan Horse strategem for misreading, by re-vision), no matter with what friendly brilliance that may be accomplished — as in Everson's appropriative explication of "Post Mortem." Rather say, at present I prefer this route, direct as possible, back into Jeffers Country because I fear how nearly we may have come to losing it — losing not only the poetry but the vital landscape of our last great transcendent vision.

Eagle and hawk with their great claws and hooked heads
Tear life to pieces; vulture and raven wait for death to soften it.
The poet cannot feed on this time of the world
Until he has torn it to pieces, and himself also.

—Robinson Jeffers, "Tear Life to Pieces"
The Beginning and the End and Other Poems

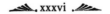

What are we doing here? Let Echo play: A good friend of mine who is also the author of this book has invited me to turn these introductory lines to some account — in fact, with the blithe valor of one certain of his own work, he has given me blank white paper to fill at will. Blank white paper is — as Robinson Jeffers knew so well, drawing his lines on the clean sides of old letters, advertisements, bills — the enemy flag to a writer. But, after scoring and losing a goodly number of flags on this course, I think I must finally decline the invitation. My reasons may or may not be of interest but time will tell them. They have to do with the work of my own poetic vision and the fact that, as an apostate Presbyterian myself — like Jeffers, I would have to apply yet another theological layer to the almost pristine, first-sight, level of Beilke's work here. And it seems to me that, if the poet's work is to see and his best critic's work is to see again, the task of Marlan Beilke has already been more than well enough accomplished.

The thing to do now, and with some urgency, is to set to use the toolings with which this book has been so well devised. I have certainly learned from using the book; and in the joy of learning it would be great fun to pick at it, argue, question — carp at, for instance, the footnotes I dropped from this writing, such as. . .

But let them alone. The poetry throbs huge as fog-caverned night over Big Sur. I'll return to it. And we'll argue again later.

Gary Elder
Portland, Oregon
December, 1976

You were never masters, but friends. I was your friend.

I loved you well, and was loved. Deep love endures

To the end and far past the end. If this is my end,

I am not lonely. I am not afraid. I am still yours.

—''The House Dog's Grave''
(Haig, an English bulldog)

Haig and Robinson Jeffers, 1939

IMPRESSIONS OF JEFFERS THE MAN

What was Robinson Jeffers like as a man, an individual, the poet who could write so eloquently both of God and the beauties of nature, as well as of the most sordid violence and cruelty? How did he seem in his daily life when met on the streets of Carmel or at small social gatherings? It was my good fortune to be with him on many occasions through the 1930's, both as a friend and as a photographer, and I am glad to record my impressions of him during a period when he was generally considered to be at the height of his creative abilities.

My first meetings with Robin and Una Jeffers occurred shortly after my marriage to Edna McDuffie. She had owned a house on Scenic Drive in Carmel for many years prior to our marriage, and we found it such a delightful place to live that we moved there permanently in 1937. Edna had known the Jeffers socially in Carmel for some time, and my first associations with them were likewise purely social, at the homes of mutual friends or over tea or port at our house or theirs. Una was immediately friendly and outgoing: vivacious, keenly intelligent, and outstanding in any company. Robin, on the other hand, was quiet and reserved, almost shy, speaking only when he had something worth saying, although never aloof or unfriendly. He had a beautifully modulated voice and a direct, penetrating gaze. He always dressed neatly, but I soon got the impression that he was none too comfortable in his party-going clothes.

I had known nothing of Robinson Jeffers' writings before I came to California to live, and when Edna gave me some of his poems to read, I found them quite beyond my grasp. It was only as I came to know the dramatic sea coast stretching from Carmel down to the Big Sur, that I began to feel the significance of his poetry. I became more and more impressed with how that magnificent grouping of mountains and sea and rocky shore must have inspired him and how deeply imbedded in that country were the very roots of his poetry.

A trip to my former home in New Jersey in 1935 revealed how little was generally known of Robinson Jeffers among my friends there. I felt that some knowledge of the rugged and beautiful country that provided the settings was quite essential to the understanding and enjoyment of his work. On my return I told Edna of my feeling. She suggested that I take photographs of some characteristic areas of the coast to show to friends who might be interested, but who, like myself, had been puzzled by Jeffers' writings.

As a lifelong dabbler in photography I was delighted with her suggestions, and on our next visit to Carmel we set to work. Some subjects were immediately obvious: the Jeffers' home, Tor House, with Hawk Tower; Point Lobos; Point Sur Rock with its lighthouse; characteristic ranch buildings under the brooding mountains; the abandoned lumber mill at Notley's landing; and Bixby Landing, featured in Jeffers' recently published "Thurso's Landing." Our interest grew with each photograph.

The results were so encouraging that we considered the possibility of putting the prints together in book form, each accompanied by a related selection from Jeffers' work. We showed the pictures to Una, telling her of our plan, and asked if we might title such a book "Jeffers' Country." She was immediately enthusiastic. She promised her cooperation in identifying other locations to be photographed and offered to help in selecting suitable passages from his poems.

We found that Una handled all matters of publishing and publicity for Robin, shielding him as much as possible from any interruptions in his work. All of our early discussions were with her, and we saw very little of him. Una showed him the photographs and told him of our plan for a book, and she told us later that he was at first quite uninterested, apparently seeing it only as a rehash of his earlier creative work. In time, however, his interest grew, and Una told us that he began to keep some of the pictures on his desk while he worked, sometimes jotting down on the backs of these prints bits of his poems which he thought suitable. On those occasions when we saw him, he would make some brief and favorable remark about the pictures, but he never went into any detail. Edna and I realized as time went on, that Robin was not inclined to discuss his writings with us or to volunteer comments on them, and we never suggested it. Una, however, would talk freely about them on any occasion.

Her quick and decisive nature demanded quick action. She would drop in at our house at any hour with some request or suggestion, or Robin would stop by to leave a scribbled note from Una, with a few soft-spoken words of explanation. The Jeffers in those days had no telephone in their home, but we would occasionally get a hurried call from Una in a phone booth or some neighbor's house. Such a call would usually send me scurrying down the coast or over to Tor House. One excited call was to say that she had just seen a crucified hawk over in the Corral de Tierra, and that I must go right over at once before it got too dark. A favorite symbol of Robin's had long been a hawk that had been shot down and then "crucified" on a fence or barn door as a scarecrow, and she had been hoping that I would find an opportunity to photograph one. This one proved to be not a hawk but an owl hung by its wings on a fence, but it would do very well and I got some effective photographs. Una was delighted.

By the time we had moved permanently to Carmel in 1937, our book project, with the wonderful cooperation of the Jeffers, was developing satisfactorily.* Because our home on Scenic Drive was a scant mile from Tor House, Una began to ask me to take simple photographs for her; views of their house with Hawk Tower; their dog and pigeons; her pet asphodel plant that had come from Greece; or pictures of their twin boys. Eventually, she asked me to try some informal photographs of Robin, something other than the formal type usually done by portrait photographers.

---

*For a number of reasons, the book was not finally published until 1971, by which time Una and Robin had both died. However, some forty of the prints, with accompanying quotations selected by the Jeffers, were shown as a set on many occasions, notably the opening of the poetry section in the Library of Congress in 1941.

Una was naturally photogenic and at ease under any circumstances. Robin, on the other hand, was almost always ill at ease and tense when the camera was pointed his way. His expression could be almost belligerent, utterly unlike his usual gentle self. I soon realized that the belligerence was directed not at me, but at the prospect of his image being held up to public gaze. It amounted to an invasion of his privacy, and even though his beloved Una had requested it, was extremely repugnant to him. The problem was to help him to relax and be himself, for the harder he tried to appear natural, the more selfconscious he became.

When Una was in the picture with Robin, he was usually much more at ease. When they were planning their trip to Ireland in 1937, Una wanted a single photograph of them both for their passport. They sat close together outside their house where the light was soft, and Robin was completely at ease and enjoying it. And why not? The camera was there that day only to help smooth their journey and add to their companionship. What the negative shows is a simple picture of a devoted couple, not a dramatic portrait of a major poet and his wife.

One day when Una wanted some photographs of Haig, their bulldog, I was able to get a charming picture of Robin as he knelt beside the dog. It was Haig who was the subject of the picture, not Robin, who was there just to see that the dog appeared at his best. Actually Haig needed no help—he was a born "ham."

On another occasion, Una wanted some pictures of herself and Robin together in their living room. I never knew what she told him or what she had in mind, but despite the fact that both Una and Haig were with him, he simply could not seem to unbend. She sat at her little desk by the window with Robin seated near her as she wrote. I made two exposures, and there is not the slightest difference in his posture or expression in the two negatives. Then she played some Irish tunes on her little old melodeon, and Robin sat on the settle by the fireplace behind her with Haig at his feet. Again Robin did not seem to move a muscle between exposures. Why was he unable to relax under those circumstances? My only guess was that he felt the camera to be an intolerable invasion of the privacy of his home. Una had asked him to do it and he did his best, but the results were only fair. I believe that Una was disappointed in the outcome.

A memorable occasion for me was when Una wanted a photograph of Robin on a grassy hillside overlooking the ocean. He and I drove down the coast to Victorine's ranch below Mal Paso Canyon, and Robin was relaxed and almost chatty on the way. He commented in his highly intelligent way on all manner of nature subjects and seemed to be thoroughly enjoying it all. However, as soon as we had climbed the grassy slopes and I unlimbered my camera, he froze. He held his knobby Irish stick and wore his usual puttees, and he tried hard to appear to be walking leisurely through the hillside pasture but he was stiff and unnatural. I made a couple of exposures that were quite unsatisfactory. All this time a light fog had been drifting in from the sea, and presently I realized that something out there was attracting Robin's attention. I could feel, rather than hear, a faint throbbing sound, unusual in its rhythm. For a matter of seconds Robin quite forgot himself in his concentration on the sound, and I snapped the shutter. As I did so he said, "It sounds like a three cylinder diesel." Robin had always had a strong feeling of kinship with the fisherfolk of Monterey and their involvement with the sea he loved, and for a few seconds he was probably with them in a passing trawler. The result was the best photograph I ever took of Robinson Jeffers, and really showed the man as I knew him. It became a great favorite of Una's.

I never attempted to photograph him without his knowledge, although there were occasions when a candid shot of him might have been very revealing. To do anything surreptitious with him, however, was unthinkable. Nor did Una ever suggest it; much as she wanted the world to know Robinson Jeffers' true self, she was too deeply devoted to him to employ any subterfuge.

He never commented to me on any photograph I took of him. Una, on the other hand, spoke freely to me about them, but never mentioned Robin's likes and dislikes. She gave prints of those she liked to anyone interested, and often used the backs for notepaper when writing to friends.

When Robin was building a stone wall for an addition to Tor House, Una wanted some pictures of him at work. He was a gifted stonemason of professional caliber, and could lay the rounded boulders from his beach to produce a wall of beauty and character. I was delighted at Una's request, as I was sure he would be relaxed and comfortable while handling the granite. I was not disappointed, although it took a bit of time. Una would make a suggestion, and he would immediately strike a stiff and unnatural pose. But with the feel of the granite and of the hammer in his hand, he would gradually relax and become his usual self. The results were good, although several times, just as I snapped the shutter, he would look up with a serious, "How am I doing," look on his face.

On another occasion Una had him stand beside an old millstone at the foot of Hawk Tower. The fine stonework, the product of his own hands, made an effective background for his strong features, but for some reason which I could never fathom, he simply could not unbend. As always when Una asked him, he made a great effort, but it just did not work out.

Probably the most delightful experience with the Jeffers was an all day visit to the limekilns back in Bixby Canyon one May day in 1937. Robin and Una had gone there many years before, and it had made a deep impression on them both. Robin later used the locale in his writings, notably "The Loving Shepherdess" and "Thurso's Landing", and he wanted photographs of the ruined kilns as they stood deep in the wooded canyon. So we packed lunches and drove in our car the twenty-odd miles to Bixby Creek, then down the old county road to its bridge over the stream. From there we scrambled on foot for a mile or so up the creek bed, crossing and recrossing it on broken logs and rocks until we came to the open space where the lime-making enterprise had been located. Over our picnic lunch, Una told us, with an occasional assist from Robin, how some hundred Chinese laborers had been employed there around the turn of the century. They mined the limestone from the surrounding hills, burned it in the kilns, and shipped the finished lime in barrels on an over-head cableway along the ridge to Bixby Landing. From there the barrels were slung out by cable to ships anchored offshore. The operation had been abandoned many years ago, and the tall kilns, cracked and broken, and the many wooden shops and cabins, mostly still intact, were now deep in a heavy growth of grass and shrubs. (Some fifteen years after our visit the entire region was swept by a forest fire, and nothing now remains but the masonry and metalwork of the kilns.)

It was still and peaceful that day in the deep canyon with its gurgling creek, and Robin was in his element. He wandered about, scrutinizing everything from the trees on the steep slopes to the locations and structural details of the wooden buildings and the kilns. His frequent comments were intensely interesting and showed the remarkable range of his know-ledge and understanding. My camera was his friend that day, never pointing its inquisitive lens at him, but recording, at his suggestion, scenes that particularly interested him. He never referred to his writings at any time that day, but Una spoke of them freely while Edna and I were with her. "The Loving Shepherdess" was obviously a great favorite of hers. How I wish I could have included one or both of the Jeffers in some of the pictures that day, for the limekilns was truly one of the "seed plots" of his poetry.

Robin's consideration for Una's comfort and safety was constantly in evidence the day of our visit to the limekilns, as he carefully and expertly guided and assisted her over the logs and boulders in the scramble along the creek bed and through the dense underbrush. On the drive home, as on other such occasions, they sat together with his arm around her. As a postscript to that happy day, Una told us some time afterward, that Robin, unbeknown to the rest of us, had found an old set of andirons in one of the houses. He had roguishly hidden it and returned next day to retrieve it. He presented the andirons as a gift to Una, and they were in daily use in Tor House for many years.

By 1939, their beloved bulldog, Haig, had aged noticeably. Una wanted some photographs of him in certain characteristic attitudes by the front door of their home. Haig, as always, was quite willing to oblige, and assumed his favorite poses under the supervision of both Robin and Una. He died shortly afterward and was buried among their flowers under a rough stone marker. Robin wrote a short poem, "The House Dog's Grave—Haig's Grave," which was published in a limited edition. The frontispiece shared one of the photographs of Haig with his nose to the door of Tor House. I am sure it had all been planned by Una when they realized that his days were numbered. Their affection for Haig was genuine, and Una told us, with some emotion, that when she and Robin looked over the prints to select one for the book, they were sitting side by side on the settle by the fireplace with tears streaming down their faces.

While most of the more detailed recollections of Robinson Jeffers relate to my attempts to photograph him, there were many other occasions when he had no reason to feel ill at ease, and I found him a delightfully interesting person. One day Edna and I drove the Jeffers down to the Jolon Valley to visit the San Antonio Mission. It was a carefree day for Robin, and we explored the old Mission building, then sadly in need of repair, and we enjoyed speculating on the functions of the outlying structures, of which little then remained but the foundation outlines. Robin was far removed that pleasant day from his intimate associations with the Carmel coast, and I found him simply a friendly and highly intelligent person in a setting of beauty and peaceful solitude.

As I saw him in his everyday life, Robin was essentially a "gentle" man. His manner, though reserved at times, was never aloof or unfriendly. I never knew him to be sharply critical or to speak disparagingly of anyone. He jealously guarded his privacy, but without giving offense. Toward Edna and me, Robin was invariably considerate and friendly in his quiet way, even when I had showed up with my inquisitive camera, and in his moments of relaxation, he could be the most delightful of companions. After all these years my lasting impression of Robinson Jeffers, the man, is of one true to himself and to his own high standard of conduct.

Horace Lyon
Carmel, California
1976

THE HOUSE-DOG'S GRAVE — HAIG'S GRAVE

by ROBINSON JEFFERS

I've changed my ways a little: I cannot now
Run with you in the evenings along the shore,
Except in a kind of dream and you, if you dream a moment,
You see me there.

So leave awhile the paw-marks on the front door
Where I used to scratch to go out or in,
And you'd soon open; leave on the kitchen floor
The marks of my drinking-pan.

I cannot lie by your fire as I used to do
On the warm stone,
Nor at the foot of your bed: no, all the nights through
I lie alone.

But your kind thought has laid me less than six feet
Outside your window where firelight so often plays,
And where you sit to read — and I fear often grieving for me —
Every night your lamplight lies on my place.

You, man and woman, live so long it is hard
To think of you ever dying.
A little dog would get tired of living so long.
I hope that when you are lying

Under the ground like me your lives will appear
As good and joyful as mine.
No, dears, that's too much hope: you are not as well cared for
As I have been,

And never have known the passionate undivided
Fidelities that I knew.
Your minds are perhaps too active, too many-sided . . .
But to me you were true.

You were never masters but friends. I was your friend.
I loved you well, and was loved. Deep love endures
To the end and far past the end. If this is my end
I am not lonely. I am not afraid. I am still yours.

Thirty copies of this poem have been printed by
The Quercus Press of San Mateo, California for
Una and Robin Jeffers in the month of June 1939,
with an original photograph by Horace Lyon.

Una asked me to take some photographs of
Craig as they realized he was nearing his
end. He died shortly after. Una told
me later than when she and Robin were
looking over the photographs to select one
for this book, they were sitting together
on a settle with tears streaming down
their cheeks. To me it was very revealing
of a little known side of two vivid
personalities.

Horace Lyon

Carmel
1973

IF SPIRITS EXIST:
Notes Concerning the First Publication of Robinson Jeffers'
"The Last Conservative" *

A mossy memory of an unpublished Robinson Jeffers poem entitled "The Last Conservative" surfaced during the writing of *Shining Clarity*. Some years ago I had seen a copy of the poem; and, in drawing this book to a conclusion, it occurred to me the poem's title might fittingly serve as a summary statement of Jeffers' final years. With this idea in mind, I wrote to The Humanities Research Center, University of Texas, Austin. In answer to my inquiry, Ellen S. Dunlap, the research librarian, assured me that "The Last Conservative" was indeed among the Texas papers.

During the time required to obtain permission to see the manuscript, I visited my dear friends of many years, Edith Emmons Greenan and her daughter, Maeve (named after Jeffers' first child, a girl who lived but one day). Both Edith and Maeve have known the Jeffers family for decades. It was, after all, Edith Emmons who, as a young woman, had married Una's first husband, Theodore Kuster. Later Edith became Una's close friend and chronicler, in her book *Of Una Jeffers* (1939). The lone dancer described by Jeffers in many of his early poems (as in "Fauna" and "Natural Music") is that same Edith Emmons. During my visit, Edith casually recalled that Robin and Una told her on several early occasions of their having seen out of the corners of their eyes the fleeting appearances of tall Indian ghosts — specters that gradually receded from sight around the corners of Tor House and vanished into thin air. The apparitions frequented the rocks and nearby shell-mounds, especially during the initial stages of the construction of Tor House.

---

*Permission to present the first appearance of "The Last Conservative" is granted through the courtesy of The Humanities Research Center, The University of Texas at Austin.

I had not seen "The Last Conservative" in fourteen years, and the enduring quality of the verse was my principal recollection of this poem concerning the agonies and solaces of Jeffers' last years. My initial reacquaintance proved astonishing! Here, still hauntingly alive in Jeffers' final memories, were those very Indian ghosts, hunched now against their fire-stained rocks, as vivid as Edith Greenan had only recently recalled them for me.

The manuscript of "The Last Conservative" has both poem and title written by Jeffers, in pencil, as was his custom. The typescript, which is numbered "III.", carries in the upper right-hand corner Melba Bennett's notation, "omit". Evidence from the Texas transcripts for *The Beginning and the End and Other Poems* (1963) suggests that the Roman numerals were added by Mrs. Bennett to designate the order of appearance of poems within the four sections of the volume. Hence, "The Last Conservative" was originally intended to be the third poem of one of these sections — probably the fourth, "Autobiographical". For one reason or another, Mrs. Bennett later chose not to include the poem. Ever helpful, she had written me long ago that there were indeed other poems from Jeffers' final years, poems omitted from the posthumous volume for various reasons. Of those omitted, only "Switzerland" and the significant short lyric "Rhythm and Rhyme" have as yet been published.

For whatever reasons it was originally excluded, "The Last Conservative" does merit the attention of anyone interested in Robinson Jeffers' poetry. Contained herein is a continuity of experience which runs the gamut of Jeffers' life and career. Much that mattered to the man is present: his scientific observation of the awesome span of geologic time, a small portion of which had created his homestead site, now a stranded beach with its sea "fifty feet lower"; the rocks which Jeffers deeply admired for their metaphorical fortitude and unswerving loyalty; the elemental purity of the poet's own place on the Tor; the quick and delicate gestures of the animal and bird prehabitants of Carmel; the poet's pride in his sons; the numbing shock of Una's early death; the squalor of the modern world, conveyed here (as elsewhere) in the form of the rotten apple simile; and finally, Robinson Jeffers' firm conviction of the solace provided by the unchanging sea, daintily restated in the patter of quail's feet on the shingles of his Tor House writing loft.

"The Last Conservative" is a characteristically comprehensive poem, pensive, full of love and disgust, loss and consolation. Nature still utters her unaltered message — even in the crowded contemporary world of streets and automobiles. The ocean, unchanging and yet the source of terrestrial life, is itself conservative and remains, in the poet's own words, "cold, grim and faithful". From this "mother", as Jeffers called the ocean in "Continent's End" (1924), the poet derives his strength; and, as venerator of the ocean, Robinson Jeffers is "the last conservative" who comprehends the true meaning of the external world, even as he proceeds in this poem from a vision of specters to the present and consolatory perception of one of nature's rather small and jaunty creatures, the California quail *(Lophortyx californica)*. If spirits exist, as Robin and Una aver, perhaps the "rock-cheeks" near Tor House now have other ghosts "beside the stones in their firelight".

My ghost you needn't look for; it is probably
Here, but a dark one, deep in the granite, not dancing on wind
With the mad wings and the day moon.

from "Tor House" (1928)

Marlan Beilke
Sutter Creek, California
April, 1977.

THE LAST CONSERVATIVE

by ROBINSON JEFFERS

The Last Conservative

AGAINST the outcrop boulders of a raised beach
　　We built our house when I and my love were young.
　　　　Here long ago the surf thundered, now fifty feet lower;
And there's a kind of shell-mound, I used to see ghosts of Indians
Squatting beside the stones in their firelight,
The rock-cheeks have red fire-stains. But the place was maiden, no previous
Building, no neighbors, nothing but the elements,
Rock, wind, and sea; in moon-struck nights the mountain coyotes
Howled in our dooryard; or doe and fawn
Stared in the lamp-lit window. We raised two boys here;
　　　　All that we saw or heard was beautiful
And hardly human.

CHAPTER ONE
The Holy Spirit Beauty

Oh heavy change.
The world deteriorates like a rotting apple, worms and a skin.
They have built streets around us, new houses
 Line them and cars obsess them – and my dearest has died.

The ocean at least is not changed at all,
 Cold, grim and faithful; and I still keep a hard edge of forest
 Haunted by long gray squirrels and hoarse herons.
And hark the quail, running on the low-roof's worn cedar shingles,
Their little feet patter like rain-drops.

—Robinson Jeffers

Poltroon Press, printers

In the years since Robinson Jeffers' death, critical commentary has begun more closely to examine the staid notion that Jeffers' ideas remained constant or static throughout his career. It is, perhaps, understandable how early commentators reached such conclusions. Jeffers' ideas were scarcely conventional, and they were repeated—with varying emphasis—throughout his mature work. The nature of the ideas, the consistent and solid backing which Jeffers gave them, and their steadfast, persistent reiteration provided the basis for the initial assumptions of arrant repetition on Jeffers' part.

That such assumptions were hasty or premature and often reflected the individual's misreading (or, still worse, distortion) of Jeffers' ideas generally passed unchallenged. Much of the inaccurate comment came from high places, and some, as Jeffers himself laconically pointed out, was even intended to be friendly. All too often the startling nature of the ideas themselves led commentators to transpose their own contorted notions for Jeffers' concepts.

In an Imagist age, few were prepared to credit the advantages to a poet of a firm ideological framework—particularly so if that framework cut across contemporary critical biases. In an age of skepticism and turmoil, a staunch poetical ideology seemed anachronistic. Some merely dismissed Jeffers as a ranting nihilist who sought to destroy all that was sacred and dear—Jeffers the poet who offered no alternatives. But with the passage of time and the arrival of more conscientious commentators, allegations of senseless nihilism and of vain repetition became increasingly less tenable.

Jeffers' mature published works span the thirty-nine turbulent years between 1924 and 1963. He witnessed two world wars, the ascendancy and triumph of modern science and technology, the Great Depression, and America's rise to status as a world power as well as myriad personal events of import. All these occurrences deeply influenced Jeffers' poetry. Ideas are affected by the events of the age in which they occur. It is a fascinating task to attempt to catalogue the flow of Jeffers' ideas and to determine whether these ideas were modified, embellished, reinforced, or clarified over the years.

If, however, the flow of his ideas is not presently obvious, in all likelihood the fault is not Jeffers'. Few modern poets employ his abiding clarity and forthrightness. *Any* volume of Jeffers' mature work contains his major ideas—openly and plainly stated. Should the ideas prove elusive, the fault is more likely in ourselves that we are the more accustomed to vagueness than to vision. Any contemporary consideration of Jeffers' ideology should seek to dispel some of the erstwhile confusion which still beclouds those ideas; as well, such a commentary should attempt to gather and summarize Jeffers' basic ideas.

Because of the remarkable scope of Robinson Jeffers' poetry, a complete study of the formulation of his ideas is a major undertaking. A partial inventory of Jeffers' ideas (as expressed in his poems) might include the following wide-ranging categories: God, man, nature, death, history (and the concept of culture-ages), science, art, the prophet in America, and the nature of human society. Although Jeffers managed— sometimes in spite of his aesthetic principles—to comment intensively upon these issues, his primary and permanent concerns were with the elemental questions of his and every age. Robinson Jeffers unremittingly sought the truth concerning the most basic questions an intelligent human being can ask: "Who is God?" and "What is man?" These were the major issues with which Jeffers wrestled throughout his long career as poet. Robinson Jeffers' ideas of God and man are cardinal to his entire career and provide, therefore, the nucleus for any study which attempts to trace the poet's central themes.

Such an ideological study, however, must be delineated still further. Should it concentrate upon Jeffers' longer narrative poems or upon the shorter so-called lyric poems? While it would be fatuous ultimately to ignore Jeffers' ideas on God and man as evinced in his narratives, Jeffers speaks more directly in the shorter poems. We may, with reasonable certitude, assume that unless Jeffers intervenes in the first person, the narratives *do* contain his ideas, but often strained through the minds of his characters. On the other hand, the shorter poems present—generally in the first person—Jeffers' immediate opinions, thoughts and observations. Thus, the shorter poems are the purer source of Jeffers' ideas.

Is it presumption to credit any modern poet with speaking unslantedly and candidly what he believes to be true in a short poem? In Robinson Jeffers' case, Hale Chatfield provides a cogent answer to this problem in his perceptive article: *"Robinson Jeffers: His Philosophy and His Major Themes."* [1]

> (Jeffers) frequently interjects comments into his dramas that indicate very effectively where his sympathies lie. Jeffers' manner of writing poetry makes it easier to distinguish his notions and opinions in his work than is the case with almost any other poet.

> He (Jeffers) wrote in 1933:
> *'I decided not to tell lies in verse. Not to feign any emotion that I did not feel; not to pretend to believe in optimism or pessimism, or unreversible progress; not to say anything because it was popular, or generally accepted, or fashionable in intellectual circles, unless I myself believed it; and not to believe easily.'*

---

[1] Hale Chatfield, "Robinson Jeffers: His Philosophy and His Major Themes", *The Laurel Review,* Volume VI, No. 2, Fall 1966, p. 58.

There is, I think, no reason to doubt the sincerity of that statement. Upon its evidence and by authority of the fact that Jeffers is without exception a solemn and serious poet, I have decided to forget some of the things we have been learning since the twenties and to operate in this study upon a conviction that everything in Jeffers' poetry that is not enclosed in quotation marks is Jeffers' honest opinion.

Moreover, although there may be some question as to the relationship between Jeffers' ideas and his characters in the narratives, there is little doubt about who is saying what in the shorter poems.

There is abundant evidence in Jeffers' writings which affirms the poet's vocational gravity and truthfulness. Recalling Nietzsche's condemnation of poets from *Also Sprach Zarathustra*("The poets lie too much"), Robinson Jeffers in his poem "Self-Criticism in February", countered: "I can tell lies in prose."[2] In his 1941 volume *Be Angry at the Sun*, Jeffers tells us that Bruce Ferguson, the principal character of his poem "Mara", is close to Jeffers himself regarding the thirst for truth:

> *Tomorrow I will take up that heavy poem again*
> *About Ferguson, deceived and jealous man*
> *Who bawled for the truth, the truth, and failed to endure*
> *Its first least gleam. That poem bores me, and I hope will bore*
> *Any sweet soul that reads it, being some ways*
> *My very self but mostly my antipodes;*[3]

[2] Robinson Jeffers, *Such Counsels You Gave To Me and Other Poems,* Random House, New York, 1937, p. 118.

[3] Robinson Jeffers, *Be Angry at the Sun and Other Poems,* Random House, New York, 1941, p. 137.

In the Foreword to *Selected Poetry* Robinson Jeffers says of his poems: "It seems to me that their meaning is not obscure."[4]

Robinson Jeffers recorded his ideas plainly, honestly, truthfully in his verse. By nature, Jeffers' poetry is free of ruse, obscurity or intentional deception. His ideas on God and man as revealed in the poems deserve reciprocal attention. A chronological study of Jeffers' ideas on God and man as recorded in his short poems should both reveal the nascence and implementation of Robinson Jeffers' ideology and simultaneously clarify those same ideas.

---

[4] Robinson Jeffers, Foreword to *The Selected Poetry of Robinson Jeffers,* Random House, Random House, New York, 1938, p. xiv.

Pan in the West

The Early Years: God
(1887 - 1923)

In retrospect, it is entirely fitting that Robinson Jeffers should have become the most theological of twentieth century American poets. His father, Dr. William Hamilton Jeffers, was a learned divine who specialized in ancient Near Eastern languages. Dr. William Jeffers also wished that one day his first son would follow in his footsteps. To this end the young future poet was carefully and ceaselessly prepared. Robinson Jeffers' father was schooling the young lad in Latin and Greek at an age when most young boys (even of Robin's day) were scarcely out of nursery school.

These sturdy lessons in language were intended to be the springboard into still other more exotic languages, languages which would one day be of inestimable value to a son who, it was hoped, would take his place among the clerical elite. This solid and rigorous preparation in languages the young prodigy was indeed subsequently to find invaluable—not in the cloth, but in poetry.

Robinson Jeffers was also schooled in the Bible by his rather elderly father. Throughout his life, Jeffers was able to locate scriptural references at will, a permanent carry-over from his training as a youth. Both his mother and father combined to provide a thorough understanding of the Old and New Testaments. The influence of his childhood intimacy with the Bible is to be found in every volume of Robinson Jeffers' poetry, so much so that a student of poetry unfamiliar with the Bible will probably find much of the verse enigmatic in its references. Theology (ultimately derived from the Presbyterianism of his youth) permeates Jeffers' work.

But of course there is more to Robinson Jeffers' religious outlook than reworked Biblical language and stories. Unlike most of the poets of his time, the early Jeffers concerned himself with important theological issues and evaluated them, summarized them, passed judgment upon them. Later, Jeffers forged ahead on the theological front by formulating a credo uniquely his own.

Jeffers' fascination with theology was not ephemeral, stale, or vapid. More than any other American poet of his day, Jeffers dared to grapple throughout a lengthy and productive lifetime with age-old theological questions. One of the most salient aspects of Robinson Jeffers' poetry is this persistent theological probing. If a complete Jeffers concordance existed, pages would be required for the listing "God".

Nor was Jeffers a mocker or an imitator in theological matters. He had no quarrel of lasting significance with any religion; neither did he espouse the tenets of one particular established religion. The opposite extreme—that of being so diffuse and eclectic that no precise theological tenets might be perceived—also does not apply to Robinson Jeffers' verse. Indeed, throughout his career, critics found fault with the specificities of Jeffers' theological views.

From childhood to old age Jeffers was fascinated by the idea of God. Accordingly, conceptions of God pervade his work. Attempts at the definition of God were one of the principal concerns of Jeffers' writing, yet there is never present the mindless and maudlin groping of less intelligent and less able versifiers of a theological bent.

Precisely what Jeffers' childhood religious training was like will probably remain a subject for inquiry. The training was thorough, basic, enlightened, broad; it was also restrictive, demanding, and rigorous. The young Jeffers was instilled with the worthy Calvinistic values of hard work and self-discipline, qualities which assured one a special place in God's world. Undoubtedly Robin found the demands placed upon him and the expectations of his parents rather confining, for evidences of his personal rebellion are already to be found in Jeffers' college verse. However, the son did not feel resentment toward either of his parents because of their expectations for or training of him. Jeffers merely felt that their goals selected for him were misplaced, that somehow he was not deserving of their care, affection and tutelage.

Robinson Jeffers refers to his father—with deep affection—in his mature verse. The son laments disappointing the father who had hoped for a theologian to follow in the father's footsteps; albeit, when it became obvious that his son was interested in poetry as a career, Dr. Jeffers vigorously championed this new vocation.

Many facets of Robinson Jeffers' early years are included in Melba Bennett's biography, *The Stone Mason of Tor House*. The usual chafings and dissatisfactions of youth were a part of Jeffers' adolescence. However, once having chosen poetry as his calling, and once his circumstances allowed him independently to produce verse, Jeffers no longer insisted upon kicking at the traces of his parental upbringing. Instead, he went on to become a successful poet using the very values, disciplines, and attitudes of mind which he had found only mildly distasteful as a youth. His beloved wife, Una, shaped him, it is true, but Jeffers' approaches to his work and life were essentially those learned in childhood from his father. A convincing case can be made that the mystique of Robinson Jeffers—poet-recluse, misanthrope, lover of nature and privacy—was merely a carry-over of his father's customs and temperament. That the son, like his father before him, should have parallel interest in theology seems singularly appropriate.

We would expect to find in Jeffers' first poems something of his Calvinistic background as well as a hint or two of his mild revolt against that background. Jeffers described his college years as "desultory". Theologically, however, Jeffers' juvenilia do not feature, as one might expect in such immature verse, a preponderant interest in God. A kernel or two, however, of Jeffers' thoughts on the topic of God is present. Reasons why Robinson Jeffers' early poems are not abundantly concerned with theology are not difficult to find. The poet was young, sensitive, and immature. A serious and personal topic such as one's theology could wait for more appropriate and more ordered days. In all likelihood, Jeffers had not yet formulated his thoughts on the topic in a fashion suitable for verse. As well, the early poems were occasional in nature, tailored for such outlets as college literary journals, annuals, magazines. The quality of the verse, as one would expect, was exploratory, often imitative and—for Jeffers—disciplinary in nature. Moreover, the early poetry (everything which predates the *Californians* volume of 1916) was not extensively edited. His juvenilia are only fragments, chips and splinters surviving from a period of thirteen years (1903-1916), valuable to us because they shed dim light on the development of a great talent. Not as theologically rich as his later work, the early poems serve as prolusion to Robinson Jeffers' mature theological persuasions.

Any commentary on Jeffers' early verse must undeniably be conditioned by familiarity with later achievement; there is, therefore, a certain danger in reading too much into these early and poetically inconsequential efforts. Nonetheless, scattered thought-initia of the mature poet are distinguishable. Perhaps the most general statement which can be made regarding Robinson Jeffers' theology as revealed in his early poems is that the God found there is strong and powerful, a solace for the poet. Two other aspects of Jeffers' conception of God are present in many of the early verses. The first attribute of God is that he is timeless, permanent, beyond the ages. *"The Measure"*, a poem written while Jeffers was a sixteen-year old college junior at Occidental College features a trinity against which one may measure the universe: "Truly great / Alone are Space, Eternity and God." God here is included as something of a third dimension: space, time, and God. Already Jeffers postulates a deity who transcends the ordinary limits of mortality and time.

The second attribute of Jeffers' God is a corollary of the first: namely that He is open to those who seek Him; that this God stands revealed in the natural world only He could create. In other words, God is omnipresent in that He presides over nature by virtue of his physical presence in things natural. This, of course, is close to the pantheist view of things. Still another 1903 Jeffers poem, *"Dawn"*, while including a conventional reference to the Hebrew conception of "Seraphim", makes allusion to a God-like sun: "The sun strides kingly forth in golden robes of pride."

Another aspect of Jeffers' early religiosity is found in two poems printed in the March 1904 edition of *The Aurora*, Occidental College's literary magazine of the day.

The first of these poems, "The Wild Hunt", is an imaginary encounter by a group of besworded horsemen with "the King of Shades" and his ominous crew. The mood is foreboding, in tone similar to the grimmer aspects of the Flying Dutchman legend, the western ballad "Ghost Riders in the Sky", or the more melancholy portions of "The Rime of the Ancient Mariner". The diction and dialogue have a distinctly Celtic air. The poem contains one of the first of Jeffers' many references to heavily oppressive evil, iniquity and sin, all but embodied in the world. Here, evil, though the horsemen would like to belittle its presence and influence, is brought before them in a most immediate manner; the mortal horsemen are entirely powerless before the black and other-worldly specters who gallop past in menacing and undeniably realistic actuality. And, significantly, the conventional religious gesture of crossing one's self when in danger or the presence of evil is dismissed as valueless: "For what is the sign of a half-made cross to fiends in *their* wood on *their* night?"

In "The Wild Hunt" then we note two new theological positions: that evil is a real and incontrovertibly fundamental force, and that mere humans seem powerless to prevent its fatalistic operation in the world. The very subject matter of the poem indicates that the young Jeffers was perhaps dabbling in extra-Christian supersititions. A 1906 poem entitled "The Forsaken Cabin" which appeared in *The University Courier*—a student weekly published at the University of Southern California, Jeffers' first graduate school—portrays Jeffers' own encounter with a presumably haunted cabin. After scrutinizing, then skirting it, Jeffers writes: "I turned with a half-whistle and a smile— / But looked across my shoulder leaving it."

The second of the March 1904 poems reinforces the contention that the young Jeffers already was exploring a theology which was at variance with Christian orthodoxy. "Witches" has distinctly Macbethan overtones (gibbets and Murderer's sweat), as well as hints of the trials at Salem. Perhaps there is a bit of humor as well:

"(And is your wife at home?)" asks the whimsical seventeen-year old versifier. And again the tone and diction are Celtic and decidedly pre-Christian.

In his senior year at Occidental College the name of the student publication was changed from *The Aurora* to *The Occidental.* "Jeff," as he was familiarly known to his classmates, was the editor of the publication, and no doubt had a hand in the change of names, for he remarked years later that it seemed inconsistent to him that a school in the West named Occidental should have a publication whose title, *The Aurora,* evoked images of the dawn in the East. The October 1904 issue of *The Occidental* carried a poem by Jeffers entitled "Mountain Pines". The mood attributed to these high-altitude trees is a somber one. Isolation and loneliness are the lot of these pines whose "gnarled roots cling / Like wasted fingers of a clutching hand / In the grim rock." It is the passing shadow of a great eagle which for a sad, all too brief time enkindles life in this "silent spectral band" of trees "...then / They find a soul, and their dim moan is wrought / Into a sighing sad and beautiful." The bright spirit of the eagle is able to breathe a fleeting life into the forest. Here Jeffers foreshadows one of his subsequent major theological tenets: that God and nature are physically one.

The bleak tones of "Mountain Pines" are matched by "The Condor", a poem which easily could pass as companion piece to its predecessor, so similar are the settings, subjects and moods of the two poems. All could not have been gloom that year, however, since the June 9, 1904 edition of *The Youth's Companion* magazine featured, complete with illustration, a new poem called "The Condor" and its editors promptly forwarded to Robinson Jeffers the first remuneration of his career, a check for fifteen dollars.

VOLUME 78   NO 23

JUNE 9. 1904

THE YOUTH'S  COMPANION

$1.75 A YEAR.

5 CTS. A COPY.

Copyright, 1903, by Perry Mason Company, Boston, Mass.

THE CONDOR

BY ROBINSON JEFFERS

My head is bald with cleaving heaven,
  And rough my feathers with the grip
Of clashing winds and clouds wind-driven.
But what of that? My wings can dare
All loneliest hanging heights of air;
Above the jagged mountain-lip
Their solemn slant and downward dip
Greet the red sun each morn and even.
The storm knows well their broad expanse,
For they can breast its pulsing power
When even the steadfast planets dance
Dizzily thro' the riotous rack
Of ruined, tattered clouds that scour
O'er heaven.   On the tempest's back
I clasp my wings, and like a horse
I rein it, mastering its force.
Then, tiring of the sport, I stretch
Upward above its region, far
As if I strove to climb and fetch
The utmost little silver star.
Then I lean low with a flat wing
Upon the lucid air, and swing
Amid the regions of pure peace.
I reck not of the earth below,
But swing, and soar, and never cease,
In circles large and full and slow,
With such a movement, such a grace,
That I forget my ugliness.

Later in his senior year at Occidental, Jeffers seems to have been much taken with the poetry of William Wordsworth. A growing naturalism is reflected even in the titles of two poems: "The Lake", which appeared in *The Occidental*, and "The Stream", printed after Jeffers' graduation from college in *Out West Magazine*. The final three lines of "The Lake" reveal a troubled young poet who turns to the solace of "a lonely lake" in his "darker hours":

> *Then, for my soul's release,*
> *Upon that lake as to my home*
> *I'll turn and find some peace.*

The final three lines of "The Stream" reflect a similar expression of the tranquility to be found in unspoiled nature:

> *One might seek peace and find her yonder,*
> *Where waters wild and wet winds wander,*
> *And having found, one might forget.*

At the age of eighteen, Robinson Jeffers is turning—not to conventional religion—but to nature as his solace in real or imagined distress.

In the autumn of 1905 Robinson Jeffers enrolled as a graduate student in world literature at the University of Southern California and lost little time in placing more of his poems in college publications. The November 1905 issue of USC's *The Cardinal* contains his poem "Steadfast Sky", the final lines of which admonish one to appreciate the fact that the physical universe is basically stable no matter how varyingly magnificent the externals may appear:

> *So imitate*
> *The eternal sky that changes not at all*
> *While ever the new splendors of it change.*

"The Moon's Girls", an unpublished but subsequently copyrighted poem of 1907, once again considers the occult and visionary as worthy subject matter for verse. The setting is long ago and far away, the notions are classic, the tone is Shelleyesque, the theme is that of the dream-swept lover, and there is no longer any hint of Christian influence in the poem.

"Pan in the West" of 1911 moves further into pagan religions and into pantheism. There is a new revelation recorded here:

> For, wandering along a rocky way
>   'Neath western pines, one unforgotten day,
> I felt thee, saw thee suddenly, and knew
>   That where white water ran,
> Where trees shook or grass grew,
>   Thou wert, too, O Cosmopolitan.

"Pan in the West" is a significant transitional piece in the theological development of Robinson Jeffers. Sometime prior to this poem, Jeffers had elected to abandon the orthodox Christianity learned so diligently in his childhood from his parents. His poetical attitude had been un-Christian, though by no means anti-Christian. Heretofore the young poet's yearnings after a deity were imitations, distant, hollow, aloof, lacking in moral weight or intensity. For the first time one catches, in "Pan in the West", a glimpse of noteworthy theological originality. Jeffers makes the observation that a nature deity (such as the classic notion of Pan) need not be relegated to bygone eras; a deity's physical presence may be detected and perceived in a fleeting, golden moment *anywhere*—even while climbing Mt. San Gabriel in southern California.

The experience described in "Pan in the West" is obviously of mystical nature—the first of those which Jeffers was to attempt to record in his poetry. By 1911, then, Robinson Jeffers had come to the realization that a God of nature was not limited to the classical world; he was omnipresent enough to be felt by a twenty-four year old poet in the West of the United States early in the twentieth century.

On December 4, 1912, a quaint little book of 46 pages was issued by the Grafton Publishing Company of Los Angeles. The title, handily abstracted from the Song of Solomon 2:5, was *Flagons and Apples;* the poet was John Robinson Jeffers, his full name appearing in book form this once in his career in deference to his namesake uncle from whom Jeffers had recently inherited sufficient funds for this first venture into print. *Flagons and Apples* [publication price: $1] was entirely financed by its author, who even wrote his own reviews. The book did not sell. His vanity satisfied by the mere act of publication, young Jeffers went back to more important things, foremost among them the courting of his already married sweetheart. 480 copies of the forgotten, neglected, thin little volume were remaindered for twenty cents each. Jeffers even advised his publisher that the book be pulped to spare a forest tree. In 1933, with his reputation established, *Flagons and Apples* sold (when rarely available) for $60; more recently, it has fetched amounts approaching $400. For all its presumed rarity, there is little lasting merit to the book other than its quaintness as a document of the poet's development. Jeffers himself was the first to realize this and say so.

A concordance to the volume indicates that Jeffers used the term "God" twenty times in *Flagons and Apples*, not insignificant since the tone of the book is almost completely amatory. One might assume, from the Biblical derivation of the title, that Robinson Jeffers in 1912 was still under considerable influence of the Bible, its teachings and literary style; however, such an assumption is only partially justified by the contents of *Flagons and Apples.*

An understanding of the theology as found in *Flagons and Apples* is facilitated by a brief account of Jeffers' circumstances at the time of publication, the book being highly biographical throughout. Since 1905 when Robinson Jeffers had first met her in a German class at USC, Una Call Kuster had haunted his life. Try as he might, there was no dismissing his fascination with this woman who was two years his senior and already happily married for three years to Theodore Kuster.

There is no blinking at the fact (despite the glosses of Jeffers' biographer) that theirs was an extremely unusual relationship. The eight long years between 1905 when they met and 1913 when they were married were years of torment for both the ill-starred lovers. Adultery, as Jeffers had been taught at home, and as he learned throughout eight years of bitter experience, was not all roses. *Flagons and Apples* stands at the near culmination of Robinson Jeffers' dolorous and unenviable circumstances as suitor to Una Kuster. It is questionable whether Jeffers ever recovered from feelings of guilt caused by this early illicit relationship.

But what do we learn of Jeffers' views of God as contained in his first book? The principal attribute of the deity found in *Flagons and Apples* is jealous vengeance. There are hints of Jeffers' adolescent nature worship in the very first poem of the book, "Her Praises"

> *Where alone in fiery-colored noontides,*
> *Hid under dreaming branches,*
> *Lurks and lives the Godhead whom we worship,—*

but the deity of *Flagons and Apples* is, by and large, a "jealous God" who, like Erinys, ceaselessly sets the world of the wrongdoer right. Jeffers may cast angelic metaphors around his loved one (presumably Una) in the first poem of the book

Then I praise you, worthy of adoration
More than any laughing springtime goddess,
But sister of the immortal
White supreme divinities of heaven

but throughout the volume there is a pervasive fear of an ominous destroying evil which in ''Nemesis'' Jeffers sees possibly as disfiguring even Una's physical beauty:

Lest evil come of your great wonderful beauty, and of
God's envy, and my surpassing happiness.

''Nemesis'' perhaps more than any other poem in *Flagons and Apples* is fraught with feelings of guilt. Guiltiness is readily transferred to others, and Jeffers transfers his guilt feelings to God himself, imagining that God is envious of the two lovers' untoward happiness. On the surface it does not occur to the poet that it is *he* who is in conflict with the decalogue, but subconsciously Jeffers is extremely fearful of divine retribution as the final four tearing lines of ''Nemesis'' reveal:

For joy is the foam of a wave that breaks on the world's low shore:
Dear and desired is that foam, but around it and underneath
What ghastly gulfs abysmal, that blacken forevermore
With death and despair and the terror of monstrous teeth!

A far less somber poem entitled ''The Quarrel'' depicts the twenty-five year old Jeffers after a petulant lover's spat magnetically attracted to what might have been Olvera Street, the oldest settled portion of Los Angeles, but he seems more attracted to the religious air of the place than to its antiquity:

> *When I left you I wandered at will*
> *Where our modern city has a*
> *Slight air of antiquity still—*
> *Down by the Mexican Plaza.*
>
> *And the bell of Our Lady with no low*
> *Tones, but with confident voice,*
> *Struck ten ....*

Possibly Jeffers at the time—whether he wandered "at will" or not—was allowing his feelings of guilt to be assuaged by casual religious association.

God "smiles bitterly" twice in the poem "And Afterward". But the increasing hopelessness of his situation culminates in Jeffers' skepticism regarding the very existence of God. The first lines of "End of Summer"

> *Let us give thanks to God, my lady,*
> *If any God at all there be,*
> *That the time coming finds us ready*
> *To sever without agony*

find Jeffers denying divine intervention in the conclusion of a love affair which probably did not involve Una, while "The Night" is authored by a poet contemplating moral relativism:

> *There is no God will tell us now*
> *If I did wrong, if I did right.*

Perhaps the truest record of Jeffers' thoughts on God in the *Flagons and Apples* period is the poem "Noon" which exposes in the heat of an oceanside sun a God-possessed, near-terrified young man who knows all too well the mighty power of an immanent God:

NOON

Hot waves of ancient waters drone
Against the shore ancestral hate.
Their dull, relentless monotone
Is as the very voice of fate.

What madness kindles in my head,
What God lays violent hands on me,
That the high sun is perfect dread,
And perfect terror the flat sea?

The blazing noon is like a load
Insufferable, too hard to bear.
O wild and cruel and occult God,
Have mercy on thy worshipper!

For the first time we have a record of one of Jeffers' most basic theological tenents: that God "is," as he was to write much later, "hardly a friend of humanity." As contrast, a poem appears below of the same title (the only time Jeffers titled two poems thus, presumably having forgotten the "Noon" of *Flagons and Apples*) which appeared in 1927, when the poet was at the height of his productive genius. The difference in merit of the two poems is immense and yet the thoughts dovetail:

NOON

The pure air trembles, O pitiless God,
The air arches with flame on these gaunt rocks
Over the flat sea's face, the forest
Shakes in gales of piercing light.

But the altars are behind and higher
Where the great hills raise naked heads,
Pale agonists in the reverberance
Of the pure air and the pitiless God.

On the domed skull of every hill
Who stands blazing with spread vans,
The arms uplifted, the eyes in ecstasy?

What wine has the God drunk, to sing
Violently in heaven, what wine his worshippers
Whose silence blazes? The light that is over
Light, the terror of noon, the eyes
That the eagles die at, have thrown down
Me and my pride, here I lie naked
In a hollow of the shadowless rocks,
Full of the God, having drunk fire.

The sea is flat, the sun is bright, the victim willingly present, but how different the quality of the poems! Terror and torture have given way to winged sacrifice to appease the awesome deity of noon.

"Another Saul" again makes Biblical reference, this time to the New Testament account of the miraculous conversion of St. Paul (Acts 9:1-22). As a relevant sidelight, S. S. Alberts on page 57 of his *A Bibliography of the Works of Robinson Jeffers* of 1933, notes that Jeffers was considering the Saul theme again in 1925 or 1926. A poem entitled "Saul" was written about this time, but was never published. As was his practice, Jeffers used the reverse side of the "Saul" poem on which to write the first draft of "The Broken Balance IV" which appeared in the *Dear Judas* volume of 1929. But in "Another Saul" from *Flagons and Apples* Jeffers again senses that

> *God mocks me in his mirth, or else*
> *Perhaps in wrath.*
>
> *God's voice was never clear, but O*
> *Sweetheart, sweetheart, your voice was clear!*

Jeffers feels that his Damascus road experience must emanate from his beloved who will clarify all things for him. But lurking in the background is the persistent prompting of his conscience and also his hostile God.

Section V of "Launcelot and Guinevere", the last regular poem of *Flagons and Apples,* (a curiously appropriate title considering the *mēnage à trois* in which he found himself) is filled with bitterness towards a God Jeffers considers responsible for his agonizing loneliness:

TO BE PUBLISHED JUNE 28*th*, 1933

A BIBLIOGRAPHY OF THE WORKS OF

ROBINSON JEFFERS

COMPILED BY S. S. ALBERTS AND APPROVED IN FULL BY MR. JEFFERS

This volume, besides being extraordinarily complete and authoritative as a bibliography, contains important unpublished material by Mr. Jeffers, including an introductory note, eight critical articles, and twenty-eight poems. It will be indispensable to every collector of Robinson Jeffers' works. ℭThe book has been designed and printed at the Walpole Printing Office, and is sturdily and handsomely bound in full cloth. ℭ There are 475 numbered copies at ten dollars each. [Ten special copies, at fifty dollars each, containing full pages of autograph manuscript, have been printed, and are fully subscribed for.] ℭPlease use the enclosed coupon and return it to Random House as soon as possible.

RANDOM HOUSE INC

20 EAST 57*th* STREET · NEW YORK CITY

Prospectus for the original issue of S.S. Alberts' *"Bibliography"*

V

When last we met!—how often
*   And often we used to meet!*
But God has trampled it all
*   Under his feet.*

God must be satisfied surely,
*   However much we have sinned,*
With your sorrow and mine
*   And the wail of the wind—*

God who has seen your beauty
*   Shine as the great stars shine,*
And your hand like a stricken bird
*   Drop out of mine.*

There is a note here of self-justification ("However much we have sinned"), a trenchant refusal to see the situation in terms of transgression and repentance. There is no denying the "sin" on Jeffers' part; he did not write "However much we *may* have sinned." Presumably the poet feels that the cards of fate have been unfairly stacked against him.

But the situation dragged on. There was no impetus (after seven years!) for Jeffers to correct the situation. He seemed resigned (because of guilt-paralysis?) to being a lover from the shadows. Indeed, when finally Una confessed to her husband that, for all of them, the situation had become an hopeless impasse, it was Mr. Kuster who recommended that Una take a year away from it all in Europe to make up her mind. During that interim, Mr. Kuster fell, conveniently for Una and Robin, in love with Edith Emmons and the situation—no thanks to Jeffers—was happily resolved for them all.

The "Epilogue" to *Flagons and Apples* features an elegant though unconvincing disclaimer by Robinson Jeffers. The poet blames his life, sorrows and sins upon the strange and enchanting atmosphere of California. Perhaps he is correct not easily to credit his situation as readily occurring in his native Pittsburgh in 1912. A note of hope appears in the "Epilogue"—the only such ray in the entire book—in that the immature young poet seems to take himself and his lot less seriously.

The final line of the book might serve as a prophetic summary of his career. In later years "The Double Marriage of Robinson Jeffers" (to his Una and to the landscape)—to borrow Lawrence Clark Powell's phrase—was to combine to create a talent unprecedented in "our country here at the west of things / ... pregnant of dreams." A substantially altered concept of his God would be one of the ground-springs of that talent.

The westward sea and the warm west wind—
It was these, not I, that wrought my rhyme.
I, that have lived, and sorrowed, and sinned,
Have spoken no word of my life as it is;
Have spoken only the ocean's abyss,
Only the open waves, that kiss,
And climb on the cliff, and fall, and climb.
Let them climb, and fall, and climb, as they will;
It is one to me, who have made what I might
Of long loves gone wrong, and light loves gone ill,
And loves of fools, forlorn and forgot,
And loves of men that witches have caught,
And loves enough, God wot; but not
The loves I have lived, nor the life I could write.

On October 11, 1916, a leading American publisher of the day, Macmillan, released to the public its printing of 1,200 copies of *Californians* by an unknown Carmel poet, Robinson Jeffers. The fact that Jeffers managed somehow to place his manuscript with the prestigious Macmillan company is significant. His publishers must have had good faith in the book; considerable numbers of advance review copies were distributed. But like the fate of *Flagons and Apples*, its predecessor, *Californians* by Robinson Jeffers of Carmel met with an indifferent reception. Jeffers himself, as before, went back to "The Homely Labors"—as one of the poems of *Californians* was suitably entitled.

Robinson Jeffers had much with which to occupy himself that year of 1916. Much of his intellectual energy was diverted to focus on the ghastly developments of World War One. The poet would soon occupy himself physically with the building of Tor House on what was then an isolated ocean front property on Carmel's Mission Point.

By 1916 Robinson Jeffers completed the three things he once quoted as the most important for a man: write a book, plant a tree, and father a child. In Jeffers' case, though, it was twins, for on November 9th, 1916, less than a month after the publishing of *Californians*, Una gave birth to Jeffers' only living children, twin boys, Garth and Donnan. (A daughter, Maeve, had been born on May 5th, 1914, but she died sadly one day later.) Obviously, Jeffers had sufficient to occupy himself that year of 1916. When it became incontrovertibly clear that the *Californians* volume was faltering, Jeffers was content to abandon it. Never again did he consider the work in *Californians* to be anything but slight and unworthy verse.

But *Californians* is valuable as a transition piece, much more so than *Flagons and Apples*. The subject matter, the setting, some of the tone, and even a few characters of Jeffers' mature poetry are to be found in *Californians*. The soul of the mature verse is not. Robinson Jeffers had found the location, but neither the form nor the spirit of his meteoric *Tamar and Other Poems* of 1924.

The theology contained in *Californians* is a giant step along the developmental path to *Tamar*. The pantheism of *Californians* is more pervasive and consequential than that of *Flagons and Apples*, so much so that Jeffers' faith in the natural world seems nearly to have eclipsed his rudimentary beliefs. Jeffers seems fascinated with earth in *Californians*; he uses the word or its compounds 46 times in the book, with the word God used 38 times, seldom in its Christian connotations.

"Stephen Brown", one of the early poems in *Californians*, finds Jeffers admiring the serene wisdom of a hermit whose eccentric habits resemble those of Jeffers' own father. Brown, a consumptive who had been given only six months to live, also came to California (the San Bernardino Mountains) for his health—and survived thirty years. In praise of the salubriousness of Brown's surroundings, Jeffers writes toward the end of the poem: "O happy earth," I cried, "O fearless, O most holy!" The young poet is gratified that the western climate has been instrumental in extending the health of the hermit, Stephen Brown; in the same manner, Jeffers' own father's health was restored by a westward move.

A Ceres-like female fertility figure appears as the persona of the poem "Emilia". Present are the classic Fauns and Satyrs, vine-leaves, wine, a bountiful garden, and the poem concludes with a sensuous dance in the gentle first rain of the season, the "Bacchanalian" Emilia gingerly stepping through her garden in the nude for the occasion. Emilia prays "not with open lips, / But longingly at heart" to the powers of nature for rain for her garden. Emilia's religion (by extrapolation Jeffers') holds "to the ancient first apocalypse" whose adherents

Prayed nor to images, nor fellowships
Of Godheads on a mountain, nor withdrawn
In heaven one God nor three; but worshipped rather
Kindlier powers,—the sun, their lofty father;

18

Deep-bosomed earth, their mother; and the wind,
The rain, the sheltering hills, the moving sea:
Even so Emilia, not with conscious mind,

I think, but by deep nature, reverently
Regarded the great elements, inclined
Her heart before the first—and verily
The only visible—Gods;—and found her prayer
As often answered as most others are.

Emilia has subconscious reverence for the forces and manifestations of nature. She has rejected idol worship, priestly organizations, asceticism, the monotheism of the Old Testament and the Trinity of the New. By the time Robinson Jeffers wrote "Emilia", he too must have come to reject these forms of religious practice. At minimum, Jeffers feels that Emilia's naturalistic religion is equally as efficacious as any codified religion.

Section 22 of "Emilia" demonstrates that her beliefs are also practical. Her prayers are answered; she can see and feel the rain in her garden: in contrast to other religions "*she* discerned / The God of her desire." Emilia expresses her devotion to the "god of her desire" in the final four sections of the poem by dancing "free and without strain, / Mixing her tender body with the rain" as a virgin "young doe-fawn ... in a lonely clearing of the wood / For love of her own lightness." "Emilia" reveals the extent of Jeffers' own rejection of conventional religions and provides us with a sensualized feminine practitioner of the more esoteric aspects of his own convictions.

"The Vardens" is a "Cawdor"-like narrative which features a prodigal son, Richard Varden, secretly loved by a stern father who none the less banishes him, leaving Richard's Esau-like brother Graham home to do the work. On his death bed, the boy's father cries out to his exiled son now encamped on the shores of Eagle Lake in northeastern California, far from Richard's native Santa Barbara. Jeffers distinctly rules out a conventional Christian afterlife for the soul of the departed aged Mr.

Varden: "To annihilation and blank vacancy / Given up, the spirit was lost." But the son, by a sort of naturalistic extra-sensory perception, detects in his sleep the remorseful, anguished keening of his father and weeps at the tidings:

> *But he, [Richard Varden] that wandering man, in grief and awe*
> *Wept silently before his lonely fire*
> *Until pale dawn with light had slain the stars.*

"The Vardens" lays bear Jeffers' disbelief in a Christian hereafter. For Jeffers, death is final. A man's spirit may wander as a ghost for a brief time, but eventually even that spirit flickers out. However, a strong spirit upon dying may be able to enlist the powers of its former abode in the natural world for a final effort at reconciling its worldly affairs. Such activity of the spirit Jeffers compares to the light of a recently extinguished star:

> *As when a star is blackened, yet its light*
> *Rains on the earth for centuries to come*
> *From the incalculable gulf and vast of heaven.*

It is only a matter of time and perspective which allows the spirit briefly to wander over the earth before "the great world that knew it not / Was emptied of a soul." The world which sustained old Mr. Varden was not even aware of his passing. It may be a man's felicity to take joy in the beauties of nature, but that felicity is not reciprocal.

Another poem which states Jeffers' view of a beautiful "but unresponsive Nature" is "Maldrove", the story of a brilliantly gifted young poet named Maldrove who stayed at Peter Graham's hermit cabin and left behind a poetic fragment before he (a casualty of World War One)

> *Fell in a skirmish by the Dardanelles*
> *(A special British blunder, God forgive them!).*

Maldrove's (Jeffers') poetic invocation is a passionate piece of pantheism:

> *Mother-country, O beautiful beyond*
> *All power of passionate verse, or dream of mine,*
> *Yet take this homeless verse; for it is thine*

and so on.   After Peter Graham allows the young Jeffers to read the treasured fragment of Maldrove's fleeting sojourn, Graham concludes:

> *Only—this world—what is there in it to love*
> *But unresponsive Nature?*

Much later in his career Jeffers will clarify his position: it is man's felicity to love the natural world which is beautiful throughout, but such a world neither notices nor needs man's devotion.

The old hermit Peter Graham makes another statement which might well serve as a concise epigram for Jeffers' efforts in *Californians:*

—He was then
Not old enough to clarify his dreams
Into a human image.

"The Three Avilas" touches on the familiar Jeffers theme of incest for the first time. Of all the poems in *Californians*, "The Three Avilas" provides the most palpable link to the romantic dilemma of *Flagons and Apples*. The theological difficulties of *Flagons and Apples* also resurface in "The Three Avilas" which tells the imagined story of an incestuous brother and sister—initially unaware of their parentage—and their ultimately successful avenging brother. "The Three Avilas" is deeply evocative of Jeffers' extraordinary courtship with all its own thorny obstacles. This narrative poem is highly biographical in nature as Jeffers writes in the prose explanation, *A Note about Places*, at the conclusion of the volume: "The story of the three Avilas, for example, grew up [as many of his future poetic narratives would] like a plant from the ravine described in it", a ravine at which Robin and Una would rest on their way home to their residence at the time, The Log Cabin, still standing at Fifth and Monte Verde streets in Carmel.

"The Three Avilas"—as does *Flagons and Apples*—features "jealous Gods". Jeffers characterizes these Gods as fickle and influence-prone:

Then think—for if we ponder long enough
On omens when the Gods are very good
It may be they'll avert them ....

"The Three Avilas" is replete with demons, fiends, and "phantoms that flock here about our bed.'' In reaction to ''lamentable demon shriek[s]'' Jeffers even ''hang[s] my [his] holstered weapon ere we sleep.'' In *Californians*, as in previous verse, abundant reference is made to other-worldly vengeance-seeking creatures.

When the avenging Avila brother is about to apprehend the two incestuous Mexican lovers, Jeffers introduces the misinterpretation that it was Christianity which forced their ''bloodhound'' brother to seek their deaths: ''both family pride / And Christian faith commanded fratricide.'' A potential correlation exists between Jeffers' adulterous love affair with Una, with its concomitant guilt feelings, and Jeffers' final rejection of Christianity, which religion he felt assessed his conduct as iniquitous. In the instance of the vengeful Avila brother, Jeffers is consciously or subconsciously conveniently interpreting the dictates of Christianity for his own ends.

In the poet's view, the incestuous Avila brother (as Jeffers surrogate) is ''more loved than the Lord Christ, and more unblest.'' True lovers here on earth receive a greater love than that of Christ himself and as a consequence are rewarded with an even crueler Calvary. When the avenging brother takes aim and kills his sister, Jeffers uses the occasion to ''prove'' that

> *...no God cares for what may be*
> *Of horrible, or out of reason done*
> *Below the foolish looks of the wide sun!*

Twisted logic and false excuses are still beclouding the facts surrounding Jeffers' courtship.

In the light of Jeffers' later work, Biblical reference in *Californians* is notably sparse. Significantly however, he includes a comparison of the surviving Avila brother covering his slain brother and sister's nakedness with a serape on Carmel Beach to the account in Genesis 9:20-27 wherein

> *...Noah's praiseworthy two sons*
> *Walked backward toward their father drunk-asleep*
> *And naked*

and covered their father.

"The Three Avilas" concludes reiterating that "to love well is to contend / With Gods vengeful and envious." Self-disenfranchised from the religion of his father, Jeffers in the final section of the narrative turns to things natural as balm and consolation:

> *But as for us, let us forget to fear,*
> *Some brief permitted while, those vengeances.*
> *The woods and shore yet shelter us; and here*
> *Where the world ends in waves and silences*
> *We may be quite as joyful as the clear*
> *Small blossoms of the beach and wilderness;*
> *Those lamps whose light is perfume, which they scatter*
> *Profuse on the wide air and the pale water.*

"The Mill Creek Farm" of *Californians* (1916) bears coincidental resemblance to Robert Frost's "Two Witches, Part I, The Witch of Coös" which appeared in his *New Hampshire* volume of 1923. Both poems deal with strong-willed country women, contain their share of gallows humor, and concern themselves with death. (This is by no means the only parallel which exists between Frost and Jeffers; a fascinating study might be undertaken on the correspondences between the two poets' lives and work.) Of the two, Jeffers' poem is, however, the heavier. The aged widow on her death-bed voices the following sentiments concerning the pointlessness of heaven:

> *... What's that?—In heaven?—*
> *A place for children to plan for; I'm eighty-seven.*
> *You'll know, when you get to be tired and sleepy and white,*
> *That the only word at the end is plain Good-night.*

Like Stephen Brown, the widow of Mill Creek Farm considers subsequent generations soft; she dies more content listening to ''the noise of the stream'' than to the imagined sounds of her dead son's voice. Jeffers once again prefers the natural world to a religious or spirit world of the hereafter.

In 1952 Robinson Jeffers wrote a reflective prose description of Point Lobos for Doubleday & Company's *The Glory of Our West*. But the first of Jeffers' numerous and eloquent canticles of that ''most beautiful union of water and earth'' appears as ''A Westward Beach'' in *Californians*. On what was already in 1916 obviously hallowed ground to him, Jeffers makes firm his vow to remain unshaken a pantheist:

> *I promise you, serene and great*
> *Ocean, and Earth, my mother,*
> *In days well-friended, fortunate,*
> *My spirit will not be other*
> *Than now it is:—I have fared not ill;*

I have known joy: yet keep my will
Austere and unsubduable!

It was a vow Jeffers was to keep for his remaining 56 years—"in days well-friended"
and in ill.

A close reading of "A Westward Beach" reveals that Jeffers in 1916 was not "a
hater of men". His view is that the natural world of beauty is capable of accepting
even man and his "dull / And outcast and unusable" discards. Ultimately Jeffers'
faith has it that the earth *is* inviolable—even at the hands of man, who can damage,
but never completely destroy the natural world.

Dear Earth, thou art so beautiful!
Lo, thou acceptest all things dull
And outcast and unusable;

Thou takest home and makest whole
The relics and discarded
Raiment of man; each toy or tool
By him no more regarded
To thee is dear, and grows to thee,
And finds acceptance full and free,
Even with the old hills and the sea.

"A Westward Beach" also begins Jeffers' dual career of poet and prophet. In this
capacity, his mission will be to plead with, cry to, or rage at humanity to return home

to the more natural life in the company of "the brown hills and the blue sky."

> *Meanwhile, my voice may reach so far*
> *As to your ears, and waken*
> *Some spark within you, the one star*
> *Your chimneys could not blacken;*
> *And I will plead and I will cry,*
> *And rage at you, and pass you by,*
> *And wander under the open sky.*

Jeffers' early theological position may be summed up with the title of one of the poems from *Californians*: "He Has Fallen in Love with the Mountains".

"The Year of Mourning" commemorates the deaths in the same year of Jeffers' father and his first child, Maeve. If anything might have rejuvenated Jeffers' Christian faith, it would have been the death of his theologian father. Instead, Jeffers again rejected the religion with which even his father had had some difficulties. The elder Jeffers had traveled to

> *The Palestinian hills where that began*
> *Which like strong poison in the sickly world*
> *Works yet for evil and good: medicinal*
> *And deadly ....*

For Jeffers, Christianity is a mixture of good and evil, a mixed blessing for the world. There is a suggestion, however, that Jeffers has not altogether dismissed an omnipotent God who presides over nature. He writes that the "lordly oaks and pines of mine own shore" are "stern; / And of their natures next to supreme God."

Section IX, the seance section of "The Year of Mourning," provides an early explanation of the origin of Gods.

> *Our baser part of consciousness flows over,*
> *And mocks us from without. Thence Gods were made.*

Apparently the Gods are imagined from man's subconscious needs; man projects the Gods from deep within his psyche. The embodiment and separation from man of such deities works for man's discomfiture.

Section X is a precursor of Jeffers' monumental poem "Night" which first appeared in *Roan Stallion and Other Poems*, 1925. The vision here is monistic, "the Protean element" (darkness) creates all things and eventually reclaims them unto itself. The stars themselves are born from and return to

> *...that one gulf*
> *Obscurest; that alone*
> *Beyond their witness opens a night*
> *Awful, discrowned of stars, naked of light.*

Jeffers characterizes a second existence for man as a physical impossibility:

> *O fools are we! who cherish*
> *Long loves in such a travelling world, who thirst*
> *For that which the stars know not, which the Gods*
> *Have not: were feigned to have:*
> *That blossom rooted in the bottomless grave,*
> *The impossible dawning of that second morn.*

A resurrection from the dead is "impossible." The finality of his father's death renders undue mourning merely a maudlin form of self-indulgence:

> *Yet he for all thy weeping, all thy love,*
> *All thy long weeping, will not wake again.*
>
> *He is gone down where Fate and adverse Gods*
> *Trample all things great, all honored things....*

The double deaths of 1914 in the Jeffers family did not leave the poet without consolation. In the final and perhaps best poem of *Californians*, "Ode on Human Destinies"—one of the few poems from the volume ever reprinted in Jeffers' lifetime—Jeffers, like the writer of Psalm 121:1, lifts up his "eyes unto the hills":

> *I lifted up my eyes and heart, to adore*
> *The inveterate stability of things.*

Guiding the "inveterate stability" of the universe is the omniscient God, Fate. Jeffers advises that a human

> *...neither tremble, neither falter*
> *In the course he cannot alter;*
> *Each walks a way long chosen, long before;*
> *That path as well as this*
> *In surest guidance is;*
> *Fate, that alone is God, can change no more*
> *Than the strong traveller may control,*
> *His necessary courses toward the timeless goal.*

The great God of the universe is Fate; section VII of "Ode on Human Destinies" opines that the Holy Spirit and hallmark of such a God is the eternal beauty of the physical world. This universal beauty is "from eternity". The stars, the human spirit, the swallows are all fuel to the great flame of the beauty of the universe. Such a deity commands and deserves our allegiance:

> *...No mean lord*
> *We serve and share with, serving thee,*
> *O twin-born bride of Destiny!*

Jeffers, his future already known to Fate and predetermined, concludes his second book, *Californians*, with the firm resolution to be guided and inspired throughout his life by Beauty, the holy spirit of Fate:

> *I, driven ahead on undiscovered ways*
> *Yet predetermined, do not fail to see,*
> *Over the fog and dust of dream and deed,*
> *The holy spirit, Beauty, beckoning me.*

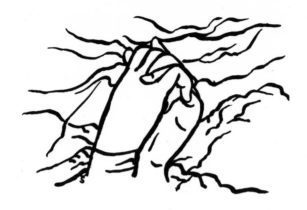

The Early Years: God
A Summary

Robinson Jeffers' early works (his juvenilia, college verse, and first two un-successful books) are largely inconsequential as poetry. The juvenilia and college verse (virtually indistinguishable from each other since Jeffers entered college at an early age) already reveal the young poet's disenchantment with the Protestant Christianity of his upbringing. The earliest extant poems are revealingly concerned with extra-Christian pursuits and naturalistic attitudes.

The quality of the verse of *Flagons and Apples* is even less (and more limited in scope) than Jeffers' juvenilia. Jeffers' guilt, derived from his unusual romantic circumstances, drives him even further from the conventional Christianity of his day. A growing sense of grim and certain retribution at the hands of a deity finds Jeffers engrafting a deity of vengeance-seeking proportions to his budding pantheism.

Robinson Jeffers' second book, *Californians* of 1916, was by far the best poetry he had written to date. The verse is disciplined, often stylistically indebted to Dante and Milton, and, more importantly, contains the initia of many of Jeffers' mature works. *Californians* (in this light) seems a somewhat underrated book. Jeffers' deity has become unabashedly pantheistic. An exhaustive study of Jeffers' theology as revealed in *Californians* might some day be attempted after the sequence of composition of the works of the volume is ascertained, *Californians* obviously containing works both of a distant and more recent composition.

Theologically, *Californians* is a vital exercise in definition of Jeffers' conception of God. The observations of the natural world Jeffers began to make in the years prior to the publication of the book were a lasting and abundant source of inspiration throughout his lifetime. After foraging through a series of pantheistic possibilities, Jeffers concluded that the world is monistic, that the single great force of the universe is Fate. Beauty is the signature of this immense power on the world. Jeffers himself had yet to experience this transcending power to be transformed into a poet of lasting merit.

To the point of the publication of *Californians* and for perhaps a few years thereafter, Jeffers was only consciously working out a definition of what he considered to be the God of the universe. Before he could write meaningfully about his investigations, he would somehow (perhaps through direct mystical encounter of his own) have to experience the *reality* of such a God. How this came about we shall probably never know. The likelihood of confirmatory evidence for mystical experience being what it is, *Californians* remains our best index to the developing thought of a poet of genius.

What but ... quotidian Sunday chicken

The Early Years: Man
(1887 - 1923)

Expressions of Robinson Jeffers' attitudes towards his fellow man are not as abundant in his early works as are his theological persuasions. Jeffers once pointed out that his parents "carried me [him] about Europe a great deal" as a child. The youthful Robinson Jeffers observed that his European counterparts were not as clean or as upright in character as he would have preferred them to be. At an early age Jeffers may have formed attitudes of suspicion towards classmates he lacked the time or inclination to learn to know.

Jeffers' father's own convictions also made an indelible impression on the young lad. From his father's Calvinistic faith Jeffers learned that man ought to humble himself before his Creator. "The Measure", printed in Occidental College's *The Aurora* in December, 1903, is Jeffers' first surviving poem which provides a clue as to his early attitudes towards man. Jeffers was sixteen at the time, and already was placing humanity in perspective:

> *And those, her [the earth's] progeny, the mighty men,*
> *Swaying her things in comradeship with fate,*
> *Seem but as worms upon a little clod.*

In relationship to the universe, man and planet earth are insignificant indeed. Underpinning this characteristic Jeffersian pronouncement is the attitude that man, powerful and influential though he may temporarily be, cannot exceed the bounds which "Space, Eternity and God" have set for him.

Next month, *The Aurora* featured a Jeffers poem with a telling title: "Man's Pride". Reminiscent of Job 40:12 which warns man of excessive self-confidence, the poem begins:

> *What is man that he should be proud?*
> *And what is the race of men*
> *That they should think high things?*

The youthful Jeffers castigates what he considers to be the vanity of human self-consciousness. Humility in place of arrogance is prescribed for the human race, then at the beginning of the scientific twentieth century. It was a message Jeffers would later reiterate with immeasurably greater skill.

A February 1904 offering, "A Hill-Top View", concludes: "The calm eternal Truth would keep us meek"—if man could seek and understand the limitations of his existence from the wholesome perspective of cosmic distance.

Robinson Jeffers' only published short story, "Mirrors", appeared in *The Smart Set* magazine in August of 1913, one year before the outbreak of World War One. It is a curious piece which features a nervously introspective young man named Adair who comes to realize that "we are all mirrors—senseless mirrors—blank spaces which reflect." By implication, human self-consciousness (with no antidote from the purgative external natural world) will ultimately turn in on itself, the results of which will be bizarre and unhealthy.

In an unpublished poem dated 1907, "North Pole", Jeffers predicts the conquering of the North Pole, which—in personification—laments that man one day will indeed subdue the earth.

> *For the thing ye [man] decide*
> *To do, in the end,*
> *Not time, not tide,*
> *Can avail to withstand.*
> *For I know ye are masters,*
> *Who cease not to dare,*
> *Whom never disasters*
> *Can bring to despair.*

Perhaps the young Robinson Jeffers had caught a bit of the contemporary optimistic fever of the triumph, through technology, of man over his surroundings. The poet, however, seems to have mixed feelings about such a triumph.

Because of the limited scope of Jeffers' first book, *Flagons and Apples*, one neither expects nor finds many sweeping pronouncements by the amorous young poet on the nature or condition of man. Perhaps the only overt and significant reference to the human race comes in the book's "Epilogue". There Jeffers admits that he has known and loved foolish people. The young versifier has now learned not to give of himself to the unworthy of his world. Clearly the writer has intentions of being more discreet with his affections in the future.

Californians of 1916 provides some concrete insight into Jeffers' perceptions of man and society. References to God outnumber those to man in the volume, but it is possible to obtain a reasonable picture of Jeffers' attitudes toward man from his second book of verse.

The first time Jeffers touches upon human freedom in a poem, he refers to his remote ancestors who migrated "Westward, free wanderers." Robinson Jeffers views himself as "the latest" of the millions who "tracked westward the wilderness." The quest for individual liberty remains one of Jeffers' most characteristic poetic themes.

"Stephen Brown", one of several hermit poems of *Californians*, includes another favorite Jeffers dictum, the necessity of one's having—insofar as one is able—beautiful surroundings. People become what their non-human environment allows them to become. If one's surroundings are beautiful and natural, then Jeffers surmises such an environment will have its wholesome impact on the individual. In the words of Stephen Brown: "We grow to be what we have loved." The conclusion of the poem seems to suggest a tangible link between the natural environment and the individual it supports. Jeffers admires individual men at peace with their chosen surroundings. The self-reliance and independence of a man like Stephen Brown, Jeffers would claim, indicate that true freedom has its birth in the open air:

A man at home in the world to live or die,
Self-stationed, self-upheld as the all-beholding sky.

But most men do not choose to live as does Stephen Brown. Peter Graham, another hermit of *Californians* who appears in the poem "Maldrove", expresses his contempt for the human situation of the day. In less than a decade, Jeffers again will take the opportunity in print to voice his own discontent with man more directly. But for the moment Jeffers describes his Peter Graham as

A jovial hermit, who professes more
Than feels contempt of man and of the time.

But Maldrove, hypothetical talented young poet and Jeffers' *doppelgänger* writes more openly, declaring that, although people will call themselves lords of the earth at the forthcoming World Fair, "I on hell ... attest I love them [the people] little, but thee [the earth] well." The young poet Maldrove later refers to "all the vermin infamies of men, / The many foulnesses" summing up his intense dislike for the many evils man seems inclined to commit.

In his early school years Robinson Jeffers was known as the "little Spartan." Peter Graham concludes "Maldrove" with the most characteristic Jeffersian summation of society present in *Californians*. Although the words are those of Jeffers' hermit friend, we may be certain—in the light of Jeffers' later caustic comments on a luxury and comfort-oriented American society—that young Jeffers found himself much in accord with Graham's judgments:

This cankered [human] world, what is there in it to love?
A world at war is well enough—but this,
Rotting in peace—commerce—and for a hope
What but the socialism we're settling to,
Quotidian Sunday chicken, and free love
High over all, the spirit of hugger-mugger,
And cosmopolitan philanthropy
With wide wings waving blessing[.]

What then, in Jeffers' view, is the best form of human society? Not the massed dependencies of modern urban civilization, but the harsh realities and isolated pastoral beauties of

...several farms, weak inroads of few men
Amid the imperturbable majesty
Of the old forest

similar to the setting of "Ruth Alison." The Jeffers of *Californians* has neither respect for nor interest in massed humanity.

A million lives like these riot and mix
About the world, and none keeps record of them.
So on a mountain-flank the rainy grass
Is new in January and lost in June,
And none keeps record of it: the blind hearts
Of men likewise renew themselves and die.

In a later poem Robinson Jeffers recoined the comparison of humanity in the mass with "all the companies of windy grasses." Ruth Alison, an individual who could not fit into the crowd, found herself betrayed and destroyed by it.

"At Lindsay's Cabin" provides further evidence of Jeffers' early, intense dislike for crowds. Lindsay, "a solitary man" with an unfortunate penchant for alcohol upon exposure to the masses of San Francisco, is shanghaied while on a necessary visit to the metropolis. The city's throngs are termed by Jeffers

> *...multitudes*
> *They moved the streets, an endless aimless throng,*
> *As in a broken anthill scurry the ants,*
> *And seem to have no aim, but everywhere*
> *In multitudinous confusion mingled*
> *Stream through the little, close, and earth ways:*
> *Even thus they swarm the city, and Lindsay felt*
> *That none among so many destinies*
> *Could be of moment, seeing so many there were,*
> *So mixed and all-inextricable.*

And in the evening Jeffers' metaphor of city inhabitants and habits becomes even less complimentary:

> *An endless aimless glitter: then indeed*
> *The fancy grew more strange, the crowd was merged*
> *Into one being unformable and huge,*
> *A monster of convulsive breath, a life*
> *Alien to man though all composed of men,*
> *Unfriendly, menacing, fearfully alive.*

. . . . . .

> ...*Lindsay groaned*
> *To be back yonder where the rivers run,*
> *And men are few,—thence individual souls,*
> *And often like the hills in dignity.*

When Lindsay awakens aboard ship and discovers that his two-year involuntary impressment ostensibly is legal and binding, we find Jeffers stating for the first time the fundamental Saxon pre-Christian advice of his ancestors:

> *Strength to desire the best, and strength to endure*
> *Albeit the worst: these both are in man's heart*
> *Borne:—happy is he who but the first of these*
> *Knows and requires: and yet not miserable,*
> *Not wholly miserable must he be named*
> *Whom the other and sadder power supports.*

The happiest individual is he who has the strength to direct his own affairs; but a man who is able courageously to endure the worst the world may hurl at him will not be discomfited altogether. The key words and ideas are, of course, strength and endurance. For the first time in verse Jeffers endorses these rock-solid, ancestral principles. Throughout his career, he will make continual reference to the ancient Saxon codes of conduct. His prosody is markedly influenced by the alliterative techniques of the Old English bards. Jeffers' graduate level study of the Old English masterpieces obviously had had a profound impact on his life and literary style. It is, therefore, astonishing that no thorough study has to date been made of this fundamental force in Robinson Jeffers' poetry.

After two years' absence, Lindsay, the persevering Saxon, returned to his beloved cabin in the Big Sur. Five years more and he was dead. Jeffers sums up Lindsay's life (and his poem) with the thought that neither usefulness nor importance to man is the criterion by which to judge a living creature. Another fundamental Jeffersian observation is also present: in the vast cosmos, man is nowhere near as important as he presumes himself to be. "What is humanity in this cosmos?" Jeffers will inquire in "Roan Stallion". What *is* important for a human is not so much his interrelationship with his fellows but his outward-directed love of the splendors of the natural world around him:

> *I think his life was largely fortunate.*
> *Useless, you say? Man, what is man to judge*
> *Of use and disuse? Are the weeds that grow*
> *Deep in the dark abysms of the eyeless wave,*
> *Yielding the fish no pasture,—are the flowers*
> *No wildbird ever saw, so buried they are*
> *In deep green hollows of the ancient wood—*
> *Are therefore these unuseful?—Man to man*

Being helpful is of worth, yet man to man
Is not the whole—perhaps is the least part
Of the infinite interrelation of all being.
This man, [Lindsay] as others love a woman, he
His chosen valley. Look! For I believe
His love hath made it the more beautiful.

The conclusion of "The Mill Creek Farm" combines Jeffers' already characteristic distaste for cities with one of his first prophetic utterances. The dying old widow of the farm foresees a dim future for a nation which recklessly sends its strong young men to the city to earn their livelihoods in a characterless manner:

Queer that a man's four boys must die, and the land
Fall from their father's into a stranger's hand!
I thought of that when I visited you in town,
Katie, and saw the people run up and down,
Trotting the streets; and young fellows busy with work
Not fit for a man to put hand to: waiter and clerk,
Poolroom loafer and barroom lapper: I thought,
Will the blessed country end like me, be caught
At the break-up time, when the world turns upside down,
With her sons all gone and rotted away in town?
Not a man with strength to keep hold of the beautiful land,
And the stranger's hulls off-shore, and the stranger's hand
Reaching up to the mountains.
                              A damnable dream
To go to sleep with.

When one considers the urban difficulties confronting contemporary America and the omnipresent Russian "fishing fleets" only a few miles westward from the Monterey Peninsula, Jeffers' predictions seem nervously appropriate.

The brief narrative poem "The Belled Doe" concludes with additional advice from Jeffers to the chiefs of men:

> *...but yet,*
> *Brief rulers, I would have you not forget*
> *The old dignity of him that drives the plow*
> *Through crumbling furrows deep, when morning's brow*
> *Flames in the orient world; and him that broods*
> *Memory of an old love under simple woods.*

Already in *Californians* the poet is devoutly concerned with the permanent and enduring occupations of men. These pursuits have an "old dignity" which the newer citified occupations lack.

"A Westward Beach" unequivocally states—for the first time—Jeffers' preference for cliffs, pines, waves, and birds rather than "human chatter":

> *How do I love these voices more,*
> *These cries remote, inhuman,*
> *These echoes of the lonely shore,*
> *Than words of man and woman?*

But feeling a tug of humanity, Jeffers realizes that man, undesirable though he may be, cannot entirely be ignored:

> *Alas, it is not well with me:—*
> *Can man wash off humanity*
> *And wed the unmarriageable sea?*

The Robinson Jeffers of *Californians* cannot yet state that he is "quits with the people." Instead, "A Westward Beach" concludes with a romantic appeal for his brethren to follow the poet's lead and unshackle themselves from their impure urbanized existences:

> *O men, my brothers! even you*
> *She [nature] would accept, unfetter.*

Never again would Jeffers refer in verse to men as his "brothers." From *Tamar* forward, he would realize that such appeals are only shallowly rhetorical. The pleading tones of "A Westward Beach" would later coalesce to become more somber predictions and warnings for the human race.

This mood of increasing pessimism in regard to the human race and its "accomplishments" already is in evidence in one of the final-poems of *Californians*, "Dream of the Future (To U. J.)". The poem is dedicated to his wife Una and optimistically predicts interstellar human colonization. But the poem also reflects Jeffers' sense of foreboding regarding the inevitable human domination of the biosphere. Jeffers requests the "men of the future" to spare the trees of his beloved region. Decades later, he would more pessimistically (and realistically, as it turned out) write: "Fire and the axe are devils." Regarding the human-dominated future Jeffers states:

> *I am ill content, I fear the too-greatness of man.*
> *Not uncorrupted the conqueror. Much is lost*
> *When the tame horse runs to the bridle, or the maid to the kiss.*

"Ode on Human Destinies", the final poem of *Californians*, has man locked into his fate and future:

> *Nothing of man's is strange to man:*
> *Who of old the course began*
> *Runs the course: he finishes.*
> . . . . . .
> *Man will change not, though all Gods*
> *Utterly change.*

Jeffers predicts eventual extinction for man:

> *Death, O Man, will reap at last*
> *All the heritage thou hast.*

Later in "Ode on Human Destinies" Robinson Jeffers plainly repeats the inevitability of man's demise:

> *...death will lay*
> *A finger on the race of man.*

The rôle that man is to play in the universe is fixed in advance:

> *Let [man] neither tremble, neither falter*
> *In the course he cannot alter;*
> *Each walks a way long chosen, long before;*
> *That path as well as this*
> *In surest guidance is;*
> *Fate, that alone is God, can change no more*
> *Than the strong traveller may control*
> *His necessary courses toward the timeless goal.*

Man's consolation in such a cosmos is not a false and fleeting feeling of superiority, but the deep repose of knowing that he is a minute but integral part of the great design:

> *...what he [man] wills*
> *Is part and substance of the immense design:*
> *He is beautiful and great,*
> *Being work and will, being child and slave, of constant Fate.*

The Early Years: Man
A Summary

It comes as no surprise that references to man in Jeffers' early works are far less numerous than his more frequent references to God. His inclination, upbringing and schooling, after all, were more theological than social in nature. Robinson Jeffers' background, by no means limited or limiting, enabled him to take the long dispassionate view of mankind so necessary in a major poet's early years. As a young man, Jeffers traveled widely in Europe, spending his boyhood years in private Swiss schools. During this time John Robinson Jeffers must have been exposed to a broad spectrum of human beings. He returned to the United States to attend a college and two universities, all three of which enjoyed a high scholastic reputation and in which Jeffers excelled as a student.

Robinson Jeffers inherited his father's dislike for unnecessary socializing; the young poet made few but lasting friendships. Jeffers, however, gladly obliged when the opportunity arose to have a few of his exploratory poems printed. College periodicals apparently were pleased to feature his verses. The publishing of *Flagons and Apples*, Robinson Jeffers' first book, was a largely self-indulgent venture. The young and love-stricken poet had as yet no comprehensive world view to set down, only a vague notion to be published for once in his life, somewhere. Under the circumstances, it is unrealistic to expect in these early verses a grand overview of the human condition.

And yet, some early evidence of Jeffers' world-view does crop up in his juvenilia. The virtues and values of solitude are present in "The Condor". Elements of Jeffers' admiration for courage are to be found in "The Wild Hunt". There are also intimations of his somber warnings to a self-satisfied human race as, for example, in "Man's Pride". Not until the publication of *Californians*, however, do we have evidence of Jeffers being forced by his surroundings categorically to assess other human beings. Previously, the poet had been able to relocate when the human scene had become for him uninviting. Faced with family responsibilities and having found his "inevitable place" in Carmel, Jeffers was forced to take a stand overagainst the encroaching human race. With his free sense of movement restricted by this new situation, Jeffers took to writing about his fellow man in the abstract and dignified mode of narrative poetry. Well over half the *Californians* volume is devoted to narrative poems which feature a personally detached view of Jeffers' contemporaries.

Besides these narratives, Jeffers designates a second poetic form found in *Californians* as "descriptive songs". These poems generally register a personal reaction to the natural phenomena of his new-found region. They are the forerunners of the lyrics which tail-ended his many volumes of verse—just as the briefer narrative poems of *Californians* foreshadow the lengthy "stories" of Jeffers' mature work.

In *Californians* one senses a strain in Jeffers' choice of poetic genre. Should he write of his intensely personal relations to the natural splendors around him and end up appealing to the limited audience who had also explored and similarly appreciated these natural wonders? This was in part the experience of George Sterling, the California poet who was Carmel's chief singer before Jeffers' arrival in 1914. Or should Jeffers write poetic narratives of present day life and affairs, gain an audience now and ultimately lose it as times changed? This later course was, no doubt, the less desirable to Robinson Jeffers who already preferred things natural to things human.

This tension in *Californians* is not resolved, for the book includes poetic narratives, personalized odes, and verse of an intimate and biographical nature. How *was* Jeffers to write of human beings when creeks and canyons, stars and the sea were really his overpowering concerns? It was a dilemma which only became evident in *Californians*. Contemporary, individual man, present and drawn from life, working in the enduring occupations *could* somehow be universalized and distilled so that stories written about such people would have more than local interest value. The narrative poems of *Californians* often deal with just such people, abstracted, isolated, fiercely defiant of urbanized society—and highly representative of what Jeffers felt was the best way for a human being to live on this planet. Quite often the values of the characters in *Californians* are the thinly disguised values of their creator.

What human values does Robinson Jeffers endorse in *Californians?* Jeffers opts for an uncluttered, uncrowded society, abundant open space, a strenuous but rewarding life, and—by implication—responsible individual liberty. Already he roundly rejects city living as unreal and depersonalizing. He laments the exploitation of nature, showing in "Ruth Alison" the tragic ends of those who do seek to plunder the land and its resources. Jeffers spurns the soft utopia of socialism while admitting to its glittering appeal and nefarious, inevitable growth.

Thus stated, Robinson Jeffers' limited prescription for society appears bucolically reactionary, but, beyond the romanticization of rural California life, he provides a wider-ranging vision of the human future. Nowhere in *Californians* does Jeffers recommend the Spartan country life for all human beings. He seems resigned—prepared even—to accept the changes and confusion the future must bring. *Californians* foresees a radically altered future—including space travel; he even predicts the human harnessing of the energy of the solar system. As a chilling, cautionary note, he also writes of the eventual extinction of the human race. This side of such a fate, Jeffers would have man realize (as he writes in "Dream of the Future") that human beings are only one small facet to a wondrously intact universe, a message the poet will incubate for eight crucible years until its full effulgence in *Tamar.*

"...this little house here

You have built over the ocean with your own hands

Beside the standing [sea-] boulders..."

—"Apology for Bad Dreams"
and
"But I Am Growing Old and Indolent"

Tor House from the North, circa 1940

CHAPTER TWO
The Splendor of Inhuman Things

Nobody Knows My Love The Falcon

The Middle Years: God
(1924 - 1940)

The advertisement in the book section of *The York Times* Sunday edition promised quality printing of author's manuscripts. The reader of the ad in Carmel was Robinson Jeffers. The time was early 1924. Nothing was promised about publishing.

After the mild disappointment of *Californians,* Robinson Jeffers eagerly set about the concerns of being father and homeowner. As Tor House gradually became furnished, Una, who had solicitously noted her husband's new-found interest in stonemasonry, cast about for another project in stone for her husband's hands. They both agreed upon a tower by the sea, something perhaps to remind them of the ancient Irish round towers. Jeffers spent four years at the task, rolling unassisted the granite boulders for the tower from the beach, then setting them in place with the aid of his crude winch. Many of the thoughts of those four laborious years were infused into a group of poems which Jeffers—this time in vain—tried to have published. Macmillan must have refused this batch, and other rejection slips found their way to the new stone house on Scenic Road, Carmel.

But this time the writer of the verses was convinced as to their quality, originality, and substance. Disillusioned with publishers, Jeffers resorted to what he had done in the past; he wrote to Peter G. Boyle (whose ad it was in *The New York Times*) as he had contacted the Grafton Publishing Company of Los Angeles in 1912. Boyle, highly enthusiastic upon reading the manuscript sent him, suggested a printing of 1,000 copies. His past experience in mind, Jeffers (who would be paying for the printing) settled for 500.

Though not a publisher, Boyle did his best to interest others in a work of which he personally thought highly. No one else, however, seemed interested. The newly completed attic on Scenic Road soon became the grand repository of a coffin-sized case of books (recently shipped from New York) by Robinson Jeffers, all of them entitled *Tamar and Other Poems*. But, three's the charm, and James Rorty took several copies East with him—to the right places it turned out—and soon Jeffers was being dubbed the poetic discovery of the decade. The case in the attic was, in turn, rapidly emptied of its contents. Returned to New York, the city of its birth, the edition of *Tamar* soon sold out. Boyle—generous as before—suggested Jeffers place the manuscript and whatever other verse he had written in the interim with a more established publisher. A leading *avant garde* publisher, Boni & Liveright of New York, eagerly agreed to a reissue of *Tamar*.

The middle of the Twenties, 1925, saw two new works offered under the Boni & Liveright imprint: Theodore Dreiser's monumental *An American Tragedy*, and the sensational *Roan Stallion, Tamar and Other Poems* by a new poet scarcely anyone knew, Robinson Jeffers of Carmel.   The age of bath-tub gin and Paul Whiteman soaked up the twelve reprintings of the Jeffers' book, four of which were completed in the first year of the serendipitous volume which reprinted all of the contents of *Tamar* plus nineteen new poems.

Theologically, there was much which was puzzling to the supposedly unshockable mid-20's readers of *Roan Stallion*. What to do with the commercial-like message which broke into the very midst of the "Roan Stallion" narrative?:

> *... not in a man's shape*
> *He approves the praise, he [God] that walks lightning-naked on the*
> *   Pacific, that laces the suns with planets,*
> *The heart of the atom with electrons: what is humanity in this*
> *   cosmos? For him, the last*
> *Least taint of a trace in the dregs of the solution; for itself*
> *   the mould to break away from, the coal*
> *To break into fire, the atom to be split.*

Robinson Jeffers of course was saying something he had said in *Californians*—but this time with genuine authority, power, and conviction. The God of the *Roan Stallion* book was no insubstantial figment of the hyper-imaginative poetic mind. Jeffers' vision of God in *Roan Stallion* was titanically energetic and vast, two of the qualities of the poems themselves. In retrospect, we can postulate that the quality of Jeffers' vigorous new poetic efforts may have stemmed directly from mystical encounter with that deity some time prior to the penning of *Tamar*.

The long narrative poems lie outside the scope of this book, but one aspect of Jeffers' concept of God is prominent in "Roan Stallion": the deity of the poem is lord of the universe, a universe which significantly includes the newly discovered scientific principles of the day. The shorter poems of the volume are also often unabashedly theological. "Gale in April", for example, contends that the beauty of the world goes on quite independently of a man's or even of man's existence:

> *O beauty of things go on, go on, O torture*
> *Of intense joy I have lasted out my time, I have thanked God*
> *and finished ....*

One of the early poems Jeffers saw fit to include in *Tamar* of 1924 was the frequently anthologized sonnet "To His Father". Again he serves notice of his rejection of Christianity:

Christ was your lord and captain all your life,
He fails the world but you he did not fail,
. . . . . .

I Father having followed other guides
And oftener to my hurt no leader at all ....

Here Jeffers records his respect for Christ as his father's inspiration, but Jeffers himself cannot accept his father's "captain." The last two lines quoted from "To His Father" indicate that the poem was written at an early date, probably shortly after the publication of *Californians* (since it was not included there)—or perhaps upon the death of his father—at a time when Jeffers was following other misleading "captains," not as yet having encountered the Presence so pervasive in poems of the *Tamar* volume.

There is, however, evidence even in *Tamar* that Jeffers was still considering and eliminating the major religions of the world. The finest poem on a purely theological topic in *Tamar* is "Point Pinos and Point Lobos". Together, these two magnificent landmarks, to the north and south respectively, framed Jeffers' physical world. Spread between them were the emerald waters of Carmel Bay. The Spaniards had been the name-givers: Point Pinos for the tortured grove of Monterey pines which grew there, and Point Lobos for the "wolves"—sea-lions actually—which frequented the rocky outcroppings of the uniquely beautiful Point Lobos peninsula. Jeffers ascribes high significance to these two promontories. The poem exists in three sections: section one focuses on Point Pinos and is only slightly longer than the second section on Point Lobos. The third division of the poem is a succinct estimation of the two major religions of the world, Christianity and Buddhism.

Point Pinos with its twisted contortions of trees and its tenebrous graveyard impressed Jeffers as a likely location for a second appearance of Christ in the western

world. Jeffers imagines Christ wandering the forest and sorrowfully asks

Which tortured trunk will you choose, Lord, to be hewn to a cross?

In contrast to the northern and European appearance of Point Pinos, Point Lobos is decidedly eastern and Oriental in aspect. In his 1952 prose selection from *The Glory of Our West*, Robinson Jeffers records his first impressions of Point Lobos:

> [*The Monterey cypress*] *look immensely old, desolate and enduring, like the ancient trees that Chinese artists love.*

> *And the granite cliffs that they grow on are like the rocks in a Chinese landscape-painting. That was my impression of Point Lobos when I first saw it—that it was Oriental, it did not belong to this country, but must have drifted, like a ship across the Pacific, from the headlands of Asia.*

Absorbed with the Eastern atmosphere of Point Lobos, Jeffers contemplates the Buddha, "Serenely smiling /Face of the godlike man made God . . . ."

Jeffers' views on Christianity and Buddhism are forthrightly recorded in "Point Pinos and Point Lobos", views which would not alter substantially in future poems. At the outset, Jeffers clarifies his personal position regarding the two religions—he writes out of respect for Christ and Buddha. Jeffers does not sneer at Christ:

> *I am not among the mockers Master, I am one of your lovers ….*

As well, Jeffers expresses his admiration for Buddha's ability to transcend the agonies of existence, to achieve Buddhahood in Nirvana:

> *He* [*Buddha*] *reunited with the passionless sky, not again to suffer The shame of the low female gate, freed, never to be born again ….*

Buddha has virtuously escaped from existence by virtue of his own Eight-fold Path.

After assiduously establishing his respect for the two great religious leaders, Jeffers presents his fundamental objection to both religions: he singles out the dichotomy of good and evil which the two religions insist upon and says it is genuinely insignificant when compared to the actual beauties and realities of the universe.

Robinson Jeffers had exhibited some monistic tendencies in *Californians.* In *Tamar* monism emerges as Jeffers' fundamental religious concept. Repeatedly in "Point Pinos and Point Lobos" Jeffers refers to "peace" by which he means a return to the one creative source of the universe. In the midst of section one of the poem, Jeffers records his adoration for this source or fountain of the universe; the hymn is a harbinger of Jeffers' intensely monistic poem "Night" which also made its first appearance in the *Roan Stallion* volume. In the following passage from "Point Pinos and Point Lobos" Jeffers attempts to define the primal monistic source of the beauties of the universe:

> *... O shining of night, O eloquence of si-*
> *lence, the mother of the stars, the beauty beyond beauty,*
> *The sea that the stars and the sea and the mountain bones*
> *of the earth and men's souls are the foam on, the opening*
> *Of the womb of that ocean.*

In Jeffers' estimation, Christ, who had known the harmonic splendors of the preexistent monistic state, forsook his abode of peace in order to have pity (like Buddha) on the human world. Pity, though, is part of dualism; its opposite is selfish cruelty. By focusing on pity and love in the world, the great mind of Christ concentrated on a dualistic half-issue and the magnificence of the primal origin of the universe was masked. Of Christ:

> *You have known this, you have known peace, and forsaken*
> *Peace for pity, you have known the beauty beyond beauty*
> *And the other shore of God. You will never again know them,*
> *Except he slay you, the spirit at last, as more than once*
> *The body, and root out love.*

In a far future world culminating with human dominance over the solar system, Jeffers imagines the spirit of Christ (and the human race captivated by it) suddenly made aware—by God—of the more mature, original deity of the cosmos:

> *O a last time in the last wrench of man made godlike*
> *Shall God not arise, bitterly, the power behind power, the last star*
> *That the stars hide, rise and reveal himself in anger—*
> *Christ, in that moment when the hard loins of your ancient*
> *Love and unconquerable will crack to lift up humanity*
> *The last step heavenward—rise and slay, and you and our children*
> *Suddenly stumble on peace?*

Jeffers believes that a dualistic religion of good and evil is *a priori* suspicious of matter. The monist, on the other hand, sees matter as enduring and renewable. Jeffers castigates Christ's inability to have faith in a physical world which, in its permanence, turns like a great wheel, recombining eternally. Ultimately, a recurrence of a world identical to ours is theoretically feasible:

> *Unhappy brother [Christ]*
> *That high imagination mating mine*
> *Has gazed deeper than graves: is it unendurable*
> *To know that the huge season and wheel of things*
> *Turns on itself forever, the new stars pass*
> *And the old return and find out their places,*
> *And these gray dead [the people buried in the Point Pinos cemetery]*
> > *infallibly shall arise*
> *In the very flesh ....*

Jeffers' position then is that in the midst of seeming change, the universe is actually steady, constant and fixed on its course when viewed *sub speciē Jeffersiensis aeternitatis.* Jeffers feels that the teachings of Christ are a step on the way of the moral exploration of the universe. As such, the teachings are valuable, but are not the ultimate source of truth.

The second section of "Point Pinos and Point Lobos" is devoted to Buddha. Of Point Lobos:

> *...there is no place*
> *Taken like this out of deep Asia for a marriage-token, this planted*
> *Asiaward over the west water.*

Point Lobos forms a physical link for Jeffers between east and west. The foreign-ness of Point Lobos prompts the poet to consider the religion Buddha founded, but here, too, Jeffers expresses his reservations concerning Buddha's dualistic assessment of the human world. Buddha strove to rid himself and his followers of "the web of human passions / As a yellow lion the antelope-hunter's net ...." But Jeffers wonders whether Buddha's escape *was* actually final:

> *... is it freedom, smile of Buddha,*
> *surely freedom? For someone*
> *Whispered in my ear when I was very young, some serpent*
> *whispered*
> *That what has gone returns; what has been, is; what will*
> *be, was; the future*
> *Is a farther past; our times he said fractions of arcs of the*
> *great circle;*
> *And the wheel turns, nothing shall stop it or destroy it,*
> *we are bound on the wheel,*
> *We and the stars and seas, the mountains and the Buddha.*
> *Weary tidings*
> *To cross the weary, bitter to bitter men: life's conqueror*
> *will not fear*
> *Life; and to meditate again under the sacred tree, and again*
> *Vanquish desire will be no evil.*

To Robinson Jeffers, Fate (as in *Californians*) is a stronger and more enduring aspect of God than is a dualistic attempt to escape from desire and matter by dividing the world into the forces of good and evil. Buddha himself would not be harmed if he should return to his earthly state to meditate once again under the Boh tree.

The third division of "Point Pinos and Point Lobos" includes Jeffers' summarization of the weaknesses of Christianity and Buddhism. Jeffers views Christ and Buddha as rebellious against the instinctive monistic God of the universe:

> *O why were you rebellious, teachers*
> *of men, against the instinctive God,*
> *One [Christ] striving to overthrow his ordinances through love and*
> *the other [Buddha] crafty-eyed to escape them*
> *Through patient wisdom: though you are wiser than all men*
> *you are foolisher than the running grass,*
> *That fades in season and springs up in season, praising whom you blame.*

Jeffers ends the poem (as he had concluded *Californians*) by reiterating his conviction that the universe is underpinned by one vital force and that beauty is "the essence and the end of God":

> *For the essence and the end*
> *Of his [God's] labor is beauty, for goodness and evil are two things*
> *and still variant, but the quality of life as of death and of light*
> *As of darkness is one, one beauty, the rhythm of that Wheel,*
> *and who can behold it is happy and will praise it to the people.*

Jeffers does not deny the existence of good and evil in the world; he recognizes them as significant moral forces, but faults Christianity and Buddhism for seizing one aspect of the moral and physical universe as the paramount theological issue.

"Point Pinos and Point Lobos" is Robinson Jeffers' most important short poem on world religions; most important, that is, until Jeffers published "Theory of Truth", the final poem in his 1938 *The Selected Poetry of Robinson Jeffers*. "Point Pinos and Point Lobos" presents the poet's thoughtful rejection of Christianity and Buddhism, Jeffers preferring his own monistic naturalism as a less distorted vision of the universe. Of the two religions considered in "Point Pinos and Point Lobos", Jeffers seems to prefer Christianity while sincerely indicating his respect for the persons and thoughts of Christ and Buddha. When, in future years, Robinson Jeffers will write of world religions, he will frequently refer to Christianity, scarcely mentioning other major religions.

The poem following "Point Pinos and Point Lobos" is "Not Our Good Luck". In it Jeffers states his conviction that God is eternally present in the world for all to see and observe. There is no excuse for following false religions—even if one should be unfortunate enough to live in an environment defiled by man such as

> *the mean mud tenements and huddle of the filth of Babylon ....*

The God of the universe does not hide himself from men:

> *God who walks lightning-naked on the Pacific has never been hidden from any*
> *Puddle or hillock of the earth behind us.*

Jeffers is echoing St. Paul who wrote in Romans 1:20-21:

> *For the invisible things of him from the creation of the*
> *world are clearly seen, being understood by the things*
> *that are made, even his eternal power and Godhead; so that*
> *they are without excuse: Because that, when they knew God,*
> *they glorified him not as God ....*

For emphasis, Jeffers repeats his message toward the end of "Not Our Good Luck":

> *But here is the marvel, he [God] is nowhere not present, his beauty,*
> > *it is burning in the midland villages*
> *And tortures men's eyes in the alleys of cities.*

Another poem of early composition Jeffers included in *Tamar* was "The Truce and the Peace (November, 1918)". In this sequence of eleven sonnets he considers the shaky peace which concluded the First World War; the poet has his suspicions as to the permanence of the war's settlement, but offers his own deeper-reaching conception of peace to the world. Obsession with human problems cannot bring the individual true peace. The First World War never troubled God who did not even bother to waken to consider it. The same kind of untroubled peace is available to those who know such a God:

11

> *Peace to the world in time or in a year,*
> *But always all our lives this peace was ours.*
> *Peace is not hard to have, it lies more near*
> *Than breathing to the breast. When brigand powers*
> *Of anger or pain or the sick dream of sin*
> *Break our soul's house outside the ruins we weep.*
> *We look through the breached wall, why there within*
> *All the red while our peace was lying asleep.*
> *Smiling in dreams while the broad knives drank blood,*
> *The robbers triumphed, the roof burned overhead,*
> *The eternal living and untroubled God*
> *Lying asleep upon a lily bed.*
> *Men screamed, the bugles screamed, walls broke in the air,*
> *We never knew till then that He was there.*

Of the nineteen poems added to the contents of *Tamar* to create the *Roan Stallion, Tamar* volume, five short poems have theological significance: 'Fog", "Phenomena", "Shine, Perishing Republic", "The Treasure", and "The Torch-bearers' Race". These five poems further elaborate the theological positions of *Tamar*.

"Fog" is a supplementary statement of Jeffers' monism. Jeffers credits the great religious and military leaders of western mankind with loving and serving ultimately the "one God". An innate passion for monism is also a quality of the creatures of nature, notably the gulls, crying out in the dense fog. Jeffers begins by addressing the gulls:

> *You dream,*
> *wild criers,*
> *The peace that all life*
> *Dreams gluttonously, the infinite self has eaten*
> *Environment, and lives*
> *Alone, unencroached on, perfectly gorged, one God.*
> *Caesar and Napoleon*
> *Visibly acting their dreams of that solitude, Christ and Gautama,*
> *Being God, devouring*
> *The world with atonement for God's sake ... ah sacred hungers,*
> *The conqueror's, the prophet's,*
> *The lover's, the hunger of the sea-beaks, slaves of the last peace,*
> *Worshippers of oneness.*

The conqueror, the prophet, the lover, and the natural birds all end up glorifying the "one God".

"Phenomena" is a serene and unified statement of the inter-relation of all the phenomena of the world. Every thing and each being in the poem as in the world fit harmoniously into the Whole. From "the navy's new-bought Zeppelin" to the sea birds, all are included within "the great frame". Although the poem appears merely to be a list of the ordinarily incongruous phenomena of a world now at peace, the poem is so cohesively constructed that it is difficult to dissect at any of the thirteen semi-colon breaks. The tightly-woven unity of the poem is patent.

PHENOMENA

Great-enough both accepts and subdues; the great frame takes all creatures;
From the greatness of their element they all take beauty.
Gulls; and the dingy freightship lurching south in the eye of a rain-wind;
The air-plane dipping over the hill; hawks hovering
The white grass of the headland; cormorants roosting upon the guano-
Whitened skerries; pelicans awind; sea-slime
Shining at night in the wave-stir like drowned men's lanterns; smugglers signaling
A cargo to land; or the old Point Pinos lighthouse
Lawfully winking over dark water; the flight of the twilight herons,
Lonely wings and a cry; or with motor-vibrations
That hum in the rock like a new storm-tone of the ocean's to turn eyes westward
The navy's new-bought Zeppelin going by in the twilight,
Far out seaward; relative only to the evening star and the ocean
It slides into a cloud over Point Lobos.

The final two lines of "Shine, Perishing Republic" underscore Jeffers' opinion that Christ, by not being "moderate as in love of man", fell into the fatal trap of embracing a dualism of good and evil:

There is the trap that catches noblest spirits, that caught—
they say—God, when he walked on earth.

Jeffers advises his sons to be more discreetly intelligent in their sympathies for humanity. Untoward love of man compromises one into an unhappy dualistic position either of loving or hating mankind.

"The Treasure" places human existence in perspective. Given the monistic view that the universe is eternally an outflowing of the process of God, the fleeting existence of the earth, a star, or a human being is important only as partial definition to "the ages of the / gulf before birth, and the gulf / After death". The purpose of being is to delineate not-being; however, "nothing / lives long". The peace of re-entering the non-existent state is the solace for the exigencies and vagaries of being. Jeffers concludes "The Treasure":

> I fancy
> That silence is the thing, this noise [existence] a found word for it;
> interjection, a jump of the breath at the silence;
> Stars burn, grass grows, men breathe: as a man finding
> treasure says "Ah!" but the treasure's the essence;
> Before the man spoke it was there, and after he has spoken
> he gathers it, inexhaustible treasure.

"The Torch-Bearers' Race" (as in "Roan Stallion") discloses that the God of the universe is not anthropomorphic:

> ... O flame, O beauty and shower of beauty,
> There is yet one ocean and then no more, God whom you [humanity]
> shine to walks there naked, on the final Pacific,
> Not in a man's form.

The westward migrations of man (''the torch-bearers' race'', to use Jeffers' terminology) and all of man's existence on the planet ''shine to'' the glory of God.

Roan Stallion, Tamar and Other Poems of 1925 reveals for the first time the active splendor and power of Jeffers' deity. Nearly all the poems of the volume have firm theological beliefs as their touchstone. Jeffers' religious convictions are indisputably basic to understanding his poetry and ideology. *Roan Stallion* is the first of many volumes which provide a revealing glimpse of Jeffers' mature conception of God.

Robinson Jeffers' next volume of poetry, *The Women at Point Sur*, was published in 1927. It is Jeffers' third major work, but this time three was not the charm, for, although the book was twice reprinted, few readers indeed understood Jeffers' intentions. Jeffers' disappointment was deep and lasting; never again did he attempt so ambitious a lengthy narrative poem with no short lyrics trailing the work. Still, ''The Women at Point Sur'' remains Jeffers' finest long narrative on a theological theme—if not his finest poem outright. The work deserves a full theological study of its own.

On August 18th, 1927, a month and a half after the appearance of his *The Women at Point Sur*, Robinson Jeffers' shorter poems written after *Roan Stallion* appeared in a unique format. That August, Harcourt, Brace and Company issued an auto-anthology assembled by Louis Untermeyer entitled *American Poetry 1927 A Miscellany* in which the various contributors selected their own previously unpublished verse. One of the stipulations was that "Each contributor is to have twenty pages completely at his disposal." Robinson Jeffers submitted fifteen short poems which took up twenty-four pages. Never again would Jeffers' short poems appear in any such quantity under another publisher's imprint. Perhaps his bitter experience with the reception of the single long narrative "The Women at Point Sur" in one volume convinced the poet to include in the future some of his brief works with the longer poetic narratives.

The poems presented for the first time in *American Poetry 1927 A Miscellany* were reprinted in 1935 when Random House devoted a volume of its new Modern Library editions to the works of Robinson Jeffers, the first modern poet to be included in the series. All fifteen of the *Miscellany* poems were reprinted in the 1935 Modern Library edition of *Roan Stallion, Tamar and Other Poems* which remained in print until a few years after 1953 when its publishers unfortunately let the helpful little volume drop out of print.

The *Miscellany* poems, as one might expect, are closest in tone and topic to those short poems which helped fill out *Roan Stallion, Tamar* of 1925, a book published only twenty-one months before. The one difference between the poems of the 1925 volume and those included in the *Miscellany* is that the later verses tend to be more topical in nature, the "Noon" poem already cited a ready example of this specificity of reference. Some of Jeffers' early sonnets are gathered from their original appearances in Monterey Peninsula newspapers—the sonnet "Compensation", for example. Later sonnets are also featured, but the outstanding poem in the *Miscellany* is Jeffers' *ars poetica*, "Apology for Bad Dreams". It is divided into four sections, the longest and most intricate of the *Miscellany* poems.

Section two of "Apology for Bad Dreams" introduces a new theological concept which gives justification for creating the long tragic verse narratives for which Jeffers had become renowned. Jeffers' conviction is that beautiful, natural places evoke from men the only human response—profound personal tragedy—which could begin to equal the natural grandeur. If God presents magnificence, then he requires the best "shining" man can muster, tragedy.

> This coast crying out for tragedy like all beautiful places:
>   and like the passionate spirit of humanity
> Pain for its bread: God's, many victims, the painful deaths,
>   the horrible transfigurements: I said in my heart,
> "Better invent than suffer: imagine victims
> Lest your own flesh be chosen the agonist, or you
> Martyr some creature to the beauty of the place."

Why does Jeffers write tragic verse? Out of necessity:

>   And I said,
> "Burn sacrifices once a year to magic
> Horror away from the house, this little house here
> You have built over the ocean with your own hands
> Beside the standing boulders: for what are we,
> The beast that walks upright, with speaking lips
> And little hair, to think we should always be fed,
> Sheltered, intact, and self-controlled? We sooner more liable
> Than the other animals. Pain and terror, the insanities of
>   desire; not accidents but essential,
> And crowd up from the core:" I imagined victims for those
>   wolves, I made them phantoms to follow,
> They have hunted the phantoms

and missed the house. It
is not good to forget over what gulfs the spirit
Of the beauty of humanity, the petal of a lost flower blown
seaward by the night-wind, floats to its quietness.

Jeffers assumed the responsibilities of a poet in a solemn and serious manner: "I can tell lies in prose." Time and again, Jeffers even in his verse, will comment on his tragic characters (chiefly Tamar Cauldwell, but others, too) in a fashion which leaves no doubt as to Jeffers' thoughts and feelings for them: the creatures are well-nigh real to Jeffers; he pities their suffering; he recalls their agonies, all in an effort to trick the "wolves" of calamity and misfortune from assaulting "this little house here". The motives are perhaps more profound than the characters; certainly they are pre-Christian in make up. Possibly, Jeffers writes his tragic verse narratives in part out of compulsion to fend off the evil which began in his mind as a result of his premarital relationship with Una. Strangely haunted by such an apprehension, the poet writes his "stories" in an effort—successful until 1950 when Una died—to divert the tragedy "all beautiful places" require.

Is Jeffers doing here what he—as a monist—promised not to do—that is, become intoxicated with a dualistic world of good and evil? The poet might explain his position thus: although he was trained as a Christian to perceive good and evil in things, and, although he experienced feelings of guilt (evil) over his early relationship with the already married Una, Jeffers' subsequent compulsion to write "stories" featuring tragic victims is an attempt to avert the coming of the opposite of his happy life. As the old German proverb has it, *Nach viele Lachenden kommt viele Sorgenden,* "After much laughing comes much sorrowing." The balanced monistic God of the universe would sometime seek to counterpoise the immoderate personal happiness which Jeffers enjoyed. To forestall such an eventuality, Jeffers writes his stories of "imagined victims".

For Jeffers, writing the tragic narratives was more than a casual occupation; it was essential to his own personal well-being. The poet painfully recognized the transience of human life and human happiness. In an effort to counter the impersonal balancing forces of God, Jeffers wrote—and built—to last. The four-foot thick walls of his Hawk Tower, built solely by the poet, stand today as mute testimony to Jeffers' temperamental necessity to meet time and transience with implacable will. Such a display of human determination Jeffers sought, but did not find, in his contemporaneous world. Later in his travels to Ireland he did find and deeply admire it in the form of the ancient stone monuments of that isle.

Yet Robinson Jeffers claims in the final lines of "Apology for Bad Dreams" not to know why God loves the ebb and flow, the creation and destruction of the worlds he builds. This is merely the way the world is. It requires more love than explanation. Who, contends Jeffers, can know the mind of God himself?

> *I have seen these ways of God: I know of no reason*
> *For fire and change and torture and the old returnings.*
> *He being sufficient might be still. I think they admit no*
> *reason; they are the ways of my love.*
> *Unmeasured power, incredible passion, enormous craft: no*
> *thought apparent but burns darkly*
> *Smothered with its own smoke in the human brain-vault:*
> *no thought outside: a certain measure in phenomena:*
> *The fountains of the boiling stars, the flowers on the fore-*
> *land, the ever-returning roses of dawn.*

God, who could be quiescent, chooses restlessness for himself in his creation. His reasons are his own. It is matter, not motives, which carry God's imprint for the human mind.

In the poems of the *Miscellany* Robinson Jeffers feels that love of God is more important to humanity than human self-love. People might mature sufficiently to realize that love for man at the expense of the adoration of God is infantile as Jeffers declares in his poem regarding thoughts of growing old, "Age in Prospect":

> *To look around and to love in his appearances,*
> *Though a little calmly, the universal God's*
> *Beauty is better I think than to lip eagerly*
> *The mother's breast or another woman's.*

Jeffers might well have written "To look *outward*", out of human self-centeredness to see God in what he had made, "his appearances".

"Pelicans" espouses another aspect of God as observed in the birds of his region. Four pelicans, awkward anachronisms of the air and all but clumsy, have flown over Tor House followed by "A lifting gale of sea-gulls," graceful as the pelicans are ungainly. The contrast stuck in Jeffers' mind and the poet concludes that God

> *The omnisecular spirit keeps the old with the new also.*
> *Nothing at all has suffered erasure.*
> *There is life not of our time. [The pelicans] He calls ungainly bodies*
> *As beautiful as the grace of horses.*
> *He is weary of nothing; he watches air-planes; he watches*
>   *pelicans.*

God neither rejects nor judges his creations. The ancient wings which "remember ... The dinosaur's day" are as welcome and proper to the air as the most recent flying contraption, a man-built air-plane. Everything proceeds from and returns to the one source.

"Credo", the fifteenth of the short poems in the *Miscellany*, considers Oriental pantheism and records Jeffers' own certitude of the reality of natural phenomena. Jeffers' Asiatic friend believes that the external world exists only because his mind makes it exist. Jeffers, an Occidental, believes rather the opposite. Reality comes not from the human mind which observes the world, but from the essence of matter itself. This frame of mind is a "harder mysticism", but one which Jeffers feels to be closer to God. The beauties of the world were present before the human mind could perceive them and will remain long after humans have vanished; a harder doctrine, but more realistic. Jeffers' own beliefs are codified in his

CREDO

My friend from Asia has powers and magic, he plucks a
        blue leaf from the young blue-gum
And gazing upon it, creates an ocean more real than the
        ocean, the salt, the actual
Appalling presence, the power of the waters.
He believes that nothing is real except as we make it. I
        humbler have found in my blood
Bred west of Caucasus a harder mysticism.
Multitude stands in my mind but I think that the ocean in
        the bone vault is only
The bone vault's ocean: Out there is the ocean's;
The water is the water, the cliff is the rock, come shocks and
        flashes of reality. The mind

> *Passes, the eye closes, the spirit is a passage;*
> *The beauty of things was born before eyes and sufficient to*
> *itself; the heart-breaking beauty*
> *Will remain when there is no heart to break for it.*

Jeffers' convictions, his credo, stipulate that reality is quite independent of man's ability to grasp it. The magnificence of "the beauty of things" goes well beyond man's meager and humble capability to appreciate what God has placed of himself in matter. Such beauty, which will survive us, is a major attribute of God.

The year after *The Women at Point Sur*, Horace Liveright released another volume of Jeffers' verse entitled *Cawdor and Other Poems*, 1928. This time the full-length narrative, "Cawdor", was followed by sixteen shorter poems. These lyrics reflect Jeffers' deepening pessimism on a variety of fronts. The joyous sense of proclaiming and praising God "to the people" present in *Roan Stallion, Tamar* is entirely absent in the short poems of *Cawdor*. No doubt Jeffers remembered the mixed reception of *The Women at Point Sur*. The optimistic excesses of everyday life in the Twenties prompted an equal and opposite reaction from the poet-builder of the Hawk Tower.

The most grim of the short poems of the *Cawdor* volume is "A Redeemer". On a hiking trip in the coast range hills Jeffers and his wife encounter "a redeemer" who had inflicted on his hands the signs of the "stigmata of crucifixion." The man explains:

> *"I pick them [the wounds] open. I made them long ago with a clean*
> *steel. It is only a little to pay—"*

The purpose of his wounds is to build up in the mind of God an antitoxin to counteract the frail happinesses of the human world which have multiplied into imbalance:

> *I am here on the mountain making*
> *Antitoxin for all the happy towns and farms, the lovely*
> *Blameless children, the terrible*
> *Arrogant cities.*

When Jeffers attempts to compare the man's wounds to those of Christ, the redeemer's reply is scathing:

> *He laughed angrily and frowned, stroking*
> *The fingers of one hand with the other. "Religion is the*
> *people's opium. Your little Jew-God?*
> *My pain," he said with pride, "is voluntary.*
> *They [the people] have done what never was done before. Not as a*
> *people takes a land to love it and be fed*
>
> . . . . . .
>
> *Oh, as a rich man eats a forest for profit and a field for*
> *vanity, so you came west and raped*
> *The continent and brushed its people to death. Without*
> *need ....*

The redeemer continues on in a haunting jeremiad against the excesses of human life in his time. "A Redeemer" reflects Jeffers' growing aversion for human disregard of what Jeffers feels to be divine. As well, "A Redeemer" castigates Christianity for its inability to redeem a society which "think[s] of nothing but happiness".

The site of the poem "Bixby's Landing" later became the locus of Jeffers' 1932 narrative "Thurso's Landing". Jeffers describes the beauties of the deserted lime-works at Bixby Creek and concludes by observing that "mother the wilderness" can return to repair the transient human despoilment of the earth with even greater beauty than before.

> *Men's failures are often as beautiful as men's triumphs,*
> *but your [nature's] returnings*
> *Are even more precious than your first presence.*

"Hurt Hawks" is perhaps Robinson Jeffers' most anthologized poem. Wildness is one of the theological and naturalistic qualities Jeffers accentuates in *Cawdor*, and in section one of "Hurt Hawks" Jeffers notes that his God is ultimately friend neither to the arrogant nor to the docile of the world:

> *The wild God of the world is sometimes merciful to those*
> *That ask mercy, not often to the arrogant.*
> *You do not know him, you communal people, or you have*
> *forgotten him;*
> *Intemperate and savage, the hawk remembers him;*
> *Beautiful and wild, the hawks, and men that are dying remember him.*

The final poem of *Cawdor*, "Meditation on Saviors", is also the most theological of the short poems of the volume. Jeffers' subject matter is the ancient human need for a savior. A savior, Jeffers opines, is easier to lean upon than truth or self-reliance. A caustic reference to institutionalized Christianity is combined with Jeffers' own suggestion for a truly efficacious savior:

> *The apes of Christ lift up their hands to praise love: but*
> *wisdom without love is the present savior,*
> *Power without hatred, mind like a many-bladed machine*
> *subduing the world with deep indifference.*
>
> *The apes of Christ itch for a sickness they have never*
> *known; words and the little envies will hardly*
> *Measure against that blinding fire behind the tragic eyes*
> *they have never dared to confront.*

"Deep indifference," the indifference of the monist who knows the world is on its fore-ordained, unalterable course. Praising love, one pole of a dualistic vision of the world, is inappropriate considering the "rottenness I smelt; / from the world...."

Jeffers, however, realizes that even humanity is needed to complete the cycle of the universe to be played out here on earth, and he does not want arbitrarily to be separated from such a drama:

> *Yet I am the one made pledges against the refuge con-*
> *tempt, that easily locks the world out of doors.*
> *This people as much as the sea-granite is part of the God*
> *from whom I desire not to be fugitive.*

Jeffers does not pity mankind; instead he realizes humanity's appropriate niche in the annals of the earth.

Fatalism re-emerges in the middle of "Meditation on Saviors". Wondering whether he could warn against the results of human folly, Jeffers realizes that anything he could say or write would already be part of the great plan:

> *The mountain ahead of the world is not forming but fixed.*
> *But the man's [a prophet's] words would be fixed also,*
> *Part of that mountain, under equal compulsion; under the*
> *same present compulsion in the iron consistency.*

Jeffers writes then, not out of an intent to save the people, but because his writing, too, is "part of that mountain". This understood, good and evil are truly perceivable only years later when they are inconsequential and past:

> *And nobody sees good or evil but out of a brain a*
> *hundred centuries quieted ....*

Do the people, in Jeffers' estimation, really need a redeemer, a savior then? Of course not, replies Jeffers, for they already have the most efficacious savior who ministers indifferently to all; they become part of God himself when their consciousness is dissolved in death:

> *And having touched a little of the beauty and seen a little*
> *of the beauty of things, [people] magically grow*
> *Across the funeral fire or hidden stench of burial*
> *themselves into the beauty they admired,*

> *Themselves into the God, themselves into the sacred*
> *steep unconsciousness they used to mimic*
> *Asleep between lamp's death and dawn, while the last*
> *drunkard stumbled homeward down the dark street.*

They are not to be pitied but very fortunate: they need no
savior, salvation comes and takes them by force,
It gathers them into the great kingdoms of dust and
stone, the blown storms, the stream's-end ocean.

Jeffers concludes *Cawdor* by touching on one of the major theological conceptions of future poems: love, when it is directed into a faith which is dualistic, is ultimately a self-seeking and self-adulatory activity. The adoration of a Christ or a Buddha (both of whom unnecessarily accentuated good and evil in the human world) is narcissistic:

Love, the mad wine of good and evil, the saint's and
murderer's, the mote in the eye that makes its object
Shine the sun black; the trap in which it is better to catch
the inhuman God than the hunter's own image.

When you love, Jeffers advises, turn your love outward away from humanity to the real "inhuman God". Wishing for himself to avoid wasting emotions on humanity, Robinson Jeffers writes in "The Bird with the Dark Plumes"

It is almost as foolish my poor falcon
To want hatred as to want love; and harder to win.

Jeffers proved to be his own best prophet. In future years he *would* win the hatred of those who disliked or misunderstood what Jeffers called his "truths".

As with "The Women at Point Sur", the two major narratives of Jeffers' 1929 volume, *Dear Judas and Other Poems,*—"Dear Judas" and "The Loving Shepherdess"—are of supreme importance for a complete understanding of Robinson Jeffers' theological *Weltanschauung.* These two poems also deserve a separate consideration as milestones of Jeffers' developing religious ideology. Both the poems develop the theme that excesses in love or compassion bring ruin to those who are imprudently enmeshed with humanity as is the case with both Judas and Clare Walker, the respective protagonists of the two poems.

The *Dear Judas* volume, with its two narrative poems of religious import, has but six short poems to end the work. Two of these shorter poems, "Birth-Dues" and "Hooded Night", are of theological interest. "Birth-Dues" echoes the thought of "Hurt Hawks" that the world's God is unreliable by human standards and inescapable:

> *The world's God is treacherous and full of unreason; a*
> *   torturer, but also*
> *The only foundation and the only fountain.*
> *Who fights him eats his own flesh and perishes of hunger;*
> *   who hides in the grave*
> *To escape him is dead; who enters the Indian*
> *Recession to escape him is dead; who falls in love with the*
> *   God is washed clean*
> *Of death desired and of death dreaded.*

Jeffers suggests that atheism, meditation techniques, and hopes of a final death and dissolution are all futile attempts to evade the God of the world. One must turn to and love the process that God has set in order, harmonize one's self to whatever manifestations the God may exhibit. This done, one need neither fear nor long for death. Death, the end of life, will come when it is ready and will be received in a neutral manner by he "who falls in love with the / God ...."

Such a person will view the universe and the human emotions from a neutral stance. Jeffers concludes "Birth-Dues" by supposing that even though he had clearly presented such a course of thought, scarcely anyone will have the "energy to hear effectively".

> *He has joy, but joy is a trick in the air; and pleasure, but*
> *   pleasure is contemptible;*
> *And peace; and is based on solider than pain.*
> *He has broken boundaries a little and that will estrange*
> *   him; he is monstrous, [to other people] but not*
> *To the measure of the God.... But I having told you—*
> *However I suppose that few in the world have energy to*
> *   hear effectively—*
> *Have paid my birth-dues; am quits with the people.*

"Hooded Night", the final poem of *Dear Judas*, is a reaffirmation of Jeffers' pantheistic faith in the forms of nature. Moved by the still pre-dawn darkness, the poet restates his faith in the "final unridiculous peace" which abides in the superb natural features of his land; the ancient granite rock, the permanent ocean, and the venerable cypresses of the Monterey peninsula. By comparison, the human world and its obsessions is "a spectral episode".

> *But here is the final unridiculous peace. Before the first man*
> *Here were the stones, the ocean, the cypresses,*
> *And the pallid region in the stone-rough dome of fog where the moon*
> *Falls on the west. Here is reality.*
> *The other is a spectral episode: after the inquisitive*

animal's [man's]
Amusements are quiet: the dark glory.

In 1932, in the throes of the Great Depression, Liveright issued its final book of Robinson Jeffers' verse, *Thurso's Landing and Other Poems*; shortly thereafter Jeffers' first major publisher became a casualty of hard times. The principal narrative of the volume, "Thurso's Landing", is followed by ten shorter poems. Jeffers' shorter narrative "Margrave" appears as the final poem of the book, an outstanding example of what the poet was able to achieve with a different class of poems, the poetic narrative of medium length.

The shorter poems of *Thurso's Landing* have little to do with Jeffers' theology. Only "The Bed by the Window", a powerfully prophetic ten-line poem which deals with the poet's chosen place of death, contains a God-related topic. Jeffers expresses his belief that God provides each life on the earth with sufficient time and opportunity to complete its predestined course:

> *We are safe to finish what we have to finish;*
> *And then it will sound rather like music*
> *When the patient daemon behind the screen of sea-rock and sky*
> *Thumps with his staff, and calls thrice: "Come, Jeffers."*

Jeffers had previously recorded his belief in predestination, but what is new here is the poet's specific reference to himself. In later years (particularly in his last three volumes of poetic narratives) Jeffers' poems will become increasingly personal in reference.

Why is the theological content of *Thurso's Landing* so meager? Guesses: perhaps the poet had written all he wished to write at the time on the topic of God; perhaps the troubles of the Depression diverted his attention to the contemporary human plight; perhaps Jeffers was more interested at the time in the many places which feature strongly in the poems of *Thurso's Landing*; perhaps Jeffers felt that he was indeed "quits with the people" at long last and had no desire to praise a God to them which they had not previously comprehended; perhaps Jeffers' travel experiences to Ireland diverted momentarily his attention from his own coast and his pantheistic devotion to it. In any event, the theological content of Robinson Jeffers' poetry reaches its lowest quantitative ebb in 1932.

In 1933 Random House issued *Give Your Heart to the Hawks and Other Poems*, its first major volume by the Carmel poet. The book is one of Jeffers' richest, for beside the lead narrative poem and the standard shorter poems following it, the book contains Jeffers' magnificent English and Irish verses (already published separately by Random House in 1931 as *Descent to the Dead* in a limited edition of 500 plus copies) as well as two medium length narratives: "Resurrection" and "At the Fall of an Age". *Give Your Heart to the Hawks* is perhaps Jeffers' most balanced single volume of verse for it contains both short and long poems of variety and intensity.

Give Your Heart to the Hawks introduces a new theological emphasis. God, as Jeffers notes in "A Little Scraping", will allow humanity to multiply to excess before dispassionately gathering it in:

God is here, too, secretly smiling, the beautiful power
That piles up cities for the poem of their fall
And gathers multitude like game to be hunted when the season comes.

The new emphasis castigates the burgeoning masses of humanity set up in millions ripe for mass death. Jeffers' monism tells him that equilibrium in populations will eventually be orchestrated by God; in this neutral view, man is little different to other over-abundant fauna.

A sense of population balance is what the poet admires in "Still the Mind Smiles". The tone of the poem is similar to that of the Preacher in Ecclesiastes; everything has its opposite, and God, "the exact poet", will return his creation to normal in a world where—once again—humans "are few":

It is necessary to remember our norm, the unaltered passions,
The same-colored wings of imagination,
That the crowd clips, in lonely places new-grown; the unchanged
Lives of herdsmen and mountain farms,
Where men are few, and few tools, a few weapons, and their dawns are beautiful.
From here for normal one sees both ways,
And listens to the splendor of God, the exact poet, the sonorous
Antistrophe of desolation to the strophe multitude.

Scarcity makes value, and Jeffers who looks down both sides of the mountain of human existence can see scarcity down the slope of the past and multitude down the grade of the future. It is the "splendor of God" which will return to "our norm" man's momentarily excessive numbers.

"Triad" associates three seemingly unrelated topics: the confusion of modern science and its inability to "understand...the nature of things", the "trap" of the Russian *coup d'état* of 1917, and the poet's sober task to deal in truths. All three components of this triad

> *... feed the future, they serve God,*
> *Who is very beautiful, but hardly a friend of humanity.*

A neutral God can scarcely be expected to be partial to the human presence in his vast universe. In Jeffers' view, God cannot be expected to save man from future mass tragedy.

"Intellectuals" is Jeffers' declaration of independence from humanity as organized in the mass around a great leader. Marx, Christ and Progress are rejected by any intelligent person who wishes not to "flock into fold" with the remainder of the human herd. Jeffers has his own view of salvation as the middle verse of the poem points out. His adoration of God is always one-sided, Jeffers to God. Reverence for outstanding humans or human ideals, Jeffers proclaims, is on the blind and circuituous path of human self-gratification and self-deification. The only solution to the human dilemma is to break out of ourselves and encounter and love "Our unkindly all but inhuman God". Jeffers implies that the human mind, the idol of intellectuals, does not contain the correct answer to the Gordian knot of human narcissism. But out-going love of the "all but inhuman" God of the world is the one activity not stained by the heady human fixation with itself. Jeffers' God is the one God who cannot be contaminated by human introversion.

INTELLECTUALS

Is it so hard for men to stand by themselves,
They must hang on Marx or Christ, or mere Progress?
Clearly it is hard. But these ought to be leaders ...
Sheep leading sheep, "The fold, the fold,
Night comes, and the wolves of doubt." Clearly it is hard.

Yourself, if you had not encountered and loved
Our unkindly all but inhuman God,
Who is very beautiful and too secure to want worshippers,
And includes indeed the sheep with the wolves,
You too might have been looking about for a church.

He includes the flaming stars and pitiable flesh,
And what we call things and what we call nothing.
He is very beautiful. But when these lonely have travelled
Through long thoughts to redeeming despair,
They are tired and cover their eyes; they flock into fold.

"Intellectuals" is the outstanding short poem of a theological nature in *Give Your Heart to the Hawks*. Its brief fifteen lines contain one of Jeffers' major definitions of his conception of God. The poem also reflects Jeffers' growing desire to be separate from the masses to whom he reluctantly (now) serves as disinterested solitary herald of the "all but inhuman God".

Written in Great Britain and Ireland, the elegiac poems of *Descent to the Dead* were, as noted, actually first printed in 1931. They were appended to the contents of *Give Your Heart to the Hawks* and are the only major portion of Jeffers' work not affected or directly influenced by Jeffers' pantheistic devotion to the inland region and coast south of Carmel. The effect of the English and Irish countryside on Jeffers was extraordinary and uniquely stimulating. The poems of *Descent to the Dead* rank among Jeffers' best, solemn and distinct in tone from the rest of the Jeffers canon. The poems are not particularly theocentric since Jeffers was concerned more with the mood of the places of his ancestors where

> *... I a foreigner, one who has come to the country of the dead*
> *Before I was called, [came]*
> *To eat the bitter dust of my ancestors;*

Jeffers is more concerned with the climate, human pre-history and background of the British Isles than with the special nature of the God of a land where by Jeffers' admission in "In the Hill at New Grange" "A foreigner I am."

Confronted in Ireland (as he was not in his own coast) with millennia of human pre-history, Jeffers concludes "The Giant's Ring, Ballylesson, near Belfast" with the charge that Christianity's hereafter is a "cheap" immortality compared to that enjoyed by the builders of the Giant's Ring,

> *...Piled up of ponderous basalt that sheds the centuries like rain-drops*

which

> *...has ear-marked already some four millenniums.*

The "very presence" of the original builder of the Giant's Ring, "thick-bodied and brutish, a brutal and senseless will-power" would

> *—Conclude that secular like Christian immortality's*
> *Too cheap a bargain: the name, the work or the soul: glass*
> *   beads are the trade for savages.*

Religious burial in Ireland is the topic of "Delusions of Saints". Jeffers repeats his contentions that Christian believers (saints)

> ...*sleep now as easily as any dead murderer*
> *Or worn-out lecher.*

From the perspective of the grave, the saints possess forever the sealed message that their faith was in vain:

> *To have found your faith a liar is no thorn*
> *In the narrow beds,*
> *Nor laughter of unfriends nor rumor of the ruinous*
> *Churches will reach you.*

When the grave inscriptions are washed from the rock by the centuries, Jeffers writes that the Christian beliefs will

> *Have shed the feeble delusions that built them,*

and

> *...stand inhumanly*
> *Clean and massive*

as their pagan predecessors do now.

The tone of Jeffers' writing on religion in *Descent to the Dead* is not so much anti-Christian as it is pre-Christian. In a land where many forms and types of religion were practiced over the centuries and where the arrival of Christianity is still a relatively recent event, Jeffers strikes contrasts among the religions, and, in passing, finds Christianity, the latest of the many faiths, wanting.

"Inscription for a Gravestone" is a personalized view of life after death. From the grave, the speaker tells of his new-found union with the natural elements and God. An attitude of final peace and lasting contentment with the prospect of death conditions the work.

INSCRIPTION FOR A GRAVESTONE

I am not dead, I have only become inhuman:
That is to say,
Undressed myself of laughable prides and infirmities
But not as a man
Undresses to creep into bed, but like an athlete
Stripping for the race.
The delicate ravel of nerves that made me a measurer
Of certain fictions
Called good and evil; that made me contract with pain
And expand with pleasure;
Fussily adjusted like a little electroscope:
That's gone, it is true;
(I never miss it; if the universe does,
How easily replaced!)
But all the rest is heightened, widened, set free.
I admired the beauty
While I was human, now I am part of the beauty.
I wander in the air,
Being mostly gas and water, and flow in the ocean;
Touch you and Asia
At the same moment; have a hand in the sunrises
And the glow of this grass.
I left the light precipitate of ashes to earth
For a love-token.

A more characteristic and succinct statement of Jeffers' thoughts on death does not exist.

Two years after *Give Your Heart to the Hawks and Other Poems* Robinson Jeffers had his eighth major volume of poetry published under the title of *Solstice and Other Poems*, 1935. It was his first book not to feature the title narrative first. With *Solstice* Jeffers rekindled his interest in writing poems of a theological nature. Six of the eighteen shorter poems are vitally concerned with God-related topics. Once again Jeffers' vision of God is at the epicenter of his work. To date, *Solstice* (with the exception of *Roan Stallion, Tamar*) was Jeffers' most theocentric volume.

Jeffers seems to have abnegated his wish to become separate from the people who are also a part of God, for in *Solstice* the poet regains something of his attitude of praising God to the world. The theologically significant short poems of *Solstice*, as those of *Roan Stallion, Tamar* had done before them, radiate Jeffers' pantheism so indelibly associated with the Sur Coast. It is as if Jeffers, "now returned home", sees with new eyes the magnificence of the region he first envisaged as a young man in love. This rising. theological exuberance will grow to find its apogee in the incomparable naturalistic beauty of the short poems of *Such Counsels You Gave to Me and Other Poems* of 1937.

Two of Jeffers' major views of God reach their culmination of expression in *Solstice*: the view that the natural world is neutral toward man and not accessory to the humanized dualism of good or evil; and the view that the real world is revealed to us by the senses and is material in nature, not idealistic or spiritualistic. This latter view Jeffers had already expressed in *Dear Judas*: "Here is reality".

"Rock and Hawk" straight-forwardly presents Jeffers' neutral view of nature in the words, "final disinterestedness". Christianity and its Mormon offshoot (the hive) are not based on the observable disinterestedness of the universe. They impose a dualistic vision of good and evil on a monistic "mysticism of stone" and clearly are not the emblems "to hang in the future sky." Look at the world for what it really is, challenges Jeffers in the poem, and you will see that truth *is* inherent in the gray rocks and the falcons, not in a fictitious spiritualization of the world.

ROCK AND HAWK

Here is a symbol in which
Many high tragic thoughts
Watch their own eyes.

This gray rock, standing tall
On the headland, where the seawind
Lets no tree grow.

Earthquake-proved, and signatured
By ages of storms: on its peak
A falcon has perched.

I think, here is your emblem
To hang in the future sky;
Not the cross, not the hive,

But this; bright power, dark peace;
Fierce consciousness joined with final
Disinterestedness;

Life with calm death; the falcon's
Realist eyes and act
Married to the massive

Mysticism of stone,
Which failure cannot cast down
Nor success make proud.

The dozen or more concrete nouns in this brief poem underscore Jeffers' concern accurately to present the real, non-human, tangible world of natural phenomena.

The neutral view of nature is prominent in another of the poems of *Solstice*, "Gray Weather". The poem praises the serene balance of nature; "no kind of excess" is evident in the Pacific Coast winter scene here described:

GRAY WEATHER

It is true that, older than man and ages to outlast him, the Pacific surf
Still cheerfully pounds the worn granite drum;
But there's no storm; and the birds are still, no song; no kind of excess;
Nothing that shines, nothing is dark;
There is neither joy nor grief nor a person, the sun's tooth sheathed in cloud,
And life has no more desires than a stone.
The stormy conditions of time and change are all abrogated, the essential
Violences of survival, pleasure,
Love, wrath and pain, and the curious desire of knowing, all perfectly suspended.
In the cloudy light, in the timeless quietness,
One explores deeper than the nerves or heart of nature, the womb or soul,
To the bone, the careless white bone, the excellence.

Beyond the froth of circumstance lies the quiet truth of the immanent God, "the careless white bone, the excellence."

Robinson Jeffers celebrates the actual, observable world in "Flight of Swans", the final poem of *Solstice*. As in "Rock and Hawk", the poet emphasizes natural occurrences (the constellation Orion, winter midnight, mountains, floods and seasons) and denigrates the illusory human invention of idealism:

> *And knows that exactly this and not another is the world,*
> *The ideal is phantoms for bait, the spirit is a flicker on a grave;—*
> *May serve, with a certain detachment, the fugitive human race,*
> *Or his own people, his own household; but hardly himself;*
> *And will not wind himself into hopes nor sicken with despairs.*
> *He has found the peace and adored the God; he handles in autumn*
> *The germs of far-future spring.*

Jeffers likens his own relationship with God to a "diamond within" which he touches to the "diamond outside"—the real God-infused world.

"Sign-Post" of the *Solstice* volume and "The Answer" of *Such Counsels You Gave to Me* answer the allegations that Jeffers' religious philosophy is cold and unliveable. Civilization, which Jeffers elsewhere had called a "transient sickness", corrupts man with false belief in mass-produced security; the lethargy which accompanies this empty security isolates man from the realities of God's existence. "Sign-Post" is a theological directive for man, written out of compassionate concern for man's present plight as Jeffers sees it. The sonnet provides modern man with the spool of thread to escape the maze he has created for himself. A variety of methods (including meditative aspects of Christianity) are recommended by the poet who has no dogma to dispense except the fundamental realization that man (who is not central either to God or the universe) *can* perceive the real world in true perspective and "love God" in the bargain.

SIGN-POST

Civilized, crying how to be human again: this will tell you how.
Turn outward, love things, not men, turn right away from humanity,
Let that doll lie. Consider if you like how the lilies grow,
Lean on the silent rock until you feel its divinity
Make your veins cold, look at the silent stars, let your eyes
Climb the great ladder out of the pit of yourself and man.
Things are the God, you will love God, and not in vain,
For what we love, we grow to it, we share its nature. At length
You will look back along the stars' rays and see that even
The poor doll humanity has a place under heaven.
Its qualities repair their mosaic around you, the chips of strength
And sickness; but now you are free, even to become human,
But born of the rock and the air, not of a woman.

Remarkable for its adroit end rhymes, the poem alludes to Christ's Sermon on the Mount and to the words of Stephen Brown in the first narrative in *Californians*: "We grow to be what we have loved." Jeffers shows that his religious beliefs are not necessarily anti-human but inhuman, in the sense that man (in Jeffers' eyes) is not what man presumes himself to be: the lord of an anthropocentric universe. Once man learns of his true stature "under heaven", he is "free, even to become human".

Even death in this attitude comes into perspective for in "Where I?" Jeffers considers the case of a woman who has terminal cancer. Her imminent death

> *...gives to her face a kind of glory.*
> *Her mind used to be lazy and heavy her face,*
> *Now she talks all in haste, looks young and lean*
> *And eager, her eyes glitter with eagerness,*
> *As if she were newly born and had never seen*
> *The beauty of things, the terror, pain, joy, the song.*
> *—Or is it better to live at ease, dully and long?*

The sonnet discloses that even a previously sluggish human life can be revitalized by contact with one of the basic realities of nature, death.

One of Robinson Jeffers' own favorite short poems, and one of his best, the most characteristic and dexterous of his sonnets, "Return", recalls the poet to the features of the earth for his pantheistic renewal.

RETURN

> *A little too abstract, a little too wise,*
> *It is time for us to kiss the earth again,*
> *It is time to let the leaves rain from the skies,*
> *Let the rich life run to the roots again.*
> *I will go down to the lovely Sur Rivers*
> *And dip my arms in them up to the shoulders.*
> *I will find my accounting where the alder leaf quivers*
> *In the ocean wind over the river boulders.*
> *I will touch things and things and no more thoughts,*
> *That breed like mouthless May-flies darkening the sky,*
> *The insect clouds that blind our passionate hawks*
> *So that they cannot strike, hardly can fly.*
> *Things are the hawk's food and noble is the mountain, Oh noble*
> *Pico Blanco, steep sea-wave of marble.*

First printed in December of 1934 (about one year before *Solstice*), "Return" is
forceful evidence of the resurgence of Jeffers' pantheism. Reverence for nature and for
nature's articulation with God are once again a major theme for Robinson Jeffers.
Rapidly accelerating toward the Second World War, the human world and its trappings
become less attractive. *Such Counsels You Gave to Me and Other Poems* appeared in
1937 containing Jeffers' finest short poems on nature and on nature's God.

Jeffers of course was not alone in sensing the oncoming, inevitable violence of
the next great conflict, but *Such Counsels You Gave to Me* emphasizes his point that,
even in a world on the brink of mayhem, God is everywhere to be found—though men,

like the drunkard in "New Year's Eve", in the stupor of their self-delusions, are unaware of God:

> *The star's on the mountain, the stream snoring in flood;*
> *the brain-lit drunkard*
> *Crosses midnight and stammers to bed.*
> *The inhuman nobility of things, the ecstatic beauty,*
> *the inveterate steadfastness*
> *Uphold the four posts of the bed.*
> *(Nobody knows my love the falcon.)*

Just as the dove is one of the symbols of Christianity, Jeffers has chosen the falcon as the appropriate bird to symbolize his conception of God.

Although gravely concerned with the burgeoning violence of his own day, Jeffers in section one of the four-part poem "Hellenistics" considers the Greeks' relationship with the God of the world.   God was well-known to the ancient Greeks, Jeffers concludes, but they did not have a monopoly on him.   His presence is everywhere to be felt, even in the scene visible from Jeffers' own house:

> *I am past childhood, I look at this ocean and the fishing*
> *   birds, the streaming skerries, the shining water,*
> *The foam heads, the exultant dawn-light going west, the*
> *   pelicans, their huge wings half folded, plunging like stones.*
>
> *Whatever it is catches my heart in its hands, whatever it*
> *   is makes me shudder with love*
> *And painful joy and the tears prickle ... the Greeks were*
> *   not its inventors. The Greeks were not the inventors*
>
> *Of shining clarity and jewel-sharp form and the beauty of*
> *   God. He was free with men before the Greeks came:*
> *He is here naked on the shining water. Every eye that has*
> *   a man's nerves behind it has known him.*

It is inevitable in this universe that man must encounter God.   If all men indeed do encounter such a magnificent God, why do so few see him lastingly in all his splendor?   In the final lines of "Hellenistics", after considering the ancient Greeks, Jeffers mentions the human condition of "the dull welter of Asia" and "the squalid savages along the Congo" as well as the precarious European situation in 1937.   Jeffers foresees the human future as a "new barbarism", warning "distant future children" against the institutionalization of their reverence for God:

> *... what power can save you from the real evils*
> *Of barbarism? What poet will be born to tell you to hate*
> *cruelty and filth? What prophet will warn you*
> *When the witch-doctors begin dancing, or if any man*
> *says "I am a priest," to kill them with spears?*

Continuing in this individualistic vein, Jeffers suggests a solution "for each man" for his own religious needs, in "Going to Horse Flats". No use trying to save the world: "it is certain the world cannot be saved." But the individual can find a manner of salvation by finding God. The method of this encounter elucidated, Robinson Jeffers concludes "Going to Horse Flats" by sadly admitting that "men instinctively rebel against" the real God who will, however, gather them in upon death.

> *... Man's world is a tragic music*
> *and is not played for man's happiness,*
> *Its discords are not resolved but by other discords.*
> *But for each man*
> *There is a real solution, let him turn from himself and man*
> *to love God. He is out of the trap then. He will remain*
> *Part of the music, but will hear it as the player hears it.*
> *He will be superior to death and fortune, unmoved by*
> *success or failure. Pity can make him weep still,*
> *Or pain convulse him, but not to the center, and he can*
> *conquer them ... But how could I impart this knowledge*
> *To that old man?*
>
> *Or indeed to anyone? I know that all*
> *men instinctively rebel against it. But yet*
> *They will come to it at last.*
> *Then man will have come of age; he will still suffer and*
> *still die, but like a God, not a tortured animal.*

As World War Two approaches, Robinson Jeffers realizes how hollow are the faiths men have institutionalized. "Air-Raid Rehearsals" gives humanity advance notification that the religious and political institutions of the day would not perform as promised: "... and neither Christ nor Lenin will save you." The poem concludes by wishing that the world could have found more secure values in time to avoid bloodshed.

> *I wish you could find the secure value,*
> *The all-heal I found when a former time hurt me to the heart,*
> *The splendor of inhuman things: you would not be*
> *looking at each other's throats with your knives.*

"Thebaid" mocks the false faiths of Jeffers' day:

> *An age of renascent faith: Christ said, Marx wrote, Hitler says,*
> *And though it seems absurd we believe.*
> *Sad children, yes. It is lonely to be adult, you need a father.*
> *With a little practice you'll believe anything.*

With the rest of the world confused by maelstroms of conflicting faiths, Robinson Jeffers imagines himself as the last man on earth to see things clearly.

> *—I see the sun set and rise*
> *And the beautiful desert sand*
> *And the stars at night,*
> *The incredible magnificence of things.*
> *I the last living man*
> *That sees the real earth and skies,*
> *Actual life and real death.*

> *The others are all prophets and believers*
> *Delirious with fevers of faith.*

Perhaps Jeffers was right, for the many "faiths" which went into the second great war's making have served only to muddy man's existence. Toward the end of his life (in the spiritual emptiness of the 1960's) Robinson Jeffers reaffirmed his early vision of himself as the lone, solitary sane figure in a deluded world by writing an unpublished poem entitled "The Last Conservative". In a world of political and environmental lunacy Jeffers foresees that his death will leave the world with no one of sound judgment. "Thebaid" presents the somber prospect of the last surviving man able to see the world neutrally in its native indifferent state.

Throughout his career, Robinson Jeffers wrote accurate poetic self-evaluations; one of the best of these occurs in *Such Counsels You Gave to Me* with the appropriate title of "Self-Criticism in February". The poem is an imagined dialogue between himself and a perceptive critic of his poetry. Jeffers places his critic's comments in italics as affirmation that his own veracity which has appeared over the years under standard type has not lost its meaning. The critic objects to the excessive violence in Jeffers' poetry — to which charge the poet replies: "But the present time is not pastoral...." The critic objects to Jeffers' too frequent use of phantom-like characters — to which Jeffers rejoins: "—how often life's are—". But the gravest fault the critic can find with Jeffers' poems is their fundamental theological premise of the existence of a neutral God:

> *And now*
> *For the worst fault: you have never mistaken*
> *Demon nor passion nor idealism for the real God.*
> Then what is most disliked in those verses
> Remains most true. *Unfortunately. If only you could sing*

That God is love, or perhaps that social
Justice will soon prevail. I can tell lies in prose.

Jeffers' intense passion for truth telling in poetry is reasserted in this poem. Out of allegiance to this truth-in-poetry principle, he is not able to feign faith in Christianity nor is he interested in the socialist-communist promise of around-the-corner utopianism. The truth lies somewhere outside of the delusory human dilemma in the "storm-beauty" of "the real God."

In 1938 Random House issued the capstone of Jeffers' career to date, a 615 page volume entitled *The Selected Poetry of Robinson Jeffers.* About one-half of Jeffers' published work is included in the book. *Selected Poetry* contains representative work chosen by Jeffers from *Tamar* of 1924 to *Such Counsels* of 1937; four new poems are also included. The book has the distinction of being the only volume of Jeffers which Random House, his publishers, kept in print over the years. By 1959 *Selected Poetry* had been reprinted (each reprinting in sizeable quantities) eleven times, a tribute to the persistent interest of American poetry readers and students.

Two of the four new poems in *Selected Poetry* are of theological interest. "Shiva" is Jeffers' last sonnet; the title refers to the Hindu goddess of destruction and of reproductive restoration. Both the attributes of Shiva are included in the poem which considers the eventual climax and conclusion of the Christian age. "Shiva" is only superficially relevant to Hinduism, as Jeffers uses the Indian deity as a vehicle for his own monistic ideas. The poet intuits the distant extermination of human liberty, appraises the vanities of human arts and sciences and predicts the end of the present universe. Already, Jeffers notes, "the hawk that is picking the birds out of our sky" has

> *...killed the pigeons of peace and security.*
> *She has taken honesty and confidence from nations and men.*

Jeffers does not gloat over the destruction of the features and foundations of the present universe, but remains steadfastly confident that his monistic conception of "empty darkness" will be able, phoenix-like, to recreate another universe in the cycles of time.

> *This is the hawk that picks out the stars' eyes.*
> *This is the only hunter that will ever catch the wild swan;*
> *The prey she will take last is the wild white swan of the beauty of things.*
> *Then she will be alone, pure destruction, achieved and supreme,*
> *Empty darkness under the death-tent wings.*
> *She will build a nest of the swan's bones and hatch a new brood,*
> *Hang new heavens with new birds, all be renewed.*

Jeffers' supreme faith in the monistic source of the universe is summed up in the final couplet of the sonnet.

One suspects that Robinson Jeffers paid careful attention to his choices for final poems in his volumes of verse. As partial confirmation of this contention, we have Jeffers' final poem in *Selected Poetry:* "Theory of Truth", one of his most memorable religious poems. To avoid ambiguity and to reiterate his personal regard for his misunderstood *Werk seines Lebens, The Women at Point Sur,* Jeffers subtitled the poem "(Reference to Chapter II, The Women at Point Sur)". The two-page poem is a painstakingly personal investigation into two fundamental human questions: how have the three most persistent and penetrating human seekers of truth arrived at their answers; and how should men live in the world.

It is significant that "Theory of Truth" does not include scientists as the most important seekers of truth. Outstanding scientific discoverers were omitted not because Jeffers had no regard for the truths of science. On the contrary, of all the modern poets of merit, he is most interested in and influenced by science. Additionally, Jeffers had studied in some depth a wide range of the sciences, was conversant with contemporary scientific advances, and had as a brother an eminent mathemtician-astronomer. For all his abiding interest in science, Jeffers penned the phrase "as unnecessary as our sciences". He felt that while science answered some important questions, the even more crucial questions of human existence were tackled by the great religious thinkers such as those identified in "Theory of Truth": Lao-tze, Jesus, and Buddha.

In Jeffers' view, these three great men did finally find truth—but only after intense personal torment. His theory of truth is that only an agonizing personal trauma (closely related to insanity) initiates the search for ultimate truth. Once found, the truth uncovered is polluted by the insanity which prompted its original discovery.

> *...Because only*
> *tormented persons want truth.*
> *Man is an animal like other animals, wants food and success and*
> *women, not truth. Only if the mind*
> *Tortured by some interior tension has despaired of happiness:*
> *then it hates its life-cage and seeks further,*
> *And finds, if it is powerful enough. But instantly the private*
> *agony that made the search*
> *Muddles the finding.*

He identifies the "private agony" of three pre-eminent world religious leaders: Lao-tze "envied the chiefs of / the provinces of China their power and pride"; Jesus "was born a bastard, and among the people / That more than any in the world valued race-purity"; Buddha was

> *A man who loved and pitied with such intense comprehension of*
> *pain that he was willing to annihilate*
> *Nature and the earth and stars, life and mankind, to annul the suffering.*

All three of the men were "powerful enough" to find God and truth. When they did, they mixed their private impurities with their new-found wisdom and bequeathed to posterity their truths, albeit flawed by the limitations of their own personalities. Jeffers concludes the poem by querying whether the search for truth is forever doomed to personal contamination:

> *Then*
> *search for truth is foredoomed and frustrate?*
> *Only stained fragments?*
> *Until the mind has turned its love from*
> *itself and man, from parts to the whole.*

As long as humans insist on living in an anthropocentric universe, man's search for God will be stained by human fixations. Jeffers' hope is that since God is eternally present in his creation, one day man will climb out of his self-made pit and encounter as best he can the ultimate truth of God. His position is deeply influenced by modern geology and astronomy, the two sciences most directly responsible for giving man a farther vision of the universe. Geological time and astronomical distance have, in Jeffers' view, made man's self-importance something less than consequential. These two insights will force future men to assess more accurately their true nature; they will experience the God who is closer to physical reality than the man-centered deities of the great religions of the Orient: Taoism, Buddhism, Christianity.

The Middle Years: God
A Summary

Robinson Jeffers' publications between the years 1924 and 1938 present a substantial, though not yet complete, consideration of his conception of God. The original pantheism present in Jeffers' *Californians* volume of 1916 is provided additional authenticity by probable mystic encounter with his God as evidenced in the poems beginning with *Roan Stallion* of 1925. Many of the basic aspects of Jeffers' conception of God in his mature works are already present as fledgling ideas in *Californians*. The poet's God does not seem to alter appreciably during Jeffers' middle years; He becomes better defined and more capably expressed in verse. During this time Robinson Jeffers had ample time and opportunity to contemplate and clarify aspects of his God. He now possessed the skill to express his theological convictions in the form of enduring poetry.

With the adverse reception of Jeffers' long theological narrative, *The Women at Point Sur*, and—more specifically—with his intensifying aversion for the mass of humanity, Robinson Jeffers, at the height of his renown in the early and mid-1930's, drastically reduced his publication of short poems of a theological nature. It was only the distant certainty of another world war which prompted the poet (out of compassion for mankind and out of personal need to express, while still he could, his faith in his God) once again to present his theological notions in verse. These shorter theological poems of the late 1930's are among Jeffers' most concise exaltations of his God. With the actual outbreak of war, his theological verse underwent a sort of paralysis. Robinson Jeffers seemed then reluctant to write of his God except to affirm God's ability to steer men through the worst hours of their folly.

Jeffers felt a more precise definition of his pantheism was in order to distinguish his from that of the Orient and, in the Library of Congress appearance in 1941, he felt constrained to make such distinction with these words, printed in 1956 as *Themes in My Poems:*

> Another theme that has much engaged my verses is the expression of a religious feeling, that perhaps must be called pantheism, though I hate to type it with a name. It is the feeling ... I will say the certitude ... that the world, the universe, is one being, a single organism, one great life that includes all life and all things; and is so beautiful that it must be loved and reverenced; and in moments of mystical vision we identify ourselves with it.

> This is, in a way, the exact opposite of Oriental pantheism. The Hindu mystic finds God in his own soul, and all the outer world is illusion. To this other way of feeling, [Jeffers'] the outer world is real and divine; one's own soul might be called an illusion, it is so slight and transitory.

His vision of reality is squarely located in this world, not in an abstract spirituality nor in a personalized other-world of spirits, demons, angels or sub-deities. Jeffers' pantheism is firmly fixed in the material, phenomenological world. Human consciousness, the only known entity substantially aware of its existence in such a world, should realize its minute importance and act in accordance with the multiform evidences of a God who, like Fate, sets the universe in motion and monitors its every activity.

Robinson Jeffers' pantheism is based firmly in the material world. Materialistic pantheism might be a designation for his religious feelings were it not for the misleading connotations of the word materialism and the conventional notions attached to the word pantheism. If a link can be made between Jeffers' form of pantheism and other pantheistic teachings, that link must not be made to Oriental pantheism; it can perhaps, be remotely identified with some of the religious aspects of American Indian nature worship.

Although not yet overtly stated, Jeffers also looks forward to a day when men will become more humble, in tune with "the beauty of things", the natural world of God's making. In his final years—sadly—Jeffers lived to see man deviate still further from such a goal.

Look—and without imagination, desire nor dream—directly

At the mountains and sea. Are they not beautiful?

. . . .

　　　　　　　　　　　　　　　　　　　　　—"is the earth

　　not beautiful?

Nor the great skies over the earth?

　　　　　　　　—"Dē Rērum Virtute"

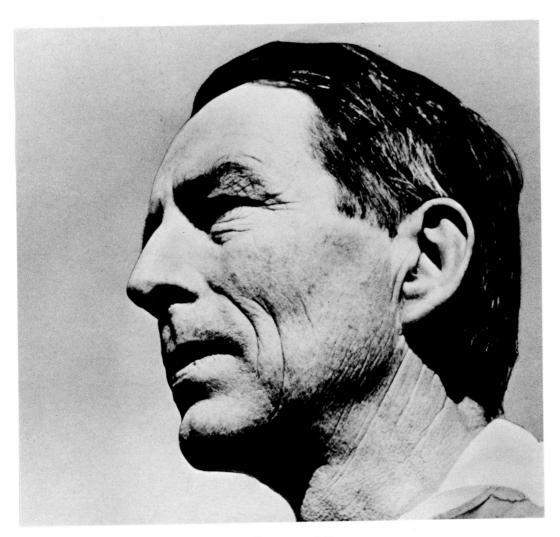

Robinson Jeffers, circa 1937

It Is Time For Us

The Middle Years: Man
(1924 - 1940)

Anyone who thinks extensively on the cardinal posit of the world, the existence and attributes of God, must invariably come to form a concomitant doctrine or opinion of man. The quantitative evidence from Robinson Jeffers' *Californians* seems to indicate that Jeffers was concerned primarily with matters theological in that volume and occupied only incidentally with penetrating thoughts on the nature and propensities of man. *Tamar* of 1924 and *Roan Stallion, Tamar* of the following year, begin to reveal more of his ideas on the subject of man's place in nature and on the purpose of human existence. What is the nature of man as seen by the mature Jeffers?

The poems of *Roan Stallion, Tamar* begin to expose aspects of Jeffers' misanthropy. The two major convictions on man in the book are those of man's comparative insignificance in the natural world, and the eventual extinction of humanity. "Granite and Cypress" introduces these themes by stressing the relative instability of man as compared to the two most impressive and lasting presences on the Monterey Peninsula:

> *(I have granite and cypress,*
> *Both long-lasting,*
> *Planted in the earth; but the granite sea-bowlders are prey*
> *to no hawk's wing, they have taken worse pounding,*
> *Like me they remember*
> *Old wars and are quiet; for we think that the future is one*
> *piece with the past, we wonder why tree-tops*
> *And people are so shaken.)*

Jeffers' *sui generis* view of humanity is that of a semi-interested yet detached outsider. He has already found his unique theological relationship with God, and it fundamentally affects his attitude toward man.

Like many of Jeffers' poems, "Boats in a Fog" strikes a contrast between the steadfastness of the natural world and the insignificance of the strictly human preoccupations. Compared to nature even the *best* man can muster is of evanescent merit:

> *Sports and gallantries, the stage, the arts, the antics of dancers,*
> *The exuberant voices of music,*
> *Have charm for children but lack nobility; it is bitter earnestness*
> *That makes beauty; the mind knows, grown adult.*

Human culture is pathetically inadequate compared to the "bitter earnestness" of nature.

> *... all the arts lose virtue*
> *Against the essential reality*
> *Of creatures going about their business among the equally*
> *Earnest elements of nature.*

The arts are a futile effort to escape from or, at best, to imitate the somber eloquence of the natural, non-human world. Culture is a cunningly decorated screen placed by man between man and nature and—ultimately—the God of nature. In the context of the real, natural world, the arts become ignoble and grotesque.

"Boats in a Fog" does not, however, denigrate simple and essential human toil. Jeffers considers human fishing activity to be as earnest and essential as the harbor fog through which the boats drift. These fishermen encounter God in their occupation and are more noble in fact than the arts which merely glorify man.

"Vices" continues the anti-culture theme. Carmel in 1925 was filling with the idle rich and the puttering artist types for which it had suddenly become notorious. "Vices" is a reaction to the feverish attempt to instil the human creator's "vices" in his works of art. Those who lack "talent" altogether merely applaud, and the whole ridiculous spectacle continues on in a vortex of generations. Distinct from the frenetic nature of local artists, Jeffers describes himself as cold, tranquil, "unagitable" and "earthfast"—everything an artist was not supposed to be in his rather frantic era.

VICES

Spirited people make a thousand jewels in verse and prose,
*   and the restlessness of talent*
Runs over and floods the stage or spreads its fever on canvas.
They are skilled in music too, the demon is never satisfied,
*   they take to puppets, they invent*
New arts, they take to drugs ... and we all applaud our vices.
Mine, coldness and the tenor of a stone tranquility; slow
*   life, the growth of trees and verse,*
Content the unagitable and somewhat earthfast nature.

Robinson Jeffers admires the ancient art of a versification fixed firmly to the natural world.

Two of the poems found in *Roan Stallion, Tamar* contemplate present and future human over-population. In "People and a Heron" Jeffers, after seeing a large crowd on Carmel Beach, later in the evening observes a solitary heron and wonders "why a lone bird was dearer to me than / many people." He concludes that "rare is dear", the bird far rarer than a throng of humans.

"Haunted Country" forecasts the growth of population in Carmel and the adjacent bit of coastline. In a note written in 1930 on the subject Robinson Jeffers wrote:

> —But this was about my own thoughts being over-populated. The growth of this village [Carmel] was forecast in "Haunted Country" in the *Roan Stallion* book — but it needed no prophet. —R.J.

"Haunted Country" surveys the future of Jeffers' region with patient dismay and with stoic resignation:

> *The inhuman years to be accomplished,*
> *The inhuman powers, the servile cunning under pressure,*
> *In a land grown old, heavy and crowded,*
> *There are happy places that fate skips; here is not one of them;*
> *The tides of the brute womb, the excess*
> *And weight of life spilled out like water, the last migration*
> *Gathering against this holier valley-mouth*
> *That knows its fate beforehand, the flow of the womb, banked back*
> *By the older flood of the ocean, to swallow it.*

Jeffers predicts that the final westering migration of man will gather on his shores and that this mass will finally be obliterated by the still "older flood of the ocean".

The poem immediately following "Haunted Country" is "Autumn Evening" With the immense natural beauties of clouds, imminent rain storms, a heron and "Jupiter ... for evening star" Jeffers expresses his supreme confidence, not in man, but in God's world:

> *The sea's voice worked into my mood, I thought "No matter*
> *What happens to men ... the world's well made though."*

The answer to manifold human problems is the native solace of the well-made world of nature.

In 1925 Robinson Jeffers' two sons were nine years of age. "Shine, Perishing Republic" admonishes his young sons to

... be in nothing so moderate as in love of man, a
clever servant, insufferable master.

Behind this warning lies Jeffers' deep distrust for men in the mass. As father, the poet cautions his boys to avoid "the trap that catches noblest spirits"—the trap of making humanity the focus of one's existence.

"Joy" records a typical reaction to Jeffers' advice against emotional excesses. The poem echoes the classical Greek admonition: Nothing too much.

JOY

Though joy is better than sorrow joy is not great;
Peace is great, strength is great.
Not for joy the stars burn, not for joy the vulture
Spreads her gray sails on the air
Over the mountain; not for joy the worn mountain
Stands, while years like water
Trench his long sides. "I am neither mountain nor bird
Nor star; and I seek joy."
The weakness of your breed: yet at length quietness
Will cover those wistful eyes.

Human vanity, in Jeffers' estimation, is bent on self-fulfilling pleasures which are not *the* foundation on which to build an intelligent life. Robinson Jeffers admires mental composure or physical and mental strength instead of solipsistic self-gratification. No matter, though, whether most humans elect joy as their life's foundation; in due course death will bring quietness to those who in life never adequately experienced a decently balanced emotional state.

"Practical People" is a criticism of misapplied and overly civilized pragmatism. The varied cycles of nature—the tides, the birth and death of stars, the waxings and wanings of human cultures "Make it a difficult world ... for practical people." The message is clear: there are magnificent natural phenomena which have nothing whatever to do with mankind; these phenomena cannot be assigned a utilitarian purpose. The world, as these phenomena demonstrate, was not made expressly for man. Should anyone be so unfortunate as to think so, he will find "it a difficult world", for he is out of tune with the world he seeks vainly to tame for humanity.

All the same, Jeffers does not characterize human lives as undirected quirks of chance. In "Woodrow Wilson (February, 1924)" the recently deceased president is having a revelatory conversation with a Presence which might be characterized as Fate. The Presence corrects the ex-president as to the real purpose of his and other men's lives:

> *...you and all men are drawn out of this depth*
> *Only to be these things you are, as flowers for color, falcons for swiftness,*
> *Mountains for mass and quiet. Each for its quality*
>
> *Is drawn out of this depth.*

People's lives do have a purpose, one known only to fate; that purpose may well be entirely different to the purpose supposed by the individual himself. Jeffers does not accept a haphazard universe; on the contrary, fate organizes things to the point of having a distinct purpose for each life.

"Science" is the first Jeffers poem to embody the idea that man is unduly preoccupied with himself. The first three words, "Man, introverted man", present

Jeffers' key doctrine that mankind is obsessed with its own successes, problems and agonies, obsessed to the point of spiritual illness. As example of this illness, Jeffers chooses modern science, which, for all its benefits to humanity, will eventually become, not man's neutral play-thing, but his painful torturer. The knowledge man has wrested from nature, the erstwhile advantage he has obtained for his species because of this knowledge, has already taken its human toll in the 1920's. Ultimately this unnatural knowledge will prove man's undoing.

> [*Man*] *Like a maniac with self-love and inward conflicts cannot*
> *manage his hybrids.* [scientific innovations]
> *Being used to deal with edgeless dreams,*
> *Now he's bred knives on nature turns them also inward: they*
> *have thirsty points though.*
> *His mind forebodes his own destruction.*

Jeffers as man and poet had an acute sense of the balance of nature. For example, on one of his visits to Ireland the poet carried with him a small pebble from the beach before Tor House. When asked about it, Jeffers explained that a friend had brought him a stone of similar size from Ireland a few years previous and now by scrupulously returning such a pebble Jeffers was ensuring that he would not leave the world in imbalance.

"Science" concludes with two lines which reflect Jeffers' deep-rooted respect for the balance of nature which man has disrupted through his scientific investigations:

> *A little knowledge, a pebble from the shingle,*
> *A drop from the oceans: who would have dreamed this*
> *infinitely little too much?*

Robert Frost's poem "There Are Roughly Zones" from his 1936 volume *A Further Range* also expresses couched alarm at man's seemingly incautious and unthinking manipulations of nature. Both poets are able to conceive of a day when these human manipulations will resoundingly backfire.

"The Torch-Bearers' Race" develops a theme already stated in "Haunted Country". Fascinated by human migrations, Jeffers considers the future of humanity in the final lines of "The Torch-Bearers' Race", wondering what will—after an unimaginably successful future—finally bring the human species to extinction. The fact that men do exist is certain evidence that one day they will not exist. The poet asks men of the future humbly to recall their origins and die nobly, returning to the "one fountain"

> *... When the ancient wisdom is*
> *folded like a wine-stained cloth and laid up in darkness.*
> *And the old symbols forgotten, in the glory of that your hawk's dream*
> *Remember that the life of mankind is like the life of a man,*
> *a flutter from darkness to darkness*
> *Across the bright hair of a fire, so much of the ancient*
> *Knowledge will not be annulled. What unimaginable opponent to end you?*
> *There is one fountain*
> *Of power, yours and that last opponent's, and of long peace.*

"Gale in April", "The Cycle", "Continent's End", and "The Coast-Range Christ" are four other shorter poems from *Roan Stallion* which also consider at length the implications of human migration over the face of the earth.

"Point Joe" comprises a more generous attitude toward mankind; the poem grants that man, when engaged in the "permanent things" of necessary food gathering, has a dignity and an assured place in the natural setting. The poem's subject is "an old Chinaman gathering seaweed / from the sea-rocks" of Point Joe, a site frequently mistaken in the sailing days as the entrance to Monterey Harbor—with fatal results. Humanity in harmony with nature has a place under the sun:

> Man gleaning food between the solemn presences of land and ocean,
> On shores where better men have shipwrecked, under fog and among flowers,
>
> Equals the mountains in his past and future; that glow from the earth was only
> A trick of nature's, one must forgive nature a thousand graceful subtleties.

"To the Stone-Cutters" is probably Robinson Jeffers' best known single poem. It was one of the poet's favorite short poems and certainly is a characteristic work. The subject of the poem is the human desire to attempt to make permanent some small aspect of one's existence before death. The search for immortality is ultimately frustrate in Jeffers' view, but there is a small hope that, for a time, one can in his chosen field extract a fragment of immortality from oblivion.

TO THE STONE-CUTTERS

> Stone-cutters fighting time with marble, you foredefeated
> Challengers of oblivion
> Eat cynical earnings, knowing that rock splits, records fall down,
> The square-limbed Roman letters
> Scale in the thaws, wear in the rain. The poet as well
> Builds his monument mockingly;
> For man will be blotted out, the blithe earth die, the brave sun
> Die blind, his heart blackening:
> Yet stones have stood for a thousand years, and pained thoughts found
> The honey of peace in old poems.

This theme of making "something more equal to the centuries" is further elaborated in the second to last poem of *Roan Stallion, Tamar and Other Poems*, "Wise Men in Their Bad Hours". The wise are judiciously disjoined from the masses of grasshopper-like humanity. The sobriquet grasshoppers alludes perhaps to Aesop's fable of the grasshopper and the ants. "In moments of mockery", even the wise may envy the mindless and easily-led masses, but the wise finally do know that personal integrity and strength are infinitely preferable to thoughtless men caught up in their "thirty-year" breeding cycles. Jeffers thought highly of this poetic assessment of the majority of humantiy—to the extent that "Wise Men in Their Bad Hours" was one of the few early poems he chose to read in his 1941 Harvard University appearance, now preserved on a 78 r.p.m. recording. (The 1937 sonnet "Hope Is Not for the Wise" also contrasts the few wise men in the world to the foolish majority.) The posture of separateness was necessary to Jeffers the poet to attain a detached yet informed critical view of humanity.

WISE MEN IN THEIR BAD HOURS

Wise men in their bad hours have envied
The little people making merry like grasshoppers
In spots of sunlight, hardly thinking
Backward but never forward, and if they somehow
Take hold upon the future they do it
Half asleep, with the tools of generation
Foolishly reduplicating
Folly in thirty-year periods; they eat and laugh too,
Groan against labors, wars and partings,
Dance, talk, dress and undress; wise men have pretended
The summer insects enviable;
One must indulge the wise in moments of mockery.
Strength and desire possess the future,
The breed of the grasshopper shrills, "What does the future
Matter, we shall be dead?" Ah, grasshoppers,
Death's a fierce meadowlark: but to die having made
Something more equal to the centuries
Than muscle and bone, is mostly to shed weakness.
The mountains are dead stone, the people
Admire or hate their stature, their insolent quietness,
The mountains are not softened nor troubled
And a few dead men's thoughts have the same temper.

The picture of man presented in *Roan Stallion, Tamar* is not a flattering one. If one seeks sympathy for humanity, it is not here. Humans in *Roan Stallion, Tamar* do figure in the poems, but more as stylized, abstracted agonists than pitiable protagonists. The real subject matter is the splendor of nature; the lessons drawn from nature may in some distant day be of humbling benefit to the race. Jeffers' underlying concern was to chronicle the truth of humanity's willfully self-distorted existence. Such a truth, he knew full well, is never relevant to "grasshopper" people for it does not tell them the things ears itch to hear. *Vis a vis* humanity, Robinson Jeffers—by nature and philosophy—is placed in a Cassandra-like position: telling the ultimate truth to incredulous "grasshoppers" who "hardly think ... / Backward but never forward". This position will become increasingly wearisome to the poet. For nearly a decade his future verse circumspectly will avoid the quantity of direct censorious reference to humanity present in *Roan Stallion, Tamar and Other Poems*.

The fifteen poems Robinson Jeffers submitted for the 1927 volume *American Poetry 1927 A Miscellany* are largely personal and topical in nature. The sonnet "Compensation" celebrates his preference for solitude in the presence of immense natural beauty. It is solitude, not loneliness, which provides Jeffers the perspective to see that even in humanity there is beauty and a measure of goodness—"from the mountain-side of solitude." The overwhelming imagery of the poem is wholesomely natural so that the final couplet, by virtue of its freshness, makes a lasting impact on the reader.

COMPENSATION

Solitude that unmakes me one of men
In snow-white hands brings singular recompense,
Evening me with kindlier natures when
On the needled pinewood the cold dews condense
About the hour of Rigel fallen from heaven
In wintertime, or when the long night tides
Sigh blindly from the sand-dune backward driven
Or when on stormwings of the northwind rides
The foamscud with the cormorants, or when passes
A horse or dog with brown affectionate eyes,
Or autumn frosts are pricked by earliest grasses,
Or whirring from her covert a quail flies.
Why, even in humanity beauty and good
Show, from the mountainside of solitude.

 Cawdor of 1928 finds Jeffers retreating increasingly to "the mountainside of solitude" from which to view man. The seven short poems which do deal with man are even more distant towards things human than Jeffers' previous poems. "A Redeemer" makes outright condemnation of the misuse of the American earth. It is also a biting statement cautioning against falsely-based human happiness. But "An Artist" contains Jeffers' most caustic comments on the human race in the *Cawdor* volume.

In many ways "An Artist" is uncharacteristic of Jeffers' work. For one thing, the poem recounts in part an obviously contrived incident, a practice Jeffers elsewhere in his verse scrupulously avoids. Thus, in spite of the intensity of feeling in the poem, there is also an air of forced and strident machination present. "An Artist", while not one of Jeffers' best poems (lacking as it does the stamp of Jeffers' personal experience), does reveal—through the protesting voice of the artist—some of Jeffers' intensifying dislike for man. The sculptor contrasts man's actuality with his potentiality:

> *What I see is the enormous beauty of things, but what I attempt*
> *Is nothing to that. I am helpless toward that.*
> *It is only to form in stone the mold of some ideal humanity that might be worthy to be*
> *Under that lightning. Animalcules that God (if he were*
> *given to laughter) might omit to laugh at.*
> . . . . . .
>
> *... I have lived a little and I think*
> *peace marrying pain alone can breed that excellence in*
> *the luckless race, might make it decent*
> *To exist at all on the star-lit stone breast.*

The artist presented here is excessive both in his desire for complete privacy and in his unmitigated contempt for man. In the prose note to the John S. Mayfield private edition of "An Artist" Robinson Jeffers points out that "The poem seems to carry that [excessive artistic] independence to its logical conclusion." While not, in all likelihood, entirely agreeing with the fictionalized sculptor of the poem, Jeffers

> *... respect[s] him enough to keep his name and the place*
> *secret. I hope that some other traveller*
> *May stumble on that ravine of Titans after their maker*
> *has died. While he lives, let him alone.*

Jeffers, too, desired his privacy. In his final years Jeffers echoed the last line of "An Artist"

>   ... *While he lives, let him alone.*

in the contents and title of his posthumously published poem "Let Them Alone", a poem which pleads the necessity of allowing the creative artist his privacy while alive.

"Ascent to the Sierras" *is* based on experience, the experience of motoring up to the Sierras (probably to Yosemite) from Carmel in the late 1920's. After imagining a fitful "thousands of years" of forays between primitive mountain and valley clansmen, Jeffers records the facts:

>   *It is not true: from this land*
> *The curse was lifted; the highlands have kept peace with*
> *the valleys; no blood in the sod; there is no old sword*
> *Keeping grim rust, no primal sorrow. The people are all*
> *one people, their homes never knew harrying;*
> *The tribes before them were acorn-eaters, harmless as*
> *deer. Oh, fortunate earth; you must find someone*
> *To make you bitter music; how else will you take bonds*
> *of the future, against the wolf in men's hearts?*

The human history of California has been peaceful in Jeffers' view. The California Indians were docile and today there exist no artificial or geographical divisions of the people, but there does exist deep within the human psyche a savagery which nature counteracts by requiring of man the "bitter music" of tragedy. "Ascent to the Sierras" contains Jeffers' first reference to a deep-seated flaw in human nature, a flaw which he feels is the root of human achievement and also the impetus for human sordidness, a flaw which the poet will continue to consider and contemplate in many of his later poems.

Closer to his American present of 1928 is the subject matter of the poem "Contrast" in which Jeffers contrasts his country (and its magnificent forests) to its paucity of great men. The poet sums up Americans of the day, concluding that the physical greatness of the land has not been matched by a similarly distinguished citizenry:

> *Our people are clever and masterful;*
> *They have powers in the mass, they accomplish marvels.*
> *It is possible Time will make them before it annuls them, but at present*
> *There is not one memorable person, there is not one mind*
> *to stand with the trees, one life with the mountains.*

In subsequent poems Jeffers will include George Washington with the names of the great champions of human freedom, but never will he retract his contention that America does not have "one mind / to stand with the trees" [the Sequoias]. Jeffers conjectures that, since America does not seem to produce great leaders in thought or politics, and since its people are more powerful "in the mass", true human freedom in such a milieu is neither secure nor assured.

"Soliloquy" is Jeffers' personal response to charges that he as poet is cruel and inhuman when writing of mankind. The poet neither apologizes for nor defends his view of man. Jeffers merely notes that a neutral view of man, however anti-human it may seem from the exterior, provides mental security and truth enough for him. Because man has become so distorted in his day, Jeffers in turn feels he must write of man in primal tragical terms in order to be understood. But writing of human beings in tragical context in the twentieth century is certain to create misunderstanding, misunderstanding to which he is resigned. Indeed, Jeffers already was misunderstood by the masses whom he no longer cared to reach. "Soliloquy" concludes with a personal prophecy which was fulfilled in his final years.

SOLILOQUY

August and laurelled have been content to speak for an age, and the ages that follow
Respect them for that pious fidelity;
But you have disfeatured time for timelessness.
They had heroes for companions, beautiful youths to dream of, rose-marble-fingered
Women shed light down the great lines;
But you have invoked the slime in the skull,
The lymph in the vessels. They have shown men Gods like racial dreams, the woman's desire,
The man's fear, the hawk-faced prophet's; but nothing
Human seems happy at the feet of yours.
Therefore though not forgotten, not loved, in gray old years in the evening leaning
Over the gray stones of the tower-top,
You shall be called heartless and blind;
And watch new time answer old thought, not a face strange nor a pain astonishing;
But you living be laired in the rock
That sheds pleasure and pain like hail-stones.

"Hurt Hawks" contains Jeffers' well-known allegation that human beings in their contemporary setting are hopelessly removed from the God of the world:

> *You do not know him [God], you communal people, or you have*
> *forgotten him.*

The second section of "Hurt Hawks" begins:

> *I'd sooner, except the penalties, kill a man than a hawk but the great redtail*
> *Had nothing left but unable misery.*

Jeffers more deeply regards the world and its inspiring creatures than man. His contention that he prefers killing a man to a hawk is not entirely rhetorical although his very nature precluded *any* wanton acts of violence. The statement is to be understood as an accurate reflection of Jeffers' scale of human and natural values. A portion of the anguish here registered is prompted by the pointless human act which wounded initially the "great redtail" hawk.

"Meditation on Saviors", the most significant short poem of *Cawdor*, includes several key comments by Jeffers on his relationship with "the people". Dictatorship and socialism are the rewards for the people who find happiness in Caesarism:

> *... As for the people,*
> *I have found my rock, let them find theirs.*
> *Let them lie down at Caesar's feet and be saved; and he in*
> *his time reap their daggers of gratitude.*

Jeffers realizes that his own people are a part of God and he has no wish to be alienated entirely from them, but neither does he feel sorry for the plight of the people—let alone attempt to love them. Their salvation has already been worked out by Fate. The poet's task is not to be reinvolved with the foolishnesses of the people, but clearly to see the present and the future unobstructed by current confusions.

> *One need not pity; certainly one must not love. But who*
> *has seen peace, if he should tell them where peace*
> *Lives in the world [in God's nature] ... they would be powerless to*
> *understand; and he [Jeffers, the poet] is not willing to be reinvolved.*

Jeffers indeed has a low opinion of the masses and he has no wish to become *re*-involved as their spiritual consultant.

The solution to each individual's spiritual dilemma is presented in the final eight lines of "Meditation of Saviors". The allusion is to the Sermon on the Mount, but the doctrine of man presented is strictly Jeffersian:

> *But while he lives let each man make his health in his*
> *   mind, to love the coast opposite humanity*
> *And so be freed of love, laying it like bread on the waters;*
> *   it is worst turned inward, it is best shot farthest.*

> *Love, the mad wine of good and evil, the saint's and*
> *   murderer's, the mote in the eye that makes its object*
> *Shine the sun black; the trap in which it is better to catch*
> *   the inhuman God than the hunter's own image.*

Cawdor and Other Poems reveals a demonstrable hardening of Jeffers' attitude toward his fellow man. If ever he had any aspirations of ennobling masses of humanity, they have permanently vanished by 1928.

In his next volume of verse, *Dear Judas and Other Poems* of 1929, Jeffers continues with persistency his demeaning of humanity. Section III of "The Broken Balance" provides a contrast between the native animals and birds of Jeffers' region and man who has choked his own being with self-love. The appraisal is scathing and historically accurate. The poet begins with an account of the fauna:

These [animals] live their felt natures; they know their norm
And live it to the brim; they understand life.
While men molding themselves to the anthill have choked
Their natures until the souls die in them;
They have sold themselves for toys and protection:
No, but consider awhile: what else? Men sold for toys.

Uneasy and fractional people, having no center
But in the eyes and mouths that surround them,
Having no function but to serve and support
Civilization, the enemy of man,
No wonder they live insanely, and desire
With their tongues, progress; with their eyes, pleasure; with their hearts, death.

Their ancestors were good hunters, good herdsmen and swordsmen,
But now the world is turned upside down;
The good do evil, the hope's in criminals; in vice
That dissolves the cities and war to destroy them.
Through wars and corruptions the house will fall.
Mourn whom it falls on. Be glad: the house is mined, it will fall.

The manuscript for the poem contains Jeffers' prose summary of these lines in the following somber thoughts:

The world turned upside down, the criminals better than the good people; and the world's hope lying in war, pestilence, corruption and vice, that they some day pull down the evil house.

The human situation is scarcely improved since Jeffers' summary of it in 1929. A significant note here is the sentiment that "civilization [is] the enemy of man". Institutions blot out opportunities to contact God.

Jeffers defines "the broken balance" in section V of the poem; the ancient balance between man and the earth has radically swung (for the moment) in favor of man. The lurch of the pendulum appears to be all in man's favor, but in the end humanity will be eliminated:

V

> Mourning the broken balance, the hopeless prostration of the earth,
> Under men's hands and their minds,
> The beautiful places killed like rabbits to make a city,
> The spreading fungus, the slime-threads
> And spores; my own coast's obscene future: I remember the farther
> Future, and the last man dying
> Without succession under the confident eyes of the stars.
> It was only a moment's accident,
> The race that plagued us; the world resumes the old lonely immortal
> Splendor; from there I can even
> Perceive that that snuffed candle had something ... a fantastic virtue,
> A faint and unshapely pathos ...
> So death will flatter them at last: what, even the bald ape's by-shot
> Was moderately admirable?

From the perspective of human extinction, man will appear "moderately admirable". The interim will make obscenities of the beautiful places of the earth which will, ultimately, outlast humanity.

Section VI of "The Broken Balance" is subtitled "Palinode" or retraction to the above. In this section Jeffers does admit to some good in man:

> ... it is barely possible that even men's present
> Lives are something; their arts and sciences (by moonlight)
> Not wholly ridiculous, nor their cities merely an offense.

Quite obviously, he considers the good in man to be as genuine as it is minute; such beauty requires the reflected light of the moon in order to appreciate it. Jeffers' retraction (palinode) is in part tongue-in-cheek.

Using the metaphor of the ever-returning generations of grasses he concludes that the broken balance will be brought back into equilibrium through natural forces already present in the non-human world, that nature herself, with the extinction of man, will be wholly victorious once again.

VII

> Under my windows, between the road and the sea-cliff, bitter wild grass
> Stands narrowed between the people and the storm.
> The ocean winter after winter gnaws at its earth, the wheels and the feet
> Summer after summer encroach and destroy.
> Stubborn green life, for the cliff-eater I cannot comfort you, ignorant which color,
> Gray-blue or pale-green, will please the late stars;
> But laugh at the other, your seed shall enjoy wonderful vengeances and suck
> The arteries and walk in triumph on the faces.

The ocean Jeffers does not care to prophesy for, but the future of humanity is more easily predicted. The grasses surrounding Tor House will long outlive the "troublesome race of man".

"Hands" is an additional consideration of the transience of man in the Big Sur region. The poem is a moving comment upon the passing of the Indian races who lived in the environs of the massive sandstone formations near "the mountain sun cup" Tassajara. Today, as in Jeffers' day, the cave paintings, white, skeletal, eerie human hands drawn in X-ray style, are clearly visible, the haunting reminder of a vanished race. The human past is but prologue to the future.

HANDS

Inside a cave in a narrow canyon near Tassajara
The vault of rock is painted with hands,
A multitude of hands in the twilight, a cloud of men's palms, no more,
No other picture. There's no one to say
Whether the brown shy quiet people who are dead intended
Religion or magic, or made their tracings
In the idleness of art; but over the division of years these careful
Signs-manual are now like a sealed message
Saying: "Look: we also were human; we had hands, not paws. All hail
You people with cleverer hands, our supplanters
In the beautiful country; enjoy her a season, her beauty, and come down
And be supplanted; for you also are human."

Herein is evinced a singular compassion for humanity which cannot, it seems, come properly to appreciate its blessings. As well, "Hands" contains one of Jeffers' oft-repeated prophecies: the present white race of man will one day be replaced in "the beautiful country", California.

The short poems of *Thurso s Landing*, 1932, reiterate two of the ideas to be found in *Dear Judas:* man can only complicate and pollute what is already natural and beautiful, and man's "great achievement", civilization, is—in Jeffers' words—only "a transient sickness".

As revealed in a number of his poems over the years, the most revered place on his beloved coast was the hill region and sea coast surrounding Sovranes Creek. This association went back for Jeffers to his early friendship with fellow poet, George Sterling, a writer whose artistic and pantheistic influence on Robinson Jeffers was profound. After a descriptive survey of the scene at Sovranes Creek, Jeffers concludes:

> *No imaginable*
> *Human presence here could do anything*
> *But dilute the lonely self-watchful passion.*

Sovranes Point, divinely sufficient unto itself, is in no need of human attention.

"November Surf" is a poem about cleansing; nature, the great heal-all, purges her coast each year with the magnificent gesture of a surf "Like smoking mountains bright from the west". Under the grind of the surf "The old granite forgets half a year's [human] filth". Metaphorically Jeffers extends the cleansing action of these tides to the entire North American continent, which, encumbered with its human contamination, "envies its cliff" on the Pacific rim. The earth dreams, prophetically, that one fine day it too will be cleansed of the human element which at present only corrupts it.

> *But all seasons*
> *The earth, in her childlike prophetic sleep,*
> *Keeps dreaming of the bath of a storm that prepares up the long coast*

> *Of the future to scour more than her sea-lines:*
> *The cities gone down, the people fewer and the hawks more numerous,*
> *The rivers mouth to source pure; when the two-footed*
> *Mammal, being someways one of the nobler animals, regains*
> *The dignity of room, the value of rareness.*

Man has possibilities of nobility in Jeffers' system of thought, possibilities which are impossible to explore under the heavy pressures of over-population.

"New Mexican Mountains" (correct title: "New Mexican Mountain") is a rare poem which resulted from Mabel Dodge Luhan's "kidnapping" of Jeffers to Taos Pueblo in New Mexico as she had previously and successfully made off with D.H. Lawrence. The poem is a description of a tribal dance of the Taos Indians. Jeffers, never impressed with the Indians ("They beat their horses"), notes that the ancient tribal traditions are breaking down; the Indians "are growing civilized".

> *Only the drum is confident, it thinks the world has not*
> *changed. Apparently only myself and the strong*
> *Tribal drum, and the rockhead of Taos mountain,*
> *remember that civilization is a transient sickness.*

Jeffers holds out the hope that the human future will not contain the demeaning and degrading elements which in a civilization preclude a natural contact with the earth.

The medium-length narrative "Margrave" from *Thurso's Landing* is the most optimistic of the pronouncements on humanity in the volume. Jeffers postulates that the fate of the world has a provision in it for the brief moment of human history:

> *It is likely the enormous*
> *Beauty of the world requires for completion our ghostly increment,*
> *It has to dream, and dream badly, a moment of its night.*

The above may have been a favorite passage because Jeffers included it with an inscribed presentation copy of his new book, *Thurso's Landing,* in May of 1932. However, the passage does not present a sanguine future for humanity whose "increment" is in reality a species of nightmare to "the enormous beauty of the world". In the light of Jeffers' other longer tragic narratives of the period, this passage is bright with faded promise.

Robinson Jeffers' prescription and prediction for the distant human future is to be found, slightly fancified, in the poem "The Stone Axe" found in his next book of poems, *Give Your Heart to the Hawks and Other Poems* of 1933. "The Stone Axe" recounts the annals of a stone axe of "clear surfaces" already two thousand years old when it was found in Scotland just prior to 1815. The axe was taken to America by an immigrant and found its way first to Michigan, then to the museum in Monterey, California, where it was "mislabelled / But sure of itself". Skilfully telescoping time, Jeffers thrusts the axe into the future, imagining an era after the collapse of western civilization. The axe, having survived the decay of two civilizations, is found by members of the latest culture, the family of a primitive named Wolf: "His beautiful naked body / Was as dark as an Indian's, but he had blue eyes." Human beings *will* survive the collapse of the present civilization to live, as their forebears once did, in widely scattered small family groups.

Appended to the *Give Your Heart to the Hawks* volume are the poems from *Descent to the Dead* of 1931. "Ossian's Grave, Prehistoric monument near Cushendall, in Antrim (Ireland)" depicts the ancient "Warrior and poet", Ossian, as weary of life and of humanity:

We dead have our peculiar pleasures, of not
Doing, of not feeling, of not being.
Enough has been felt, enough done, Oh and surely
Enough of humanity has been.

Ossian's is the alluring call to rest, away from the feverish activities of human existence.

"No Resurrection" presents Jeffers' estimation of "the good life." Just as "The Stone Axe" revealed that Jeffers was perhaps more interested in the human future that the human present, so "No Resurrection" shows Jeffers' great regard for the past as opposed to a slovenly, eviscerated present. More than any other of his volumes, *Give Your Heart to the Hawks* reflects Jeffers' abiding fascination with the human past and future. As implied in "No Resurrection", Jeffers was cut out for another century:

Friendship, when a friend meant a helping sword,
Faithfulness, when power and life were its fruits, hatred, when the hatred
Held steel at your throat or had killed your children, were more than metaphors.
Life and the world were as bright as knives.
But now, if I should [be resurrected] ...
. . . . . .

... I should find the old human affections hollowed.
Should I need a friend? No one will really stab me from behind.
The people in the land of the living walk weaponless.
Should I hate an enemy? The evil-doers
Are pitiable now. Or to whom be faithful? Of whom seek faith?

. . . . . .

... A fool of a merchant, who'd sell good earth
And grass again to make modern flesh.

The speaker from the grave desires "no resurrection"—at least not into "modern flesh", a blurred and gray manner of existence compared to that he had known in the lambent days of the past, "bright as knives".

"Ghosts in England" recounts a monologue of the dead addressed to the living. Fate, the dead reveal, controls the living as well as the dead; death will be welcome in its day:

> ... *"We also,"* they say, *"trembled in our*
> *time. We felt the world change in the rain,*
> *Our people like yours were falling under the wheel. Great*
> *past and declining present are a pitiful burden*
> *For living men; but failure is not the worm that worries the*
> *dead, you will not weep when you come,"*
> *Said the soft mournful shadows on the Dorset shore.*

The English of the 1930's were losing their Empire, soon to join the legions underground which were the beckoning voices of *Descent to the Dead.*

With *Solstice and Other Poems* of 1935 Robinson Jeffers returned once again to the American present and, as the hand writing on the wall, he found modern life wanting. "The Cruel Falcon" initiates his criticism of modern life by noting:

> *In pleasant peace and security*
> *How suddenly the soul in a man begins to die.*

The body of a man may thrive under conditions of peace and plenty, but it is the soul that withers.

By 1935 Franklin Roosevelt was entrenched in the White House, the "first hundred days" were history, and there was constant talk (with little actual result) about revitalization of the economy. "The Trap" lampoons the type of mentality which prefers ignoble plenty, what President Franklin Roosevelt in a speech called "the new abundance", to personal integrity and individual freedom from statism.

THE TRAP

I am not well civilized, really alien here: trust me not.
I can understand the guns and the air-planes,
The other conveniences leave me cold.

"We must adjust our economics to the new abundance ..."
Of what? Toys: motors, music-boxes,
Paper, fine clothes, leisure, diversion.

I honestly believe (but really an alien here: trust me not)
Blind war, compared to this kind of life,
Has nobility, famine has dignity.

Be happy, adjust your economics to the new abundance;
One is neither saint nor devil, to wish
The intolerable nobler alternative.

Jeffers, "really alien here: trust me not", maintains his preference for another time, another place. He senses the purpose of the guns and air-planes—conveniences for the war that is already being calculated elsewhere as well as in Washington—but the domestic conveniences of the soft utopia "leave me cold." The nobler alternative of neutrality in European wars and personal integrity at home is the poet's prescription for an ideal, upright, lasting freedom for America.

Although Jeffers would have preferred to remain silent and thus be more readily understood in the future, in the late 1930's he was drawn to comment increasingly on political matters. His fear for the long-term future of the republic increased. "Shine, Republic", a sequel to "Shine, Perishing Republic" of *Roan Stallion, Tamar* of 1925, is a refutation of the idea that the "new abundance" of Franklin Roosevelt's New Deal is what free men in a free country truly need. Social prosperity, Jeffers reveals, is actually the enemy of freedom. Unhappily, minions of luxury will win out over the champions of liberty, and only future free societies will profit by America's errors, edging "their love of freedom / with contempt of luxury."

"Shine, Republic" widens a concept found in "Life from the Lifeless":

> *Men suffer want and become*
> *Curiously ignoble; as prosperity*
> *Made them curiously vile.*

Neither "Shine, Republic" nor "Life from the Lifeless" advocates ignoble poverty as a prerequisite to freedom any more than Jeffers suggests that luxury breeds free men. Rather, Jeffers wishes for the "intolerable alternative" of a middle way: men having enough goods for sustenance, but not a glut of possessions which tend to make men vile and corrupt. Under the circumstances (likely, in Jeffers' opinion, to accelerate) outlined in "Shine, Republic", the collapse of a free America is inevitable. These lines, while not yet fully realized, are now closer to fulfilment:

SHINE, REPUBLIC

The quality of these trees, green height;
    of the sky, shining; of water, a clear flow; of the rock, hardness
And reticence: each is noble in its quality.
    The love of freedom has been the quality of Western man.

There is a stubborn torch that flames from Marathon
    to Concord, its dangerous beauty blinding three ages
Into one time; the waves of barbarism
    and civilization have eclipsed but have never quenched it.

For the Greeks the love of beauty, for Rome
    of ruling; for the present age the passionate love of discovery;
But in one noble passion we are one; and
    Washington, Luther, Tacitus, Aeschylus, one kind of man.

And you, America, that passion made you. You
    were not born to prosperity, you were born to love freedom.
You did not say "en masse," you said "independence."
    But we cannot have all the luxuries and freedom also.

Freedom is poor and laborious; that torch is not
    safe but hungry, and often requires blood for its fuel.
You will tame it against it burn too clearly, you
    will hood it like a kept hawk, you will perch it on the wrist of Caesar.

But keep the tradition, conserve the forms,
    the observations, keep the spot sore. Be great, carve deep your heel-marks.
The states of the next age will no doubt remember
    you, and·edge their love of freedom with contempt of luxury.

Caesar, in Jeffers' usage, is symbolic of enslavement and dictatorship. It was Jeffers' conviction that only an intense and concentrated national conserving of ideals might preserve the country prior to inevitable demise.

"Ave Caesar" affords a precedent for dictatorship—the northern Europeans who willingly placed themselves under the Roman yoke for "love of luxury". It is not possible simultaneously to be a nation devoted to luxuries and a free nation.

AVE CAESAR

> *No bitterness: our ancestors did it.*
> *They were only ignorant and hopeful, they wanted freedom but wealth too.*
> *Their children will learn to hope for a Caesar.*
> *Or rather—for we are not aquiline Romans but soft mixed colonists—*
> *Some kindly Sicilian tyrant who'll keep*
> *Poverty and Carthage off until the Romans arrive.*
> *We are easy to manage, a gregarious people,*
> *Full of sentiment, clever at mechanics, and we love our luxuries.*

Characteristically, Jeffers avoided the "luxuries" of electricity and a telephone in his Tor House until the late 1940's when Una became too ill to be without them. "Ave Caesar" predicts a spate of socialism for America ("some kindly Sicilian tyrant") before the betrayal and final loss of its freedom.

Neither "Ave Caesar" nor "Shine, Republic" refers to the end of the world. Jeffers postulates a new set of "Romans" to rule after the collapse of imperial America. Even more distant, "the states of the next age" will establish their freedoms on a firmer foundation than America's. Human history has chapters yet unwritten.

If Jeffers terms modern day Americans "a gregarious people", in "Rearmament" the poet characterizes modern man in an equally disparaging light. The masses of humanity, even in Jeffers' day numbering in their billions, are easily swayed by mass movements.

> *The beauty of modern*
> *Man is not in the persons but in the*
> *Disastrous rhythm, the heavy and mobile masses, the dance of the*
> *Dream-led masses down the dark mountain.*

Here Jeffers is not championing the Communist terror in Russia, the Nazi tyranny in Germany, nor any contemporary reactionary fervor in the United States. He simply states that if there is any beauty in modern man at all it is to be found—not in individuals who are smothered in "the molten mass"—but in the pathetic delusions of millions who unwittingly play out the roles which a detached God has prepared for them long in advance.

And what purpose is there in such mass delusion and mass destruction? Jeffers, who relished cities as well as he enjoyed wars, provides his answer in "What Are Cities For?" Without the destructions and delusions, the earth, "crying out for tragedy", would be deprived of its due, the "many beautiful [human] agonies." Perhaps, as Jeffers proposed in *Thurso's Landing*, God also requires this aspect of our "ghostly increment".

WHAT ARE CITIES FOR?

The earth has covered Sicilian Syracuse, there asphodel grows,
As golden-rod will over New York.
What tragic labors, passions, oppressions, cruelties and courage
Reared the great city. Nothing remains
But stones and a memory haunting the fields of returning asphodel.
You have seen through the trick to the beauty;
If we all saw through it, the trick would hardly entice us and the earth
Be the poorer by many beautiful agonies.

"Praise Life" is a short poem from *Solstice* in which Jeffers reminds us that anguish and human life go hand in hand. No utopian delusion will disguise that fact, although America has come closest to countermanding human suffering. He is a fool who promises total release from the pain and toil which give life meaning.

PRAISE LIFE

This country least, but every inhabited country
Is clotted with human anguish.
Remember that at your feasts.

And this is no new thing but from time out of mind,
No transient thing, but exactly
Conterminous with human life.

Praise life, it deserves praise, but the praise of life
That forgets the pain is a pebble
Rattled in a dry gourd.

The final short poem of *Solstice*, "Flight of Swans", repeats the assertion that Jeffers has seen through the trick to the real state of things. The poet

> ... *knows that exactly this and not another is the world,*
> *The ideal is phantoms for bait,*
>   *the spirit is a flicker on a grave;—*

Jeffers' solution for "the fugitive human race" is to find the peace and to adore the God of the world's beauties. It is not likely men will do this, but it is long overdue. There is, in Jeffers' view, no other alternative:

> ... *Sad sons of the stormy fall,*
> *No escape, you have to inflict and endure; surely it is time for you*
> *To learn to touch the diamond within to the diamond outside,*
> *Thinning your humanity a little between the invulnerable diamonds,*
> *Knowing that your angry choices and hopes and terrors are in vain,*
> *But life and death not in vain; and the world is like a flight of swans.*

The phrase "sad sons of the stormy fall" alludes only superficially to the original fall of Adam. Jeffers refers primarily to the gulf which human consciousness has created in the human mind between the necessity for survival and the truer instinct to appreciate God's splendors in the world.

The solution of the human dilemma is to thin human nature a little with the real presences of the swan-flight world. "Sign-Post", Jeffers' "great ladder out of the pit of yourself / and man", advises men to "Love God" and eventually they will be

> ... *free, even to become human,*
> *But born of the rock and the air, not of a woman.*

Such Counsels You Gave To Me and Other Poems of 1937 is Robinson Jeffers' last volume prior to World War Two. Many of the themes relating to man in Jeffers' previous volume, *Solstice*, are reworked and reconsidered in *Such Counsels*. In this latest book, Jeffers was interested in defining what his idea of the best life for a man actually was. A second theme in *Such Counsels* is related to political theory: how would the politics of the world affect the chances of freedom for man in the future? Jeffers' answer is as bleak in *Such Counsels* as it was in *Solstice*, although he never prophesied an immediate collapse of individual liberty, thinking rather that freedom would crumble slowly away from those who were careless as to its maintenance.

The first short poem of *Such Counsels*, "The Coast-Road", sets the tone for the volume. Jeffers combines the two themes on man in one poem. He feels civilization, "like an old drunken whore", will come to destroy the free life of independent men, bringing with it the tyrannies, wars, degeneration, and false education which cut one's roots to the earth. Civilization, as Jeffers had written previously, is the enemy of man:

> *I too*
> *Believe that the life of men who ride horses, herders of*
> *cattle on the mountain pasture, plowers of remote*
> *Rock-narrow farms in poverty and freedom, is a good*
> *life, At the far end of those loops of [coast] road*
> *Is what will come and destroy it, a rich and vulgar and*
> *bewildered civilization dying at the core,*

A world that is feverishly preparing new wars, peculiarly
vicious ones, and the heavier tyrannies, a strangely
Missionary world, road-builder, wind-rider, educator,
printer and picture-maker and broad-caster,
So eager, like an old drunken whore, pathetically eager to
impose the seduction of her fled charms
On all that through ignorance or isolation might have
escaped them. I hope the weathered horseman up yonder
Will die before he knows what this eager world will do
to his children. More tough-minded men
Can repulse an old whore, or cynically accept her drunken
kindness for what they are worth,
But the innocent and credulous are soon corrupted.

A life of isolation and self-sufficiency is the best bet in a world socially, culturally and politically "dying at the core".

"Going to Horse Flats" presents a Robert Frost-like encounter by Jeffers with a news-starved old hermit. After Jeffers purposely proposes some naïve solutions to the world's problems (Christian love and savage extermination of one's foes), the hermit decamps in anger, leaving the solitary Jeffers to ponder the nature of the human world. The world, concludes Jeffers, was not made for man, but the individual can survive intact if his heart is not beclouded with human considerations but filled with the love of God.

... Man's world is a tragic music
and is not played for man's happiness,
Its discords are not resolved but by other discords.
But for each man
There is real solution, let him turn from himself and man
to love God. He is out of the trap then. He will remain
Part of the music, but will hear it as the player hears it.

He will be superior to death and fortune, unmoved by
success or failure. Pity can make him weep still,
Or pain convulse him, but not to the center, and he can conquer them ....

Occasionally, Jeffers' ideas on man have been misinterpreted as blind hatred of mankind. Jeffers' "Going to Horse Flats" corrects this mistaken simplification by demonstrating that his ideas on man would only serve to make one *more*, not less, humane. A "hater of men" simply would not take the thought to write "Going to Horse Flats."

But Jeffers cherishes no illusions about the human species. "Hellenistics" lauds the Greek thinkers for their wisdom in identifying the "three vices natural to man and no other animal". Instead of parroting the customary definitions that man is the only creature who thinks, walks upright, uses tools, has an articulate language and what not, Jeffers identifies man's unique "qualities" on the other side of the ledger:

II

I think of the dull welter of Asia. I think of squalid
savages along the Congo: the natural
Condition of man, that makes one say of all beasts "They
are not contemptible. Man is contemptible." I see

The squalor of our own frost-bitten forefathers. I will
praise the Greeks for having pared down the shame of three vices
Natural to man and no other animal, cruelty and filth and
superstition, grained in man's making.

This is no social Darwinism. The Greeks only "pared down" man's unique vices; they did not eliminate them, and civilization, though it tries to disguise them, only succeeds in making man's vices more insidiously practicable.

But how to avoid the vices and lead the best life? "The Wind-Struck Music" chronicles a ranching incident in the life of "old Tom Birnam", a cattleman friend of Jeffers. The poem concludes with Jeffers' enthusiastic appraisal of Tom Birnam's life:

> *... this old man died last winter,*
> *having lived eighty-one years under open sky,*
> *Concerned with cattle, horses and hunting, no thought*
> *nor emotion that all his ancestors since the ice-age*
> *Could not have comprehended. I call that a good life,*
> *narrow, but vastly better than most*
> *Men's lives, and beyond comparison more beautiful; the*
> *wind-struck music man's bones were moulded to be the harp for.*

The happiest, best adjusted man is one whose occupation is compatible with his ancient nature. Clearly, Jeffers is not fascinated with novel human occupations.

"The Beaks of Eagles" concludes with a thought related to "The Wind-Struck Music": man has not changed in the centuries since the ice-ages which helped to produce him. Jeffers realizes that man will and must attempt all that is possible for him, but notes that it is also true that man was formed by and is inalterably tuned to other times and different conditions.

> *It is good for man*
> *To try all changes, progress and corruption, powers,*
> *peace and anguish, not to go down the dinosaur's way*
> *Until all his capacities have been explored: and it is good for him*
> *To know that his needs and nature are no more changed*
> *in fact in ten thousand years than the beaks of eagles.*

The present and future are best experienced with firm contact on the human past.

The human world presents many choices most of which must be refused by an individual who wishes to retain his integrity. As compensation for human treacheries, Jeffers would have man remember God's beautiful presence as praised in the final lines of "Nova":

> *... We cannot be sure of life for one moment;*
> *We can, by force and self-discipline, by many refusals*
> *   and a few assertions, in the teeth of fortune assure ourselves*
> *Freedom and integrity in life or integrity in death. And*
> *   we know that the enormous invulnerable beauty of things*
> *Is the face of God, to live gladly in its presence, and die*
> *   without grief or fear knowing it survives us.*

Just as "Sign-Post" in *Solstice* is Jeffers' most concise theological dictum for man, so "The Answer" from *Such Counsels You Gave To Me* gives man "the answer" to social confusions and deceptions. Jeffers advises a firm neutrality when dealing with "open violence" and a sense of proportion and balance when in the midst of calamity. Man has his rightful place and truly knowing it, can maintain his personal integrity in the days of mass confusion and despair. "The Answer" ranks as one of Robinson Jeffers' clearest estimations on the conduct of human life.

THE ANSWER

Then what is the answer? —Not to be deluded by dreams.
To know that great civilizations have broken down into
*   violence, and their tyrants come, many times before.*
When open violence appears, to avoid it with honor or
*   choose the least ugly faction; these evils are essential.*
To keep one's own integrity, be merciful and
*   uncorrupted and not wish for evil; and not be duped*
By dreams of universal justice or happiness. These
*   dreams will not be fulfilled.*
To know this, and know that however ugly the parts
*   appear the whole remains beautiful. A severed hand*
Is an ugly thing, and man dissevered from the earth
*   and stars and his history ... for contemplation or in fact ...*
Often appears atrociously ugly. Integrity is wholeness,
*   the greatest beauty is*
Organic wholeness, the wholeness of life and things, the
*   divine beauty of the universe. Love that, not man*
Apart from that, or else you will share man's pitiful
*   confusions, or drown in despair when his days darken.*

A sense of intense sorrow is prevalent in "The Purse-Seine", the first of the short poems of *Such Counsels* which touches on Jeffers' view of the socio-political scene of his day. Recalling the panorama of a great city (San Francisco?) by night, Jeffers' thoughts run to the end-time of the civilization which produced the city:

> *I cannot tell you how*
> *beautiful the city appeared, and a little terrible.*
> *I thought, We have geared the machines and locked*
> *all together into interdependence; we have built the great cities; now*
> *There is no escape. We have gathered vast populations*
> *incapable of free survival, insulated*
> *From the strong earth, each person in himself helpless,*
> *on all dependent. The circle is closed, and the net*
> *Is being hauled in. They hardly feel the cords drawing,*
> *yet they shine already. The inevitable mass-disasters*
> *Will not come in our time nor in our children's, but*
> *we and our children*
> *Must watch the net draw narrower, government take all*
> *powers—or revolution, and the new government*
> *Take more than all, add to kept bodies kept souls—or*
> *anarchy, the mass-disasters.*

"The Purse-Seine" makes striking comparison between the harvesting of Monterey Bay sardines and the in-gathering of civilized man. Jeffers is thinking of the collapse of the republic at a time well after what would be World War Two—perhaps 1990 or so. The startling nature of the prophecies is surpassed only by the time-table-like accuracy of their subsequent partial fulfillment. In 1937, the end of a free America was in the long sight of Robinson Jeffers.

In the gathering storms of the late 1930's, Jeffers' immediate concern was to maintain his neutrality in tricky times. The last two lines of "The Great Sunset" announce Jeffers' intent meticulously to remain neutral:

> *"To be truth-bound, the neutral*
> *Detested by all the dreaming factions, is my errand here."*

Jeffers purposes to remain neutral—in spite of temptations and pressures to become identified with one ideology or another.

The poet's neutral stance is best exemplified in "Thebaid", a poem which stresses the moral immaturity of man.

> *How many turn back toward dreams and magic, how many children*
> *Run home to Mother Church, Father State,*
> *To find in their arms the delicious warmth and folding of souls.*
> *The age weakens and settles home toward old ways.*
> *An age of renascent faith: Christ said, Marx wrote, Hitler says,*
> *And though it seems absurd we believe.*
> *Sad children, yes. It is lonely to be adult, you need a father.*
> *With a little practise you'll believe anything.*

"Thebaid" chastises man for his gullibility and credulousness. The only hope for men seeking truth in the future may be to become hermits isolated away somewhere in a "cave in the mountain" or in a cell in "the red desert". Truth, in Jeffers' reckoning, will go a-hungering while men flock to the same empty shrines they habitually seem eager to call upon in times of distress.

One of the three false shrines debunked in "Thebaid" is examined in detail in "Blind Horses". Communism (one version of Caesarism) is analyzed for what it is, "not quite a new" concept. The bankrupt notions of a state-provided security perennially attract those greedy for power. Jeffers sees through the illusory Communistic idealization of the masses who, after all, lack the intelligence to conduct the most basic of activities in their own best interest. It is ironic that while Robinson Jeffers in 1937 in Carmel could see Joseph Stalin's grave errors, these same excesses could not safely be denounced until N. Khrushchev's reign decades later.

In the 1930's when tribes of the "leading intellectuals" were blissfully fellow traveling, Robinson Jeffers wrote "Blind Horses", the objectivity and accuracy of which is best evidenced by citing the complete veracious poem.

BLIND HORSES

The proletariat for your Messiah, the poor and many
    are to seize power and make the world new.
They cannot even conduct a strike without cunning
    leaders: if they make a revolution their leaders
Must take the power. The first duty of men in power: to
    defend their power. What men defend
To-day they will love to-morrow; it becomes theirs,
    their property. Lenin has served the revolution,
Stalin presently begins to betray it. Why? For the sake
    of power, the Party's power, Caesarean power.

    This is not quite a new world.
The old shepherd has been known before; great and
    progressive empires have flourished before; powerful bureaucracies
Apportioned food and labor and amusement; men have
    been massed and moulded, spies have gone here and there,
The old shepherd Caesar his vicious collies, watching
    the flock. Inevitable? Perhaps, but not new.
The ages like blind horses turning a mill tread their own
    hoof-marks. Whose corn's ground in that mill?

Jeffers correctly identifies Marxism-Leninism as a state religion founded upon some of the treasured ideas of Christianity and Judaism. Age after age experiences, almost as clock work, the returning destructions of freedom through collectivism. "Whose corn's ground in that mill?" Jeffers implies it is God's, God whose cycles—even in human folly—are perceptible and, from a distance, beautiful.

Section III of "Hellenistics" is Jeffers' peek at the future of a collectivist society. Perversion of freedom is inevitable, but, just as sure, men who "have tough hearts" will survive group nonsense to recreate somewhere once again a free identity for themselves. First World War Two approaches:

III

The age darkens, Europe mixes her cups of death, all the
*   little Caesars fidget on their thrones,*
The old wound opens its clotted mouth to ask for new
*   wounds. Men will fight through; men have tough hearts.*

Men will fight through to the autumn flowering and
*   ordered prosperity. They will lift their heads in the great cities*
Of the empire and say: "Freedom? Freedom was a fire.
*   We are well quit of freedom, we have found prosperity."*

They will say, "Where now are the evil prophets?" Thus
*   for a time in the age's after-glow, the sterile time;*
But the wounds drain, and freedom has died, slowly the
*   machines break down, slowly the wilderness returns.*

Freedom, the causative agent of a notable society, eventually dies and with it the society itself—not at once, but slowly and with certainty.

Section IV of "Hellenistics" finds Jeffers directly addressing the "distant future children" in the beginning of a new age. He tells them they are lacking nothing that the previous civilization's glutted citizens enjoyed. "Freedom is laborious". But most important, the people of the new age are whole once again, not dependent upon the mind-twisters of collectivist terror. The poet promises them neither ease nor relaxation, but their world will shine anew "in earnest".

IV

Oh distant future children going down to the foot of the
  mountain, the new barbarism, the night of time,
Mourn your own dead if you remember them, but not for
  civilization, not for our scuttled futilities.

You are saved from being little entrails feeding large
  brains, you are saved from being little empty bundles of enjoyment,
You are not to be fractional supported people but
  complete men; you will guard your own heads, you will have proud eyes.

You will stand among the spears when you meet; life will
  be lovely and terrible again, great and in earnest;
You will know hardship, hunger and violence; these are
  not the evils: what power can save you from the real evils

Of barbarism? What poet will be born to tell you to hate
  cruelty and filth? What prophet will warn you
When the witch-doctors begin dancing, or if any man
  says "I am a priest," to kill them with spears?

The trinity of uniquely human evils (cruelty, filth, and superstition) unless checked early on in the next age will, as in all the others, eventually bring man's greatest prospect, freedom, to its knees.

"Night Without Sleep", the final poem of *Such Counsels You Gave To Me,* provides a resolution to the social and political difficulties of the human species. Jeffers' deep faith in the cycles of his God leads him to conclude that even the present and future evils of man will, in time, heal. There is little use in fighting what amounts to predestination.

> *The world's as the world is; the nations rearm and*
> *prepare to change; the age of tyrants returns;*
> *The greatest civilization that has ever existed builds*
> *itself higher towers on breaking foundations.*
> *Recurrent episodes; they were determined when the*
> *ape's children first ran in packs, chipped flint to an edge.*

Jeffers thinks too of the incomparable Ventana country sunk in darkness with the rain gouging at the canyons, and is concerned about the damage done there too. The effects of erosion, he concludes, will be covered in time, and man's current disasters will someday also be soothed.

> *These wounds will heal in their time; so will humanity's.*

One year after *Such Counsels* Jeffers had a new volume at press, *The Selected Poetry of Robinson Jeffers* of 1938. Only four new poems were included in the compilation; they continue chronicling the decay of the age, admire uncorrupted contemporary life, and present Robinson Jeffers' ideas on how humans may arrive at truth.

"Decaying Lambskins" compares our age to others. In engineering, astronomy and military science our age has far excelled the ages of China, Rome or Egypt. But do we have much of which lastingly to be proud?

> *So boastful?*
> *Because we are not proud but wearily ashamed of this peak of*
> *time. What is noble in us, to kindle*
> *The imagination of a future age? We shall seem a race of cheap*
> *Fausts, vulgar magicians.*
> *What men have we to show them? but inventions and appliances.*
> *Not men but populations, mass-men; not life*
> *But amusements; not health but medicines. And the odor: what*
> *is that odor? Decaying lambskins: the Christian*
> *Ideals that for protection and warmth our naked ancestors ...*
> *but naturally, after nineteen centuries ....*
> . . . . . .

> *Our civilization, the worst it can do, cannot yet destroy itself;*
> *but only deep-wounded drag on for centuries.*

The Christian age seems to prefer to borrow the great men of antiquity rather than produce new equivalents. Jeffers sums up his age as that of the tinkerer. The age was founded on ancestral hopes for a life of comfort, and that mistaken notion has stained the entire epoch. Now "after nineteen centuries" the manuscripts and palimpsests of vellum are beginning to rot under our noses. Nonetheless, end-time is centuries off.

After a journey to Ireland, Jeffers wrote "Now Returned Home", a memoir of his travels which would not fit properly into *Descent to the Dead*. The vision of man here presented is sad and pathos-charged. An orphaned infant in precarious health is traveling to his new home to live on an isolated and cold island with his aunt. The little family is transferred from the steamer to a curragh and the islanders recede on the waves toward their home. A sad, gray picture, but also one of humans content with their lot, making a living in immense natural beauty and unwitting isolation from the corruptions of cities. Jeffers' memory of it all:

> *Now, returned home*
> *After so many thousands of miles of road and ocean, all the hulls*
> *   sailed in, the houses visited,*
> *I remember that slender skiff with dark henna sail*
> *Bearing off across the stormy sunset to the distant island*
> *Most clearly; and have rather forgotten the dragging whirlpools*
> *   of London, the screaming haste of New York.*

Man among the elements is man at his best.

"Theory of Truth" is the last poem of Jeffers' "middle years". In many ways it is one of his best for it combines his views of man and God in one thought-provoking poem. The view of man presented in the poem is deterministic. Jeffers asserts that man's search for truth cannot be satisfying or successful unless men first learn to uncenter their fascination with themselves. The Reverend Arthur Barclay of Jeffers' neglected *The Women at Point Sur* asked himself the three great questions which Christ, Lao-tze and Buddha must have asked:

> *I remember*
> *This is the very place where Arthur Barclay, a priest in revolt,*
> *   proposed three questions to himself:*

First, is there a God and of what nature? Second, whether there's
anything after we die but worm's meat?
Third, how should men live?

The three religious leaders found their truths but also, in Jeffers' theory of truth, stained their results with personal impurities. Their common error was the conception that man was the center of the universe. When this idea is finally eradicated, man will have a better opportunity to incorporate truth.

Then
search for truth is foredoomed and frustrate?
Only stained fragments?
Until the mind has turned its love from
itself and man, from parts to the whole.

The Middle Years: Man
A Summary

In the decade and a half between 1924 and 1940, Robinson Jeffers wrote much of his finest poetry. The poet's view of man during this time was faithfully recorded in harmony with Jeffers' guideline for versification, "I can tell lies in prose." Accordingly, Jeffers does not, in these or in any other poems, flatter mankind into thinking it is on the road to spiritual recovery from the disasters which would accompany the end of the Christian age. It is Jeffers' intention to tell the truth of human existence in the twentieth century. He does so from the perspective of the neutral observer who has the vistas of the past and the future before him to make more meaningful the human events of the immediate present. As poet, Robinson Jeffers takes the long view of man.

While Jeffers never wrote wildly adulatory poems in praise of man, there is in the later poems of his middle years a subtle change in emphasis from some of his ideas on man as expounded in *Roan Stallion, Tamar.* Though Jeffers preferred a goodly separation from most men in order to write his poetry, he did not, in the early years of his mature verse, become as incisive in his criticisms of human shortcomings as in later years. The poet was still interested in ordering his theological universe and, to a lesser degree, in presenting that world in his long narratives. Humanity, while it had never recovered from the gaping wounds of the Great War, did proceed fopishly to revel in the trivia of the times.

In those early days, Robinson Jeffers sought to present a more sober view of the human prospect, an anti-toxin to all the frivolous happinesses of a people living like grasshoppers in fragile little circles of sunshine. Those early poems seek in part to correct this short-sighted approach to life. Beneath their crusty exterior, the poems reveal a native concern by the poet for the ultimate shabbiness of men's brief lives and an even more basic love for the entire nursery of life on earth. Jeffers seeks to right the broken balance of man's disassociation from the provident earth. His approach, while at times caustic, is a well-intentioned and overdue purgation of human self-centeredness. In these early poems the poet has made his diagnosis of the human condition and applies the most appropriate means at his disposal to rectify the situation. It is only in the works of 1935 and after that Jeffers, his diagnosis now strongly reinforced by a cyclic view of history, finally is forced to conclude that the prognosis for humanity is—as he had expected in his youth—grim indeed.

But Jeffers' mature view of man is not all self-fulfilling vitriolic prophecy. The poet takes pride and comfort in the well-integrated lives of men whose occupations are conducted in accord with man's ancient nature. These fortunate few huntsmen and herdsmen are "well-buttoned in their skins" and demonstrate that humanity has not outgrown its dim origins. Robinson Jeffers does not glorify man's past. Instead, Jeffers' contention is that the lives of these men-in-nature have a message for all men, a message to avoid or at least to understand the pitfalls of much of contemporary life in order to remain whole.

The middle 1930's find Jeffers realizing that precious few people actually desire the truth about themselves, let alone are prepared to live in consonance with the truth. The poet begins to address—more realistically—a limited audience who might partially understand the poet's intentions. Jeffers begins to write of the individual maintaining his personal wholeness in the midst of impending mass disaster. The poet's view of most of humanity grows darker. Looking into the future, Jeffers realizes that the past will repeat itself and men will sell their greatest heritage, freedom, for socialized security and the "new abundance" of mass-produced trinkets.

Through it all, Robinson Jeffers holds out three hopes for man. Even in the midst of the creepingly socialized masses there are individuals who maintain their integrity as an inspiration for all of mankind. "Corruption is not compulsory". Second, the individual has the comfort of knowing that man's enemy, civilization, will not hold up under the increasing centuries of human corruption. Eventually, after generations of turmoil and suffering, mankind will again emerge uncivilized and free. And third, since there is no changing or helping the decay of the present and immediate future, the individual who has uncentered himself from humanity and its self-obsession has the greatest comfort of all, the certain knowledge that the beauties of the natural world are serenely ambivalent to human misfortune and serve to remind man that he himself is but a transient creature in the vast natural process.

Robinson Jeffers is concerned with human overpopulation since he realizes that more humanity means increased agony and accelerated corruption, "You making haste haste on decay." But the poet's single most important doctrine on man as evidenced in the poems of his productive middle years is the conviction that man is not the center of the universe. Time and again, Jeffers seeks to locate man, not out of any vindictiveness or malice, in his proper place—for mankind's ultimate good. Man is merely another creature of the world; at rare times a special creature, but nevertheless a creature dependent on his world and one who must act accordingly if he is ever to come of age or to fulfill his potential. Jeffers' view of man, then, is not negative in the wider sense. True, he does not seek to ennoble man through social action or through the use of ready-made package-plan salvation schemes. But Jeffers intends something fundamentally more beneficial for the race. He attempts to teach a few individuals the truth of man's existence, a truth based on facts which—in Jeffers' view—finally are available through the discoveries of modern astronomy, biology and geology.   These facts would—if recognized and assimilated—at long last make something noble of "that doll humanity."

Robinson Jeffers' vision of humanity is not idealistic. His human system allowed for short-term folly. He recognized that it might require the collapse of the Christian age for his vision ever to come to fruition, and he knew, agonizingly, that the remaining decades of his life ("Truthbound and neutral" as he planned it) would run flagrantly amuck and in violation of the best hopes he had for humanity.

Lend me the stone strength of the past and I will lend you

The wings of the future, for I have them.

How dear you will be to me when I too grow old, old comrade.

—"To The Rock That Will Be A Cornerstone Of The House"

Robinson Jeffers atop his Tor, 1937

CHAPTER THREE
All Things Are Full of God

When Man Stinks, Turn to God

The Final Years: God
(1941 - 1962)

More than any other factors, two disasters influence Robinson Jeffers' final four volumes of poetry. (*Medea* of 1946 is not considered here as it was a printing of Jeffers' successful free translation of Euripides' drama.) The first disaster was the Second World War which left its mark on *Be Angry at the Sun,* 1941, and *The Double Axe,* 1948. Jeffers' second poignant misfortune was the death of his wife, Una, in 1950. *Hungerfield,* 1954, the memorial volume for Una, and even his posthumous *The Beginning and the End,* 1963, are profoundly overcast with the specter of Una's death. These two disasters condition Robinson Jeffers' last poems.

Permeated with the twin sorrows of war and death, the poems of Jeffers' final years differ in tone and topic from his earlier work. The tone of Jeffers' last four volumes of verse is often that of a poet with clenched teeth "steering through hell."

The hallmark of Jeffers' personal code in his final years is endurance: endurance to watch his country win the war and lose its purpose; and endurance after Una's death to persevere in life until he too could join her in death. Jeffers' last volumes of poetry are more obsessed "with contemporary history" than any of his other poems. Public and personal events occupied the verse increasingly, and as they did so the quality of the verse—as Jeffers himself acknowledged—sometimes suffered. The introductory "Note" to *Be Angry at the Sun and Other Poems*, 1941, laments this tendency in his recent verse:

> ... but I wish also to lament the obsession with contemporary history that pins many of these pieces to the calendar, like butterflies to cardboard. Poetry is not private monologue, but I think it is not public speech either; and in general it is the worse for being timely....
>
> Yet it is right that a man's views be expressed, though the poetry suffer for it. Poetry should represent the whole mind; if part of the mind is occupied unhappily, so much the worse. And no use postponing the poetry to a time when these storms may have passed, for I think we have but seen a beginning of them; the calm to look for is the calm at the whirlwind's heart.
>
> R. J.

Although the poems of Robinson Jeffers' final four volumes are often concerned with human affairs, they are not mediocre verse. Each volume of Jeffers' mature work has something distinct to recommend it. For example, while the lead narrative of the *Such Counsels You Gave to Me* does not possess the vitality of some of Jeffers' previous narratives, the lyric poems of that volume more than compensate for this variation. The contemporaneousness of Jeffers' final four books of poetry is offset by two redeeming factors. First, many of the poems which deal with ephemeral historical events accurately predict the future instead of merely chronicling the present. Often the actual dates of composition are included to lend prophetic authenticity; in employing this approach, Jeffers often vindicates his earlier less specific, but heavily prophetic poems. Second, the poet becomes more personal in his later poems. The "real Robinson Jeffers" is, perhaps, more present in his final posthumous poems than in any others. Jeffers' final volumes of poetry give us his personal thoughts, feelings and reactions to the hardships of age, war and death.

In his later poems Jeffers' praise of his God is often diminished, but confidence in his now-established theological position remains supremely unshaken. Jeffers, it is true, does praise his God in *Be Angry at the Sun* with a single poem ("The Excesses of God"), but this work actually appeared two years earlier in Edith Greenan's *Of Una Jeffers*, 1939, a fond tribute to the poet's wife. Actually, "The Excesses of God" is as old or older than 1924 when that title appeared in a proposed table of contents for Jeffers' unpublished precursor to *Tamar, Brides of the South Wind*. "The Excesses of God" is a fundamental theological statement by Jeffers, but its topic and tone are out of context in the 1941 volume, *Be Angry at the Sun*. Similar publishing incongruities are not rare in Jeffers' volumes of poetry; he was characteristically indifferent to a strictly chronological presentation of his poems. Robinson Jeffers was more interested in the essential and mundane task of merely presenting his works, some of which, he anticipated, might "stick in the world's thought". This poetic long view in no way detracts from the simple grace and theological insight of the chronologically misplaced poem.

THE EXCESSES OF GOD

Is it not by his high superfluousness we know
Our God? For to equal a need
Is natural, animal, mineral: but to fling
Rainbows over the rain
And beauty above the moon, the secret rainbows
On the domes of deep sea-shells,
And make the necessary embrace of breeding
Beautiful also as fire,
Not even the weeds to multiply without blossom
Nor the birds without music:
There is the great humaneness at the heart of things,
The extravagant kindness, the fountain
Humanity can understand, and would flow likewise
If power and desire were perch-mates.

God is known by the superabundance of excellences he leaves behind in everything from the iridescent abalone shell to a moonrise. This attitude of heart-felt praise for God is far more in tune with the poems of *Roan Stallion, Tamar* than those found in *Be Angry at the Sun.*

"Faith" is a poem representative of Jeffers' thoughts on God and man in the early 1940's. The poem is filled with Jeffers' rejection of faith, the adhesive used by men to bind themselves together in common activity. As well, "Faith" is a comment on the origin and function of conventional religion. The glue of faith, Jeffers asserts in the poem, is slowly becoming unstuck and civilization as a result is decaying. Lies are required to make men work together. Is it possible, the poet asks in the final line of the poem, at last to choose a better bond for human conduct, a faith founded not on lies, but on truth, truth which would not come undone or tumble its adherents periodically into war?

FAITH

Ants, or wise bees, or a gang of wolves,
Work together by instinct, but man needs lies.
Man his admired and more complex mind
Needs lies to bind the body of his people together,
Make peace in the state and maintain power.
These lies are called a faith and their formulation
We call a creed, and the faithful flourish,
They conquer nature and their enemies, they win security.
Then proud and secure they will go awhoring
With that impractical luxury the love of truth,
That tries all things: alas the poor lies,
The faith like a morning mist burnt by the sun:
Thus the great wave of civilization
Loses its forming soul, falls apart and founders.
Yet I believe that truth is more beautiful
Than all the lies, and God than all the false gods.
Then we must leave it to the humble and the ignorant
To invent the frame of faith that will form the future.
It was not for the Romans to produce Christ.
It was not for Lucretius to prophesy him, nor Pilate
To follow him....Or could we change at last and choose truth?

The poem "Birthday" holds out the guarded hope that men of the future may choose truth over the historical sequence of ignorance, faith, religion, civilization and decadence. Truth, says Jeffers, is always at hand:

Girls that take off their clothes, and the naked truth,
Have a quality in common: both are accessible.

Jeffers' slim hope is that mankind may one day base its associations on the readily available truth of God.

The falsehoods, propaganda and false faiths flaunted in the early 1940's make it difficult for Jeffers to praise his God as he had done in more steady times. One of the prophetic poems of *Be Angry at the Sun*, "Contemplation of the Sword (April, 1938)", predicts that only the outright violence of general war will resolve the conflicts present in the human world. Jeffers addresses his complaint to his God:

> *Dear God, who are the whole splendor of things and the*
> *sacred stars, but also the cruelty and greed, the treacheries*
> *And vileness, insanities and filth and anguish: now that*
> *this thing [war] comes near us again I am finding it hard*
> *To praise you with a whole heart.*
> *I know what pain is, but*
> *pain can shine. I know what death is, I have sometimes*
> *Longed for it. But cruelty and slavery and degradation,*
> *pestilence, filth, the pitifulness*
> *Of men like little hurt birds and animals ... If you were only*
> *Waves beating rock, the wind and the iron-cored earth,*
> *the flaming insolent wildness of sun and stars,*
> *With what a heart I could praise your beauty.*
> *You will not repent*
> *nor cancel life, nor free men from anguish*
> *For many ages to come. You are the one that tortures him-*
> *self to discover himself: I am*
> *One that watches you and discovers you, and praises you*
> *in little parables, idyl or tragedy, beautiful*
> *Intolerable God.*

The above selection from "Contemplation of the Sword" serves as the best introduction to Jeffers' theological attitudes in both *Be Angry at the Sun* and *The Double Axe*. The other side of God, the violence with which God discovers himself and the human cruelty, filth and superstition unleashed on mankind and the world for a second time in his life, makes Jeffers' praise of his God a difficult task.

Be Angry at the Sun does not counsel despair, but two poems ("The Soul's Desert" and "Drunken Charlie") advocate the individual's enlightened disassociation from the follies which mankind is about to perpetrate on the earth. "The Soul's Desert (August 30, 1939)" is Jeffers' prologue to the long six years of war ahead. Man is thoroughly discredited as a source for anyone's faith; only God is left:

> *... Clearly it is time*
> *To become disillusioned, each person to enter his own soul's desert*
> *And look for God—having seen man.*

The only counsel Jeffers has to offer to man in a world of human madness is the individual's retreat to God.

"Drunken Charlie" concludes with the rhymed plaintive sentiment that the things worth fighting for are the pantheistic things of God, not man. Human notions of a sacred war are ill-informed.

> *Oh my dear, there are some things*
> *That are well worth fighting for.*
> *Fight to save a sea-gull's wings:*
> *That would be a sacred war.*

One of the final poems of the volume, "The Bloody Sire", suggests that the origin of religions is "stark violence." Christianity, thinks Jeffers, is on a rapid downward course, but a new seminal violence will, in the wake of its shock waves, create a new system of values.

> Who formed Christ but Herod and Caesar,
> The cruel and bloody victories of Caesar?
> Violence, the bloody sire of all the world's values.

"The Bloody Sire" of *Be Angry at the Sun* serves as a link to Jeffers' other volume concerned with the Second World War, *The Double Axe and Other Poems*, 1948. Jeffers' choice of controlling symbol for the book—the double axe of ancient Crete with its dual connotations of destruction and regeneration—is evocative of his ability to view the war from more than one vantage point. The long two-part poem which begins the volume, "The Double Axe", is Jeffers' last substantial narrative. It is Jeffers' finest philosophical poem and one of his most important theological poems as well. The work has been singularly neglected and grossly misunderstood. More than any other major work of Robinson Jeffers, "The Double Axe" cries out for intelligent criticism. The second division of the poem subtitled "The Inhumanist" is stylistically influenced by Nietzsche's *Also Sprach Zarathustra*. But the first division, "The Inhumanist" is the final eloquent statement regarding Jeffers' God immediately prior to Una's death.

A cluster of twenty-seven lyrics tail *The Double Axe*. These short poems like those of *Be Angry at the Sun* are frequently topical in nature. "Quia Absurdum" is, however, not topical except in its rejection of the two faiths which, in Jeffers' view, helped prepare the Second World War: Christianity and Communism. In the poem, Robinson Jeffers gives intentionally conflicting advice in the hope that people will see out of themselves through to the God of the stars. Jeffers expands one of the themes of *Such Counsels:* man has foolishly insulated himself from God's earth and from God.

QUIA ABSURDUM

Guard yourself from the terrible empty light of
*   space, the bottomless*
Pool of the stars. (Expose yourself to it: you might learn something.)

Guard yourself from perceiving the inherent nastiness of
*   man and woman.*
(Expose your mind to it: you might learn something.)

Faith, as they now confess, is preposterous, an act of will.
*   Choose the Christian sheep-cote*
Or the Communist rat-fight; faith will cover your head
*   from the man-devouring stars.*

The poem is an expose of misplaced faith in God and man. Jeffers identifies the faults of both false religions—Christianity and Communism—as their refusal to expose themselves either to the truth of the monistic, pantheistic world (Christianity) or to the truth of the nasty nature of man (Communism). In Jeffers' estimation, Christianity makes a religion of hating the world in order to find its God, while Communism makes a religion out of deifying man in order to avoid God. Both are crying need of the right kind of "exposure."

"Pearl Harbor" confidently predicts an American victory in the conflict to follow. The final lines of the poem, however, turn from the "ridiculously panicked" activity of war preparations to contemplate the methods of finding God in a confused world. The poet walks at night in the midst of the newly-proclaimed black-out and thinks of his God:

*   Walk at night in the black-out,*
The firefly lights that used to line the long shore
Are all struck dumb; shut are the shops, mouse-dark the

> *houses. Here the prehuman dignity of night*
> *Stands, as it was before and will be again. O beautiful*
> *Darkness and silence, the two eyes that see God; great staring eyes.*

Jeffers' theological monism appears in this quotation with the mention of the "beautiful darkness" which antedated man and which will claim him at last.

"Teheran" is a remarkably accurate assessment of the pathetic sellout of much of the European continent to Communism. Jeffers prophetically notes that after the Second War there will be only "two powers alone in the world", America and Russia. The poet is concerned that the agreements reached at Teheran are shot through with falsity and deceit, a fact obvious enough even at that time.

> *Observe also*
> *How rapidly civilization coarsens and decays; its better*
> *qualities, foresight, humaneness, disinterested*
> *Respect for truth, die first; its worst will be last.—Oh*
> *well: the future! When man stinks, turn to God.*

It, of course, was neither humane nor far-sighted to deliver Eastern Europe to Communism; stark evidence of civilization's modern-day decay. The human world "stinks" there already. Jeffers' religious vision and allegiance to truth tower wholesomely and beautifully against the backdrop of that enslaved portion of the world.

The coming Allied invasion of northern France is the topic of "Invasion (written May 8, 1944)". Jeffers maintained a strict personal neutralism in the conduct of the war and steadfastly desired the United States also to remain neutral in the European war.

> *Let no one believe that children a hundred years from*
> *now in the future of America will not be sick*
> *For what our fools and unconscious criminals are doing today.*

"Europe has run its course," wrote Jeffers and it was America's duty to "feed and defend" the lamp of freedom, not attempt to redeem the irredeemable. But the poet also sees the invasion from a religious standpoint. From his neutral stance he observes the "enormous weight" of western civilization beginning to slide to its doom. From this vantage "it is ghastly beautiful". Humanity should look for the beauty of God in things—even in the tragic moments of the beginning of the loss of man's freedom in this age. The poem concludes:

> *I believe that the beauty and noth-*
> *ing else is what things are formed for. Certainly the world*
> *Was not constructed for happiness nor love nor wisdom.*
> *No, nor for pain, hatred and folly. All these*
> *Have their seasons; and in the long years they balance*
> *each other, they cancel out. But the beauty stands.*

"Greater Grandeur" is Jeffers' theological summation of the Second World War. Having already endured one war to make the world safe for democracy, Jeffers did not subscribe to the conventional notions of the justness or worthiness of the second victory. But this time the victory will be different. Fate and God now have the human world in tow and the individual can only observe the tragic drama grind on to grim conclusions. Jeffers looks for the long-range beauty in the process of things and refuses to swim in subjective pity or terror.

GREATER GRANDEUR

Half a year after the war's end, Roosevelt and Hitler
dead, Stalin tired, Churchill rejected—here is the
Triumph of the little men. Democracy—shall we say?—
has triumphed. They are hastily preparing again
More flaming horrors, but now it is fate, not will; not
power-lust, caprice, personal vanity—fate
Has them in hand. Watch and be quiet then; there is
greater grandeur here than there was before,
As God is greater than man: God is doing it. Sadly, im-
personally, irreversibly,
The tall world turns toward death, like a flower to the sun.
It is very beautiful. Observe it. Pity and terror
Are not appropriate for events on this scale watched from
this level; admiration is all.

Jeffers predicts that what would become known as the Cold War would not only be a jockeying for power but also a protracted struggle with fate as the referee and final victor. During and after the Second World War the human world was often choked with cruelties and agonies. In *The Double Axe* Robinson Jeffers, who never forgot the beauties of the natural world, extended his theological admiration for beauty—not to the cruelties of war which he profoundly abhorred but—to the strange beauty of the process man was acting out. That manner of uncommon beauty could only come from God. Even the tragic beauty of God is worthy of "admiration".

By the end of the war Jeffers was thoroughly disillusioned with dishonest human governments. "New Year's Dawn, 1947" discredits respected human institutions and redefines the conscience. Jeffers eliminates as unreliable the state, the church, human customs and traditions, scriptures and creeds, even aspects of the conscience which might have been contaminated with human falsehoods. The best guideline for man is an intuition or conscience thoroughly exposed to the transhuman magnificence of God's creation.

> *The state is a blackmailer,*
> *Honest or not, with whom we make (within reason)*
> *Our accommodations. There is no valid authority*
> *In church or state, custom, scripture nor creed,*
> *But only in one's own conscience and the beauty of things.*
> *Doggedly I think again: One's conscience is a trick oracle,*
> *Worked by parents and nurse-maids, the pressure of the people,*
> *And the delusions of dead prophets: trust it not.*
> *Wash it clean to receive the transhuman beauty: then trust it.*

After the war Robinson Jeffers stood alone as never before. His younger twin son, Garth, had been a military policeman in Germany, but had—to the great relief of his parents—returned safely with his German bride. Jeffers had his family intact after the war, but his neutral stance had cost him dearly. He was scrutinized by the government during the conflict and with the publishing of *The Double Axe* long after the war's conclusion in 1948, the poet's tepid publisher repudiated Jeffers' opinions and work in an unprecedented publisher's retraction printed both within *The Double Axe* and boldly on the book's dust wrapper. All this Jeffers took in stride for it was exterior and passing in nature. What happened in 1950—Una's death—was not exterior and from it he was never to recover.

Robinson Jeffers' idea of the beauty of God helped him bear up under the loss of his wife as it had supported him in dark days of the Second World War. There was no attempt to gloss over the gaping loss; Jeffers would never be entirely himself again. But the poet's supreme confidence in all aspects of the natural universe—including death—kept him from despair. "Hungerfield", the narrative poem of *Hungerfield and Other Poems*, 1954, was first published in the May 1952 issue of *Poetry Magazine*. "Hungerfield" is not as long or developed as Jeffers' standard narratives and is intended to be a loving tribute to his wife. The poet chose the narrative poem as his best vehicle for tribute and grief. As such, it is a deeply touching and successful comment on a unique personal and literary partnership.

Besides the lead narrative, *Hungerfield* contains one play and fourteen shorter poems, only two of which further help to clarify Jeffers' relationship with his God. "Dē Rērum Virtute" is titularly indebted to Lucretius and in the poem Jeffers takes a similarly fatalistic view of the world. In everything God has left his mark:

> *I believe the first living cell*
> *Had echoes of the future in it, and felt*
> *Direction and the great animals, the deep green forest*
> *And whale's-track sea; I believe this globed earth*
> *Not all by chance and fortune brings forth her broods,*
> *But feels and chooses. And the Galaxy, the firewheel*
> *On which we are pinned, the whirlwind of stars on which our sun*
>   *is one dust-grain, one electron, this giant atom of the universe*
> *Is not blind force, but fulfills its life and intends its courses.*
> *"All things are full of God.*
> *Winter and summer, day and night, war and peace are God."*

Jeffers' fatalism is not guided by "blind force", but carries on in accordance with a deterministic blue-print of the future. Once again he rejects a world of pure chance.

The phenomena of the world, including man, inherit a collective consciousness which communicates to itself the direction of its future. The process, magnificently self-tuned, is compellingly beautiful.

This process is the subject of "The Beauty of Things". Jeffers considers the true subject matter for poetry to be the praise of the beauties which God has instilled in everything in the universe. Great poetry, he contends, is holistic in that it stresses the relationships of things, it makes an intelligent, truthful whole of aspects of the universe. The real reason for the existence of poetry is the unification of the world in truth.

THE BEAUTY OF THINGS

To feel and speak the astonishing beauty of things—earth, stone and water,
Beast, man and woman, sun, moon and stars—
The blood-shot beauty of human nature, its thoughts, frenzies and passions,
And unhuman nature its towering reality—
For man's half dream; man, you might say, is nature dreaming, but rock
And water and sky are constant—to feel
Greatly, and understand greatly, and express greatly, the natural
Beauty, is the sole business of poetry.
The rest's diversion: those holy or noble sentiments, the intricate ideas,
The love, lust, longing: reasons, but not the reason.

In his final years, Robinson Jeffers—in spite of innate comprehension of the evil man is capable of—attempted through the use of his theological insight to unify the world of nature and of man. Previously Jeffers had written of the beauties of nature and even of man; now he understood their interrelation as purposeful effulgences of God.

Nature provided an unusually beautiful gesture on Jeffers' death in January of 1962. The entire coast, headlands to mountains, was covered with a mantle of snow that January 20th when the seventy-five year old poet died peacefully asleep in "The Bed by the Window" precisely where, three decades earlier, he had forecast he would die. The storm of white diminished with the human world scarcely aware of the poet's passing.

In the year following Jeffers' death, members of his family and his biographer and friend, Melba Berry Bennett, assembled and transcribed the poems Jeffers had left behind, poems which spanned the long, lonely and comparatively unproductive years since *Hungerfield* of 1954. There were sufficient poems to make a thin seventy-four page volume—nearly one page for each of Jeffers' seventy-five years—*The Beginning and the End and Other Poems* of 1963. Aside from the minor difficulties in the transcription of Jeffers' occasionally cryptic handwriting, the contents are authentically his. The views have not changed nor has the style. No long narratives are present; Jeffers' health and lack of subjects precluded sustained effort in his final years. The pall of Una's death and the poet's profound loss provide the backdrop for the work; yet these short poems of Jeffers' final years are some of his most lucid and arresting works. Shortly before his death Jeffers was asked if he wished to write anything further. His response was, "No, I have said it all."

The Beginning and the End contains some of Jeffers' most deeply theological poems. The first poem of the volume, "The Great Explosion", provides a definition of God:

> *He is no God of love, no justice of a little city like*
> *Dante's Florence, no anthropoid God*
> *Making commandments: this is the God who does not*
> *care and will never cease. Look at the seas there*

> *Flashing against this rock in the darkness—look at the*
> *tide-stream stars—and the fall of nations—and dawn*
> *Wandering with wet white feet down the Carmel Valley*
> *to meet the sea. These are real and we see their beauty.*
> *The great explosion is probably only a metaphor—I know*
> *not—of faceless violence, the root of all things.*

Jeffers repudiates the Gods of Moses and Dante and reaffirms the innate creative violence of his God. This is the God who tortures himself—chiefly through violence—to discover himself. These violences are beautiful in that they are a magnificent part of the ceaseless cyclic monistic nature of God.

Several poems of *The Beginning and the End* forthrightly reject false conceptions of God. "The Beginning and the End" observes that the religions of love cannot conceal man's blood-thirsty nature; in fact, Jeffers contends that man's viciousness helped create these very religions:

> *[Men are] —Blood-snuffing rats:*
> *But never blame them: a wound was made in the brain*
> *When life became too hard, and has never healed.*
> *It is there that they learned trembling religion and blood-sacrifice,*
> *It is there that they learned to butcher beasts and to slaughter men,*
> *And hate the world: the great religions of love and kindness*
> *May conceal that, not change it. They are not primary but reactions*
> *Against the hate: as the eye after feeding on a red sunfall*
> *Will see green suns.*

The religions of man's past have been negligent in dealing with the brain wound which eventuated as men attained the conscious state. They have merely sought to compensate for man's evil by projecting it on the world, using beasts and victims as scapegoats. Jeffers advises man to see himself for what he is (blood-snuffing rat) and *then* think about the real God.

"The Great Wound" rejects and discredits one of the religions of man's past, Christianity.

> *And that a wandering Hebrew poet named Jesus*
> *Is the God of the universe. Consider that!*

Likewise, "Unnatural Powers" concludes with Jeffers' rejection of religions of love. Contemporary man's predicament is paradoxical. For "fifty thousand years" man has dreamt of doing the impossible (human flight, breathing under the seas, flights to the moon) and now that he has accomplished these things, truth reveals that the God who has aided man is a fiction. Of man:

> *How little he looks, how desperately scared and excited,*
> *like a poisonous insect, and no God pities him.*

"Animula" provides Jeffers' view of the doctrine of the soul's immortality. He does not deny the existence of the soul in a living man, but Jeffers finds the notion of the immortality of the soul merely another of man's braggadocian fictions.

ANIMULA

> *The immortality of the soul—*
> *God save us from it! To live for seventy years is a burden—*
> *To live eternally, poor little soul—*
> *Not the chief devil could inflict nor endure it. Fortunately*
> *We are not committed, there is no danger.*
> *Our consciousness passes into the world's perhaps, but that*
> *Being infinite can endure eternity.*
> *—Words, theological words—eternal, infinite—we dream too much.*
> *But the beauty of God is high, clear and visible,*
> . . . . . .
>
> *Man's world puffs up his mind, as a toad*
> *Puffs himself up; the billion light-years cause a serene and wholesome deflation.*

Man will be reabsorbed like other occurrences in a world composed of matter—and hence eternal.

"But I Am Growing Old and Indolent" records the results of Jeffers' interrupted and discontinued creation of vicarious narrative poem victims. The poet addresses himself and recalls his vows of the past, vows which, ruefully, he was unable at the last to keep.

BUT I AM GROWING OLD AND INDOLENT

I have been warned. It is more than thirty years since I wrote—
Thinking of the narrative poems I made, which always
Ended in blood and pain, though beautiful enough—my pain, my blood,
They were my creatures—I understood, and wrote to myself:
"Make sacrifices once a year to magic
Horror away from the house"—for that hangs imminent
Over all men and all houses—"This little house here
You have built over the ocean with your own hands
Beside the standing sea-boulders..." So I listened
To my Demon warning me that evil would come
If my work ceased, if I did not make sacrifice
Of storied and imagined lives, Tamar and Cawdor
And Thurso's wife—"imagined victims be our redeemers"—
At that time I was sure of my fates and felt
My poems guarding the house, well-made watchdogs
Ready to bite.
*   But time sucks out the juice,*
A man grows old and indolent.

In his final years Jeffers retained feelings of guilt. He interpreted his inability to continue writing narratives as the cause for the misfortunes which befell him in his age.

Robinson Jeffers' latter-day poetic inactivity was offset by the intensity of his adoration of the beauties of God in nature. At least seven of the poems of *The Beginning and the End* are concerned with praising the beauty of God. The poet's grandchildren who lived with him in his last years are included in two of his poems lauding God's beauty. Jeffers holds guarded hopes in "To Kill in War Is Not Murder" that, in spite of the corruption and vulgarity of modern man, his grandchildren may live to appreciate "the beauty of God".

> *As for me, I am growing old and have never*
> *Been quite so vulgar. I look around at the present world*
> *   and think of my little grandchildren*
> *To live in it. What? Should I cut their throats?*
> *The beauty of men is dead, or defaced and sarcophagussed*
> *Under vile caricatures; the enormous inhuman*
> *Beauty of things goes on, the beauty of God, the eternal*
> *   beauty, and perhaps they'll see it.*

With human dignity truncated by the vagaries of modern existence, the only beauty to turn to is that of God.

"Granddaughter" expresses the fervent wish that his granddaughter "in her quiet times" will also have the capability to love God.

> *When she is eighteen*
> *I'll not be here. I hope she will find her natural elements,*
> *Laughter and violence; and in her quiet times*
> *The beauty of things—the beauty of transhuman things,*

> *Without which we are all lost. I hope she will find*
> *Powerful protection and a man like a hawk to cover her.*

The one hope for humanity is its contact with God in nature. "Nightpiece" reaffirms his old confidence in nature, whatever the situation may be with man:

> *The elements thank God are well enough,*
> *It is only man must be always wakeful, steering through hell.*

"Vulture" finds Jeffers on an early morning hike. He "lay down to rest" and while motionless was inspected by a vulture wheeling overhead. Jeffers regretfully reports that he

> *...was sorry to have disappointed him. To be eaten*
> *by that beak and become part of him, to share those wings and those eyes—*
> *What a sublime end of one's body, what an enskyment; what a life after death.*

Jeffers longs to share a cyclic eternity through the reuse of his body by the ordinary creatures of God. The poet's pantheism includes deep regard for the less attractive albeit essential of God's creatures. While writing "Vulture" Jeffers may have recalled his first publishing success, "The Condor", another poem about a vulture-like creature written over fifty years in the past.

"My Loved Subject" reveals that although Jeffers had aged, he had no intention of lessening his praise of the beautiful regions of which he wrote in the past.

> *Old age clawed with his scaly clutch*
> *As if I had never been such.*
> *I cannot walk the mountains as I used to do*
> *But my subject is what it used to be: my love, my loved subject:*
> *Mountain and ocean, rock, water and beasts and trees*
> *Are the protagonists, the human people are only symbolic interpreters—*
> *So let them live or die.*

Jeffers' main concern as poet was not faithful rendition of all aspects of human nature, but the truthful and heart-felt praise of the God found in nature.

"Fierce Music" recounts Jeffers' forty years' experience with the sounds of the ocean at Tor House. The poem regrets the human penchant for disregarding or not perceiving the beautiful sights and sounds of God.

FIERCE MUSIC

All night long the rush and trampling of water
And hoarse withdrawals, the endless ocean throwing his skirmish-lines against the granite,
Come to my ears and stop there. I have heard them so long
That I don't hear them—or have to listen before I hear them—How long? Forty years.
But that fierce music has gone on for a thousand
Millions of years. Oh well, we get our share. But weep that we lose so much
Because mere use won't cover up the glory.
We have our moments: but mostly we are too tired to hear and too dull to see.

More than most men Robinson Jeffers did hear and see the splendors of God and endeavored in his art to record his feelings of devotion and love for natural grandeur.

The most devout praise of the beautiful things of God in *The Beginning and the End* is the poem "Look, How Beautiful". The God of the poem is monistic in will and act; he creates and destroys out of no humanly identifiable motive. He is recognized by the immense beauty of "all the things that He does."

LOOK, HOW BEAUTIFUL

There is this infinite energy, the power of God forever
working—toward what purpose?—toward none.
This is God's will; he works, he grows and changes, he has no object.
No more than a great sculptor who has found a ledge
fine of marble, and lives beside it, and carves great images,
And casts them down. That is God's will: to make great
things and destroy them, and make great things
And destroy them again. With war and plague and hor-
ror, and the diseases of trees and the corruptions of stone
He destroys all that stands. But look how beautiful—
Look how beautiful are all the things that He does. His signature
Is the beauty of things.

A true understanding of such a God does not, Jeffers implies, attempt to interpret God's acts as good or evil. The creative and destructive acts of God—unlike corresponding human activity—are both worthy of adoration. As Jeffers points out in ''See the Human Figure'', ''To see the inhuman God is our health.'' Man, if he is to become whole as a species or as an individual, must seek the God inherent in the world.

Beside the beauty of God, the second major theological theme in *The Beginning and the End* is Jeffers' monistic vision of that God. Four poems lay particular stress upon the idea that God is (in Jeffers' old age as he had described Him in earlier years) one source, one energy, one entity. The longest poem of the volume, ''The Beginning and the End'', suggests that the reason all things are full of God and beautiful is that all things *are* God. Each aspect of the universe is a work of God and is connected and interrelated through a type of consciousness. Nowhere does Jeffers make this clearer than in these lines from ''The Beginning and the End'':

I think the rocks
And the earth and the other planets, and the stars and galaxies
Have their various consciousness, all things are conscious;
But the nerves of an animal, the nerves and brain
Bring it to focus; the nerves and brain are like a burning-glass
To concentrate the heat and make it catch fire:
It seems to us martyrs hotter than the blazing hearth
From which it came. So we scream and laugh, clamorous animals
Born howling to die groaning: the old stones in the dooryard
Prefer silence: but those and all things have their own awareness,
As the cells of a man have; they feel and feed and in-
    fluence each other, each unto all,
Like the cells of a man's body making one being,
They make one being, one consciousness, one life, one God.

"Monument" underscores the importance of thinking of God as "One flowing life." The life sciences with their Linnaean binomial nomenclature system and carefully constructed phylogenies of descent are really only paralleling the truth that all life is interrelated. The gaps separating creatures postulated by man do not really exist in God's world. Ultimately there is no gap between the living and the non-living.

Erase the lines: I pray you not to love classifications:
The thing is like a river, from source to sea-mouth
One flowing life. We that have the honor and hardship of being human
Are one flesh with the beasts, and the beasts with the plants
One streaming sap, and certainly the plants and algae
    and the earth they spring from
Are one flesh with the stars. The classifications
Are mostly a kind of memoria technica, *use it but don't be fooled.*
It is all truly one life, red blood and tree-sap,
Animal, mineral, sidereal, one stream, one organism, one God.
There is nothing to be despised nor hated nor feared.

Jeffers' vision of God is monistic; he allows no divisions in the nature of his God—or in his adoration of Him.

HE IS ALL

> *There is no God but God; he is all that exists,*
> *And being alone does strangely.*
> > *He is like an old Basque shepherd,*
> *Who was brought to California fifty years ago*
> *And has always been alone, he talks to himself,*
> *Solitude has got into his brain,*
> *Beautiful and terrible things come from his mind.*
> > *God is a man of war,*
> *Whom can he strike but himself? God is a great poet:*
> *Whom can he praise but himself?*

Because God is one, he is utterly alone; no companions to relate to; the supreme monistic source and fountain. God's two main attributes, violence and beauty, Jeffers translates into two corresponding human occupations: war and poetry. Having no real adversaries, God fights himself and appears violent; receiving no sufficient praise, God lauds himself and appears incomparably beautiful in all his works.

The eventual extinction of man has no bearing on the unity of the universe nor on other life in it. The God of the universe who *is* the universe goes on blaringly forever, nothing diminished. For those who have "the honor and hardship of being human" and can comprehend the beauties of God's activities, the planet which sustains human life and the portion of the universe surrounding it are astonishingly beautiful—precisely as the earth was perceived to be by the first men who left it to travel to the comparative void of the moon.

HOW BEAUTIFUL IT IS

It flows out of mystery into mystery: there is no beginning—
How could there be? And no end—how could there be?
The stars shine in the sky like the spray of a wave
Rushing to meet no shore, and the great music
Blares on forever, but to us very soon
It will be blind. Not we nor our children nor the human race
Are destined to live forever, the breath will fail,
The eyes will break—perhaps of our own explosive bile
Vented upon each other—or a stingy peace
Makes parents fools—but far greater witnesses
Will take our places. It is only a little planet
But how beautiful it is.

The Final Years: God
A Summary

Robinson Jeffers' last four volumes of poetry were deeply influenced by two sad events: the Second World War and the death of his wife, Una. Jeffers had realized that his God could destroy as well as create; poems to this effect had appeared in previous volumes. But the bitter test of Jeffers' faith in the neutral God of the world came first with the acceleration of the destruction of the world's greatest civilization by war and again with the death by cancer of his dearly loved wife. These two stark and adverse realities forced the poet to live stringently in accordance with his ideas of God.

The neutral monistic God of these final poems plays no favorites with humanity. But it is Jeffers' conviction—more than ever before—that if ever man is to fulfill his potential, he must turn away from mankind as an object of adoration to the real God of the world. The God who figures so largely in the last four volumes has the same attributes as the God of Jeffers' first mature poems. However, the poems of the post-humous *The Beginning and the End and Other Poems,* define Jeffers' God with utmost clarity.

The four attributes of God as found in his last poems are not new to Jeffers' verse. The poet views his God as beautiful in the signature of his power on the universe, monistic in his presence in all matter, entirely alone in his glory and in his agony, and violent in his inexplicable creative energies. Jeffers rejects for a final time the anthropoid religions of the past, assuming that some completely new culture-age of the future will build itself up on the firm knowledge of a truer vision of God.

But when man himself perishes, God in his violent surgings will bring forth even more perceptive creatures to praise "the beauty of things". Taken thus, Jeffers' view of God is apocalyptic. The poet hopes for a reversal of man's ancient animosity to God through encountering the real God in nature. But Robinson Jeffers realizes that this will not come about in our present dying age; accordingly, he frequently addresses the people of God of the future.

I have much in common with these old rockheads.

Old comrades, I too have escaped and stand.

I have shared in my time the human illusions, the muddy foolishness

And craving passions, but something thirty years ago pulled me

Out of the tide-wash; I must not even pretend

To be one of the people. I must stand here

Alone with open eyes in the clear air growing old,

Watching with interest and only a little nausea

The cheating shepherds, this time of the demagogues and the docile people, the shifts of power,

And pitiless general wars that prepare the fall;

But also the enormous unhuman beauty of things; rock, sea and stars, fool-proof and permanent

The birds like yachts in the air, or beating like hearts

Along the water; the flares of sunset, the peaks of Point Lobos;

And hear at night the huge waves, my drunken quarrymen

Climbing the cliff, hewing out more stones for me

To make my house. The old granite stones, those are my people;

Hard heads and stiff wits but faithful, not fools, not chatterers;

And the place where they stand today they will also stand tomorrow.

—"The Old Stonemason"

Robinson Jeffers in front of Tor House, 1937

The Last Conservative

The Final Years: Man
(1941 - 1962)

One of the factors which went into the making of Robinson Jeffers, the poet, was the First World War. Neither Western Civilization nor Jeffers himself ever recovered from the impact of that war. It was six long years after the Great War that he was to emerge as a significant voice in American poetry. During his middle years Jeffers was partially able to shelve the implications of that conflict in the hope that America would remain strictly neutral in the future. In his final years Robinson Jeffers was to re-encounter the terrible consequences of total war, and, consequently, scuttle the fragile hope he had had of America's remaining splendidly neutral.

Under these circumstances, Jeffers' already cautious view of man became increasingly guarded. For a poet who had held out a frail and tenuous hope that mankind might at last become rational in the conduct of its international affairs, the actions of the leading nations from the mid 1930's forward were a final straw. In

Jeffers' view, mankind had hopelessly discredited itself with such shoddy activity. Jeffers, who himself remained staunchly neutral, wished only to disengage himself from the certain folly of the machinators of the second great conflict in his lifetime.

The dismayed poet felt bitter anguish at the impending confrontation, so much so that he could scarcely refrain from commenting on the major developments as the debacle unfolded. Buttressed by his neutral position, Jeffers was able to see through the smoke of battle with perspicuity to the eventual outcome and beyond. The observations and predictions which the poet made before, during and after the war stand singularly untarnished.

Besides personally feeling the burden of the war, Jeffers found that his isolationist and neutral stand was interpreted by individuals and some in government as unpatriotic and, at least once, even—ludicrously—pro-German. Jeffers' neutrality left him in an unenviable position: National Socialist sympathizers realized they could not claim Robinson Jeffers as literary ally; the millions loyal to the Roosevelt regime which had helped to foment American involvement in the war condemned Jeffers as un-American; and the fellow-travelers of Communism were eager to make negative value judgments about a man who was not avidly in favor of the total destruction of their illegitimate ideological cousins, the Nazis. As a result, Jeffers' always small but devoted audience dwindled—a fact which led myopic and jejune critics to attack Jeffers in his later years as a poet without either talent or an audience—a sad comment itself on the degeneracy of American literary criticism subsequent to World War Two.

The poet's neutrality is crustily expressed in "The Stars Go over the Lonely Ocean" from *Be Angry at the Sun,* the first of two volumes scarred by the war. In an interview with one of the feral Russian boars which years ago escaped from a private game preserve in the Santa Lucia Mountains, the ancient, gamey boar voices Jeffers' neutralist sentiments.

THE STARS GO OVER THE LONELY OCEAN

Unhappy about some far off things
That are not my affair, wandering
Along the coast and up the lean ridges,
I saw in the evening
The stars go over the lonely ocean
And a black-maned wild boar
Plowing with his snout on Mal Paso Mountain.

The old monster snuffled, "Here are sweet roots,
Fat grubs, slick beetles and sprouted acorns.
The best nation in Europe has fallen,
And that is Finland,
But the stars go over the lonely ocean,"
The old black-bristled boar
Tearing the sod on Mal Paso Mountain.

"The world's in a bad way, my man,
And bound to be worse before it mends;
Better lie up in the mountain here
Four or five centuries,
While the stars go over the lonely ocean,"
Said the old father of wild pigs,
Plowing the fallow on Mal Paso Mountain.

> *"Keep clear of the dupes that talk democracy*
> *And the dogs that talk revolution,*
> *Drunk with talk, liars and believers.*
> *I believe in my tusks.*
> *Long live freedom and damn the ideologies,"*
> *Said the gamey black-maned wild boar*
> *Tusking the turf on Mal Paso Mountain.*

Jeffers admires the smashed neutrality of Finland, the natural independence of the old boar—freedom uncollared by ideology—while despising the National Socialist and Communist revolutionaries and the cumbrously propagandized dupes of democracy.

How should men live for the next "Four or five centuries"? The poem "Battle (May 28, 1940)" provides a solution:

> *...It would be better for men*
> *To be few and live far apart, where none could infect*
> *   another; then slowly the sanity of field and mountain*
> *And the cold ocean and glittering stars might enter their minds.*
> *   Another dream, another dream.*
> *We shall have to accept certain limitations*
> *In future, and abandon some humane dreams; only hard-*
> *   minded, sleepless and realist can ride this rockslide*
> *To new fields down the dark mountain; and we shall have*
> *   to perceive that these insanities are normal;*
> *We shall have to perceive that battle is a burning flower or*
> *   like a huge music, and the dive-bomber's screaming orgasm*
> *As beautiful as other passions; and that death and life are*
> *   not serious alternatives. One has known all these things*
> *For many years: there is greater and darker to know*
> *In the next hundred.*

The ideal human life here suggested is identical to that set forth in *Californians* of 1916, but the Jeffers of 1940 realizes that the heavy pressures of population and politics will make an isolated life impossible for centuries to come. Adjust, if you can, and keep freedom alive until the next age, is Jeffers' advice. Many of the poems of *Be Angry at the Sun* forecast that the end of civilization is a long way off. The final lines of "Battle":

> *If civilization goes down—that*
> *Would be an event to contemplate.*
> *It will not be in our time, alas, my dear,*
> *It will not be in our time.*

From the Second World War and on, western civilization can only decline. Jeffers does not favor such disintegration, but, having to choose, he would prefer a clean and immediate collapse of civilization to creeping degradation and cruel slavery which come in the final time of a dying civilization.

A vista of the human future is found in section three of "I Shall Laugh Purely". Clearly the end time of a civilization is centuries off:

> *But this, I steadily assure you, is not the world's end,*
> *Nor even the end of a civilization. It is not so late as you*
> *   think: give nature time.*
> *These wars will end, and I shall lead a troupe of shaky old*
> *   men through Europe and America,*
> *Old drunkards, worn-out lechers; fallen dictators, cast*
> *   kings, a disgraced president; some cashiered generals*
> *And collapsed millionaires: we shall enact a play, I shall*
> *   announce to the audience:*
> *"All will be worse confounded soon."*

We shall beware of wild dogs in Europe, and of the police
in armed imperial America:—
For all that pain was mainly a shift of power:— we shall
enact our play: "Oh Christian era,
Make a good end," but first I announce to our audiences:
"This play does not represent the world's end,
But only the fall of a civilization. It is not so late as you
think: give nature time."

The poem concludes with the conviction that the next age will not be centered around man, but on the beauty of the non-human world and its God.

...I shall laugh purely, knowing the next age
Lives on not-human beauty, waiting on circumstances and
its April, weaving its winter chrysalis;
Thin snow falls on historical rocks.

"Prescription of Painful Ends" chronicles the future degeneration of the Christian era:

...the progress of Europe and America
Becomes a long process of deterioration—starred with
famous Byzantiums and Alexandrias,
Surely—but downward.

Eventually, only a matter of a long time, the era will end in collapse.

In the interim, Jeffers reconsiders the quality of human life in deteriorating times in "The Sirens". In those days, humans will still be excessively turned in on themselves, rejecting the substantial blessings of the angels of life. This personal deterioration, too, is entirely inevitable given man's present and past.

THE SIRENS

Perhaps we desire death: or why is poison so sweet?
Why do the little Sirens
Make kindlier music, for a man caught in the net of the world
Between the news-cast and the work-desk—
The little chirping Sirens, alcohol, amusement, opiates,
And carefully sterilized lust—
Than the angels of life? Really it is rather strange, for the angels
Have all the power on their side,
All the importance:—men turn away from them, preferring their own
Vulgar inventions, the little
Trivial Sirens. Here is another sign that the age needs renewal.

"Contemplation of the Sword (April, 1938)" begins with a listing of the mass horrors of war. In April of 1938, the Second World War seemed inevitable to Jeffers but the impending incredible suffering of millions is a festering source of agony to the poet. Men strangely seem to prefer these mass agonies to sanity and reason.

Reason will not decide at last; the sword will decide.
The sword: an obsolete instrument of bronze or steel,
    formerly used to kill men, but here
In the sense of a symbol. The sword: that is: the storms
    and counter-storms of general destruction; killing of men.
Destruction of all goods and materials; massacre, more or
    less intentional, of children and women;
Destruction poured down from wings, the air made
    accomplice, the innocent air
Perverted into assassin and poisoner.

The sword: that is: treachery and cowardice, incredible
baseness, incredible courage, loyalties, insanities.

The sword: weeping and despair, mass-enslavement, mass-
torture, frustration of all the hopes
That starred man's forehead. Tyranny for freedom, horror
for happiness, famine for bread, carrion for children.
Reason will not decide at last, the sword will decide.

A few years and these dreadful predictions could serve as graphic descriptions of Dresden and Stalingrad; little wonder Jeffers hoped his country would remain neutral and aloof from such contagion! If anything, Jeffers' pacifism was more intensely patriotic than the effusive propaganda emanating from the national capital.

What of the great men of the human world? In order to become great, a man must have a following and a man's following ultimately corrupts him and his ideas. Isolation from men is better for a would-be great man than erstwhile fame or even posthumous recognition.   Humans tend to corrupt the few truly great men they produce.

GREAT MEN

Consider greatness.
A great man must have a following, whether he gain it
Like Roosevelt by grandiose good intentions, cajolery
And public funds, or like Hitler by fanatic
Patriotism, frank lies, genius and terror.
Without great following no greatness; it is ever the greedy
Flame on a wick dipped in the fat of millions;
No man standing alone has ever been great;
Except, most rarely, his will, passion or intellect
Have come to posthumous power, and the naked spirit
Picked up a crown.
                  Yes. Alas then, poor ghost,
Nietzsche or Jesus, hermit, martyr, starved prophet,
Were you honest while you lived? You are not now.
You have found your following and it corrupts you; all greatness
Involves betrayal, of the people by a man
Or of a man by the people. Better to have stood
Forever alone. Better been mute as a fish,
Or an old stone on the mountain, where no man comes
But only the wilderness-eyeing hawk with her catch
And feeds in peace, delicately, with little beakfuls,
While far down a long slope gleams the pale sea.

"Great Men" provides a harsh view of most of humanity. The masses either support a man of base qualities or corrupt a man of worthy talents. As stated in "Faith", men can be held together only by outright lies: "Man ... / Needs lies to bind the body of his people together." Humans, as Jeffers had observed elsewhere, are "slavish in the mass."

If men must use hatred and lies to bind themselves together, there is also a compensatory and salutary exterior tension in the world which "hates humanity". Accordingly, the world of man is becoming increasingly conditioned by mass anxiety and insanity.

NERVES

You have noticed the curious increasing exasperation
Of human nerves these late years? Not only in Europe,
Where reasons exist, but universal; a rope or a net
Is being hauled in, a tension screwed tighter;
Few minds now are quite sane; nearly every person
Seems to be listening for a crash, listening...
And wishing for it, with a kind of enraged
Sensibility.
         Or is it that we really feel
A gathering in the air of something that hates
Humanity; and in that storm-light see
Ourselves with too much pity and the others too clearly?

Well: this is February, nineteen-three-nine.
We count the months now; we shall count the days.
It seems time that we find something outside our
Own nerves to lean on.

"Shine, Empire" is the last of three prophetic poems which deal with the future of the United States. With the American entry into the war, Jeffers foresaw a divided post-war world, half of which would become America's onerous defensive obligation in order to ensure her own survival. The poem seethes with Jeffers' intensely disappointed patriotism over the fateful decision to enter into the war. The poet's estimation of his countrymen slips to an all-time low. Because Americans largely assented in the decision to become involved with the war, Jeffers sees them as lower than most of "the natural run of the earth."

> *Powerful and armed, neutral in the midst of madness,*
> *we might have held the whole world's balance and stood*
> *Like a mountain in a wind. We were misled and took sides.*
> *We have chosen to share the crime and the punishment.*
>
> *Perhaps justly, being part of Europe. Three thousand*
> *miles of ocean would hardly wash out the stains*
> *Of all that mish-mash, blood, language, religion, snobbery.*
> *Three thousand miles in a ship would not make Americans.*
>
> *I have often in weak moments thought of this people as*
> *something higher than the natural run of the earth.*
> *I was quite wrong; we are lower. We are the people who*
> *hope to win wars with money as we win elections.*
> *Hate no one.*

But hate was ground out by government propagandists—enough of it to stir the people into action, victory and consequent bankruptcy.

Jeffers, who had spent considerable time in Europe, also had a low opinion of the Europeans' ability to retain liberty. Freedom was America's special custody and it was squandered to resurrect the dead soul of Europe.

> *All Europe was hardly worth the precarious freedom of*
> *one of our states: what will her ashes fetch?*

Jeffers feels that Americans of the future must hold up their empire or be doomed in its collapse. The American empire, foredestined to be weak and ill-administered, is deftly compared to previous empires:

> *Now, thoroughly compromised, we aim at world rule, like*
> *Assyria, Rome, Britain, Germany, to inherit those hordes*
> *Of guilt and doom. I am American, what can I say but*
> *again, "Shine, perishing republic?" ...Shine, empire.*

This pall of doom and fate Jeffers was never able to lift from his mind or future verse. The isolation he had recommended for men and nations was now a hopeless dream in an increasingly insane world.

But there was one glimmering hope in Jeffers' world—he believed that old personal allegiances still held. In "The House Dog's Grave (Haig, an English bulldog)" Jeffers celebrated the death of a favorite pet with the lines:

> *You were never masters, but friends. I was your friend.*
> *I loved you well, and was loved. Deep love endures*
> *To the end and far past the end. If this is my end,*
> *I am not lonely. I am not afraid. I am still yours.*

The old fidelities still counted for something in a human world gone irretrieveably wrong.

The final poem of *Be Angry at the Sun* gives the book its title. In it Robinson Jeffers reaffirms his neutral position in a senselessly committed world. The wheel of fate grinds those unable to sense its turning. Jeffers remains separate, his "cold passion for truth" more important than any allegiance to a human "pack."

BE ANGRY AT THE SUN

That public men publish falsehoods
Is nothing new. That America must accept
Like the historical republics corruption and empire
Has been known for years.

Be angry at the sun for setting
If these things anger you. Watch the wheel slope and turn,
They are all bound on the wheel, these people, those warriors,
This republic, Europe, Asia.

Observe them gesticulating,
Observe them going down. The gang serves lies, the passionate
Man plays his part; the cold passion for truth
Hunts in no pack.

You are not Catullus, you know,
To lampoon these crude sketches of Caesar. You are far
From Dante's feet, but even farther still from his dirty
Political hatreds.

Let boys want pleasure, and men
Struggle for power, and women perhaps for fame,
And the servile to serve a Leader and the dupes to be duped.
Yours is not theirs.

Against a world on fire, Robinson Jeffers retained his integrity and character. For seven years the oracle of Jeffers' neutrality would remain shut. When it reopened in 1948, the poet's view of man would be as grimly forthright as ever.

Many of the poems found in Robinson Jeffers' 1948 volume, *The Double Axe,* were written during the course of the Second World War. Jeffers had no reason and little opportunity to publish the poems during the years of the conflict; the poems stirred up enough controversy as it was when published three years after the war. Jeffers persisted in his firm neutral stance and explained his historical position in the Preface to *The Double Axe:*

> ...But I believe that history (though not popular history) will eventually take sides with me in these matters. Surely it is clear even now that the whole world would be better off if America had refrained from intervention in the European war of 1914; I think it will become equally clear that our intervention in the Second World War has been—even terribly—worse in effect. And this intervention was not forced but intentional; we were making war, in fact though not in name, long before Pearl Harbor. But it is futile at present to argue these matters. And they are not particularly important, so far as this book is concerned; they are only the background, or moral climate, of its thought and action.
>
> R.J.

The poet's Preface was in part a mild response to his publisher's unprecedented retraction (which boldly appeared on the page opposite the author's Preface) of Jeffers' opinions on the war.

The attitudes toward man in *The Double Axe* are reminiscent of similar opinions expressed in *Be Angry at the Sun.* In "Cassandra" as in "Faith" Jeffers remarks that men prefer lies to the truth:

> *Truly men hate the truth; they'd liefer*
> *Meet a tiger on the road.*

The closing lines of the poem compare Jeffers to Cassandra and her sad plight:

> *No: you'll still mumble in a corner a crust of truth, to men*
> *And Gods disgusting.—You and I, Cassandra.*

In contrast, government, in its massive propaganda campaigns to convince people of the rectitude of its provocations, openly dispenses lies.

INK-SACK

> *The squid, frightened or angry, shoots darkness*
> *Out of her ink-sack; the fighting destroyer throws out a smoke-screen;*
> *And fighting governments produce lies.*
> *But squid and warship do it to confuse the enemy, governments*
> *Mostly to stupefy their own people.*
> *It might be better to let the roof burn and the walls crash*
> *Than save a nation with floods of excrement.*

The poem is one of Jeffers' shortest and most vitriolic directed against the Roosevelt regime's hierarchy which was responsible for mobilizing the masses with mendacious hate campaigns.

As in *Be Angry at the Sun*, Robinson Jeffers commends those who had the courage to remain neutral during the Second World War. With the war drawing to a close, Jeffers has praise only for a trio of the nations of Europe. "The Neutrals" provides a clear view of Jeffers' dashed hopes for the proper kind of allegiances between men and nations.

THE NEUTRALS

Now the sordid tragedy crashes to a close,
Blood, fire and bloody slime, all the dogs in the kennel
Killing one dog: it is time to commend the neutrals.
I praise them first because they were honest enough
Not to be scared nor bought, and then I will praise them
That their luck held. I praise free Ireland, horse-breeding, swan-haunted,
And high Switzerland, armed home of pure snows, and Sweden,
High in the north, in the twice-hostile sea: these three hold all
That's left of the honor of Europe.
                                    I would praise also
Argentina, for being too proud to bay with the pack,
But her case is not clear and she faced no danger. I will praise Finland—
In one poem with the peace-keepers unhappy Finland—
For having fought two wars, grim, clean and doomed.

In "Fourth Act (written in January, 1942)", less than two months after Pearl Harbor, Jeffers summarizes the American people:

Because you are simple people, kindly and romantic,
      and set your trust in a leader and believed lies;
Because you are humble, and over-valued the rat-run his-
      torical tombs of Europe: you have been betrayed

A second time into folly.

The naïve American, to the detriment of his own land, had false confidence in his president and in the worn-out values of Europe. Jeffers likens the war to a five-act play (entitled "The Political Animal") being staged by God in an effort to make man see his own self-centeredness. Admittedly, the play is an inferior one since it can never succeed in this limited objective, but the war, after all, is only a minor event in the history of God's earth.

> *Not a good play, but you can see the author's intention:*
> *to disgust and shock. The tragic theme*
> *Is patriotism; the clowning is massacre. He wishes to turn*
> *humanity outward from its obsession*
>
> *In humanity, a revider le stelle. He will have to pile on*
> *horrors; he will not convince you*
> *In a thousand years: but the whole affair is only a hare-*
> *brained episode in the life of the planet.*

Jeffers' view of man is still the same, for man has not changed. Man is as caught up as ever with that least admirable facet of the world—himself.

"Calm and Full the Ocean" reveals deep-felt compassion for

> *Not a few thousand but uncounted*
> *millions, not a day but years, pain, horror, sick hatred;*
> *Famine that dries the children to little bones and huge*
> *eyes; high explosive that fountains dirt, flesh and bone-splinters.*

Human hatred in war produces these ghastly results, results which Jeffers wants no part of personally since his nation might have aided the victims rather than add to their numbers. The horrors are shocking and it seems that for the moment man's world has become unstuck from the world of nature: "As if man's world / were perfectly separate from nature's, private and mad. / But that's not true." The abnormality of man's acts appears monstrous, but Jeffers avers that human actions in reality are "Too small to produce any disturbance" in the natural world.

"What of It?" suggests that what is wrong with man can be cured by nature.

> *—what of it? What is not well? Man is not well?*
> *What of it?*
> *He has had too many doctors, leaders and saviors: let him*
> *alone. It may be that bitter nature will cure him.*

Given time and exposure to nature, man may be cured of his narcissism by his God.

Alone in a sea of indignant poems "Their Beauty Has More Meaning" once again registers Robinson Jeffers' faith—not in man—but in the beauties of God in nature. Humanity will one day become extinct, but that loss to the natural world will be infinitesmal. The lasting qualities of the natural world far exceed the few humanity had to offer.

THEIR BEAUTY HAS MORE MEANING

> *Yesterday morning enormous the moon hung low on the ocean,*
> *Round and yellow-rose in the glow of dawn;*
> *The night-herons flapping home wore dawn on their wings.*
> > *Today*
> *Black is the ocean, black and sulphur the sky,*
> *And white seas leap. I honestly do not know which day is more beautiful.*
> *I know that tomorrow or next year or in twenty years*
> *I shall not see these things—and it does not matter, it does not hurt;*
> *They will be here. And when the whole human race*
> *Has been like me rubbed out, they will still be here: storms, moon and ocean,*
> *Dawn and the birds. And I say this: their beauty has more meaning*
> *Than the whole human race and the race of birds.*

A similar sentiment is expressed in "The Eye" in which Jeffers contrasts the war to the Pacific Ocean: "It is half the / planet." The great eye of the greatest ocean watches things of importance, but "what it watches is not our wars."

Three of the poems of *The Double Axe* correctly predict the end and consequences of the Second World War. "Eagle Valor, Chicken Mind" speaks of "the bloody / and shabby / Pathos of the result" of the war. "Teheran" lists the principals to survive the war:

> *The future is clear enough,*
> . . . . . .
>
> *there will be Russia*
> *And America; two powers alone in the world; two bulls*
> *in one pasture. And what is unlucky Germany*
> *Between those foreheads?*

"Teheran" concludes with a sage observation: "When man stinks, turn to God." The gullibility so in evidence at the Teheran conference elicited such pointed advice.

But it is "Historical Choice (written in 1943)" which foreshadows the post-war era with the most astonishing clarity and accuracy. America had made its decision to lead the war effort two years before the poem's composition. The results of that choice—for America—would be sorry. History has vindicated the predictions of this remarkable poem whose subject is human folly.

HISTORICAL CHOICE
(*written in 1943*)

Strong enough to be neutral—as is now proved, now American power
From Australia to the Aleutian fog-seas, and Hawaii to
      Africa, rides every wind—we were misguided
By fraud and fear, by our public fools and a loved leader's ambition,
To meddle in the fever-dreams of decaying Europe. We
      could have forced peace, even when France fell; we chose
To make alliance and feed war.
                  Actum est. There is no returning now.
Two bloody summers from now (I suppose) we shall have
      to take up the corrupting burden and curse of victory.
We shall have to hold half the earth; we shall be sick with self-disgust,
And hated by friend and foe, and hold half the earth—
      or let it go, and go down with it. Here is a burden
We are not fit for. We are not like Romans and Britons—
      natural world-rulers,
Bullies by instinct—but we have to bear it. Who has kissed
      Fate on the mouth, and blown out the lamp—must lie with her.

''We Are Those People'' forecasts what must come to all empires, defeat.

I have abhorred the wars and despised the liars,
    laughed at the frightened
And forecast victory; never one moment's doubt.
. . . . . .

        ... it becomes clear that we too may suffer
What others have, the brutal horror of defeat— ....

To see the American future, Jeffers advises his countrymen to watch the now-defeated Germans: "therefore watch Germany / And read the future." Defeat is indeed ignominious. Like Germans after World War Two, Americans of the future will one day have to play the ragged part of the vanquished:

> *Our men will curse, cringe, obey;*
> *Our women uncover themselves to the grinning victors for bits of chocolate.*

"Diagram" depicts another view of the human future. There are two curves in the historical firmament: that of "the Christian culture-complex" and the aeronautical curve of the future "that began at / Kittyhawk." When the two curves cross in the sky Jeffers predicts dire things for the human future:

> *But watch when the two curves cross: you children*
> *Not far away down the hawk's-nightmare future: you will see monsters.*

Another theme which touches on humanity in *The Double Axe* is Jeffers' contention that man is the only creature unworthy to inhabit the earth. "Orca" contains the most pellucid statement of this position.

> *The earth is a star, its human element*
> *Is what darkens it. War is evil, the peace will be evil,*
> *cruelty is evil; death is not evil. But the breed of man*
> *Has been queer from the start. It looks like a botched*
> *experiment that has run wild and ought to be stopped.*

"The King of Beasts" reiterates Jeffers' view of human cruelty and also registers the resultant human unhappiness.

THE KING OF BEASTS

Cattle in the slaughter-pens, laboratory dogs
Slowly tortured to death, flogged horses, trapped fur-bearers,
Agonies in the snow, splintering your needle teeth on chill steel—look:
Mankind, your Satans, are not very happy either. I wish
*   you had seen the battle-squalor, the bombings,*
The screaming fire-deaths. I wish you could watch the
*   endless hunger, the cold, the moaning, the hopelessness.*
I wish you could smell the Russian and German torture-
*   camps. It is quite natural the two-footed beast*
That inflicts terror, the cage, enslavement, torment and
*   death on all other animals*
Should eat the dough that he mixes and drink the death-
*   cup. It is just and decent. And it will increase, I think.*

With the horrors of the war, human savagery has been cruelly turned in on man.

"Original Sin" recalls man's barbarous past, a past which Jeffers feels is worth recalling from time to time, if only to provide perspective to the present. Jeffers pictures human predecessors gleefully dancing about a pit in which they are slowly roasting to death a mammoth. The poet concludes with characteristic disavowal of the human species:

*   These are the people.*
This is the human dawn. As for me, I would rather
Be a worm in a wild apple than a son of man.
But we are what we are, and we might remember
Not to hate any person, for all are vicious;
And not be astonished at any evil, all are deserved;
And not fear death; it is the only way to be cleansed.

For man, the only solution to his blood-thirsty and cruel nature is the final escape, death—the sole method of being washed clean of the original sin of being born a man.

The final poem of *The Double Axe*, ''The Inquisitors'', is an eerie hypothetical account of a judgment on man by a race of giant hills who frequent the Santa Lucia Mountains south of Carmel. They examine representative samples of the human species on a ''table-topped rock''. The hills discuss the apparent harmlessness yet obvious noxiousness of the creatures and even peel one human to examine the brain, the supposed source of the contagion of the earth. They ponder the human possession of the newly discovered secret of nuclear energy and consider exterminating the species but decide that man is ultimately not nearly as dangerous as assumed:

"It is not likely they can destroy all life: the planet is
    capacious. Life would surely grow up again
From grubs in the soil, or the newt and toad level, and be
    beautiful again. And again perhaps break its legs
On its own cleverness: who can forecast the future?"

Humanity—with its apparently monumental difficulties—is inconsequential when compared to the earth's energetic thrust for life.

Jeffers presents his best possible counsel in "Advice to Pilgrims". Humans are guided by unreliable pilots, their minds. The senses are slightly more reliable, but intuition remains the most trustworthy guide—if it has been properly exposed to the beautiful natural qualities of the world. The poet's advice is succinct. Mankind can have its minor beauty only when insulated, not from nature, but from other men.

ADVICE TO PILGRIMS

That our senses lie and our minds trick us is true, but in general
They are honest rustics; trust them a little;
The senses more than the mind, and your own mind more than another man's.
As to the mind's pilot, intuition—
Catch him clean and stark naked, he is first of truth-tellers; dream-clothed, or dirty
With fears and wishes, he is prince of liars.
The first fear is of death: trust no immortalist. The first desire
Is to be loved: trust no mother's son.
Finally I say let demagogues and world-redeemers babble their emptiness
To empty ears; twice duped is too much.
Walk on gaunt shores and avoid the people; rock and wave are good prophets;
Wise are the wings of the gull, pleasant her song.

The redeeming world of nature is the heal-all for humans making the pilgrimage through life who wish to remain in contact with the true goal of their journey, individual reunion with God.

The Double Axe was written by a poet who felt and saw clearly the unpleasant realities of human behavior during a terrible time in human history. The poems are not complimentary to man. Robinson Jeffers' deep dejection at seeing some of the most cherished and precious of human achievements—entities such as freedom, human dignity and integrity, honesty, personal decency and kindness—defaced and degraded is reflected in the short poems of *The Double Axe*. The war ground down to its heavy conclusion, and the heavy peace fell as Jeffers had predicted it would.

At a time when the rest of the world was busy trying to get back on its feet, Robinson Jeffers had to face the grim prospect that Una's cancer (which had been successfully treated in 1941) had now become malignant. The death of his wife would stifle significant publication by the poet (with the exception of *Hungerfield* of 1954) for the remainder of his life.

Five of the thirteen short poems of *Hungerfield* deal directly with Jeffers' view of man. They reinforce his concepts of the nature and definition of man, the limited beauty of humanity, and the best way for a man to live. The longest of the lyrics of *Hungerfield* is "Dē Rērum Virtute" which, along with other topics, considers the limited beauty of man. Jeffers, fully convinced that man is part of God in nature, writes of the beauty of the human species—in its proper setting. It is difficult to see through to the real beauty that is man's, suggests Jeffers, since the quality and quantity of beauty present in all of humanity is eclipsed by the brilliance of God and of nature.

> ... *Indeed it is hard to see beauty*
> *In any of the acts of man: but that means the acts of a sick microbe*
> *On a satellite of a dust-grain twirled in a whirlwind*
> *In the world of stars ....*
> *Something perhaps may come of him; in any event*
> *He can't last long.—Well: I am short of patience*
> *Since my wife died ... and this era of spite and hate-filled half-worlds*
> *Gets to the bone. I believe that man too is beautiful,*
> *But it is hard to see, and wrapped up in falsehoods.*
> *Michangelo and the Greek sculptors—*
> *How they flattered the race! Homer and Shakespeare—*
> *How they flattered the race!*

> ## V

> *One light is left us: the beauty of things, not men;*
> *The immense beauty of the world, not the human world.*
> *Look—and without imagination, desire nor dream—directly*
> *At the mountains and the sea. Are they not beautiful?*

> . . . . . .

> *The beauty of things means virtue and value in them.*
> *It is in the beholder's eye, not the world? Certainly.*
> *It is the human mind's translation of the transhuman*
> *Intrinsic glory. It means that the world is sound,*
> *Whatever the sick microbe does. But he too is part of it.*

Jeffers writes searchingly of the real but limited significance of man.

The human population explosion, which for Carmel had begun in the early 1920's and in Jeffers' day was still nowhere near culmination, is what prompted "Carmel Point", an expression of pity for the beautiful places of the earth befouled with human habitation. However, man will soon (in geological terms) vanish from the face of the earth and Carmel Point will beautifully regain its patient, pristine loveliness.

CARMEL POINT

The extraordinary patience of things!
This beautiful place defaced with a crop of suburban houses—
How beautiful when we first beheld it,
Unbroken field of poppy and lupin walled with clean cliffs;
No intrusion but two or three horses pasturing,
Or a few milch cows rubbing their flanks on the outcrop rockheads—
Now the spoiler has come: does it care?
Not faintly. It has all time. It knows the people are a tide
That swells and in time will ebb, and all
Their works dissolve. Meanwhile the image of the pristine beauty
Lives in the very grain of the granite,
Safe as the endless ocean that climbs our cliff.—As for us:
We must uncenter our minds from ourselves;
We must unhumanize our views a little, and become confident
As the rock and ocean that we were made from.

The theme is the insignificance of man—and the remote possibility of man becoming tranquil at last under the sure influence of nature.

Man sprang from nature and is part of nature still. Jeffers' definition of man ("man, you might say, is nature dreaming") from his brief poem "The Beauty of Things" emphasizes the special abilities and mission of man. It is man's destiny to "break the somnambulism of nature" with his consciousness—not an important task as things go, but nevertheless a unique one. If only, Jeffers hopes, one day man would be able to transcend the scars of the wound caused by his emerging from that sleep and duly act out his destined role in the natural world. At present, regretably, man is merely a "spoiler".

Most of humanity is dangerously unstable as indicated in the autobiographical "The Old Stonemason". Jeffers' communion is not with fickle men, but with the conservative and unchanging "people" of his avocation and inspiration, the "people" of "Hard heads and stiff wits", the faithful, rocky "people" of Jeffers' stonemasonry. The poet's position is purposefully distant and remote from the "popular drift" of humanity.

THE OLD STONEMASON

Stones that rolled in the sea for a thousand years
Have climbed the cliff and stand stiff-ranked in the house-walls.
Hurricane may spit his lungs out they'll not be moved.
They have become conservative; they remember the endless
Treacheries of ever-sliding water and slimy ambushes
Along the shore; they'll never again give themselves
To the tides and the dreams, the popular drift,
The whirlpool progress, but stand steady on their hill—
At bay?—Yes, but unbroken.
*   I have much in common with these old rockheads.*
Old comrades, I too have escaped and stand.
I have shared in my time the human illusions, the muddy foolishness
And craving passions, but something thirty years ago pulled me
Out of the tide-wash; I must not even pretend
To be one of the people. I must stand here
Alone with open eyes in the clear air growing old,
Watching with interest and only a little nausea
The cheating shepherds, this time of the demagogues and the
*   docile people, the shifts of power,*
And pitiless general wars that prepare the fall;

But also the enormous unhuman beauty of things; rock, sea and
    stars, fool-proof and permanent,
The birds like yachts in the air, or beating like hearts
Along the water; the flares of sunset, the peaks of Point Lobos;
And hear at night the huge waves, my drunken quarrymen
Climbing the cliff, hewing out more stones for me
To make my house. The old granite stones, those are my people;
Hard heads and stiff wits but faithful, not fools, not chatterers;
And the place where they stand today they will stand also tomorrow.

Humanity being what it was, Jeffers looked elsewhere for honest companionship and steadfastly refused to relinquish his scournful view of the masses of humanity.

Nor did Jeffers abandon his personal position of neutrality in human factions and wars. "Time of Disturbance" restresses the old stonemason's code of non-alignment with men. Inured feelings of good and evil, of love and revenge, are out of place in a neutral world. The poet advises man to preserve at all costs a separate, uncontaminated neutral stance in causes, crises, organizations, and human quarrels.

TIME OF DISTURBANCE

The best is, in war or faction or ordinary vindictive
     life, not to take sides.
Leave it for children, and the emotional rabble of the streets, to
     back their horse or support a brawler.

But if you are forced into it: remember that good and evil are as
     common as air, and like air shared
By the panting belligerents; the moral indignation that hoarsens
     orators is mostly a fool.

Hold your nose and compromise; keep a cold mind. Fight, if needs
     must; hate no one. Do as God does,
Or the tragic poets: They crush their man without hating him,
     their Lear or Hitler, and often save without love.

As for these quarrels, they are like the moon, recurrent and fan-
     tastic. They have their beauty but night's is better.
It is better to be silent than to make a noise. It is better to strike dead
     than to strike often. It is better not to strike.

This personal ethic is an adaptation of older codes of human behavior tempered with Jeffers' own neutrality and pacifism. Human violence and war were ingrained activities of man. If a man must kill, he should do so dispassionately—not hardened with hatred—but Jeffers thought it far better, to avoid altogether situations of potential viciousness.

The poems of *Hungerfield* reveal a solitary, uncommitted, aging man in permanent anguish at the loss of his wife. Jeffers' commentary on man in *Hungerfield* is ideologically similar to that of previous volumes, with the tone, perhaps, being somewhat less bitter and biting. His advice on the conduct of human life was addressed to a narrow band of those capable of listening. Age, sorrow, grief and loss have tempered the man, but the crisp clarity of diction and the same old allegiance to truth are present in full vigor in the handful of poems from the last volume to appear in Jeffers' lifetime. After 1954 and *Hungerfield,* the aging widower had another eight years to live. The sparse poetic fruit of those years is mute tribute to his departed Una.

Although Robinson Jeffers' posthumous *The Beginning and the End* is the shortest book of his mature poems, eight years of life went into the forty-eight poems collected in the little volume. Jeffers devotes considerable attention in these poems to man. As the volume's title suggests, Jeffers' observations on man range from the hypothetical origin of man to the final extinction of the species.

The title poem, "The Beginning and the End", hypothesizes the origin of man. Man, originally a northern forest ape, was forced to take up the bipedal state when the great northern forests were decimated through climatological change. Early man lived in constant fear of other more sizeable and ferocious creatures. Man had to perfect alertness in the form of consciousness, fire, and weapons in an effort to survive. But in so doing, man also made

> *a wound ... in the brain*
> *When life became too hard, and [it] has never healed.*

Jeffers expresses the hope that slowly one day man may become accustomed to his own nature and live in accordance with it.

>   *That ancient wound in the brain*
> *Has never healed, it hangs wide, it lets in the stars*
> *Into the animal-stinking ghost-ridden darkness, the human soul.*
> *The mind of man ....*
> *Slowly, perhaps, man may grow into it—*
> *Do you think so? This villanous king of beasts, this deformed ape?—He has mind*
> *And imagination, he might go far*
> *And end in honor. The hawks are more heroic but man has a steeper mind,*
> *Huge pits of darkness, high peaks of light,*
> *You may calculate a comet's orbit or the dive of a hawk, not a man's mind.*

In Jeffers' final opinion, the future of man is open either to honor or shame. Given the long view of things, "The Beginning and the End" is a reasonably optimistic assessment of man's future. Man's steep mind cannot be predicted, channeled, or calculated. Perhaps there are fine things in store for man. There is, however, no cause for glorying in man's past; men have been and still are in Jeffers' view "Blood-snuffing rats".

What function does man serve in God's ordering of things?

>   *The human race is one of God's sense-organs,*
> *Immoderately alerted to feel good and evil*
> *And pain and pleasure. It is a nerve-ending,*
> *Like eye, ear, taste-buds (hardly able to endure*
> *The nauseous draught) it is a sensory organ of God's.*
> *As Titan-mooded Lear or Prometheus reveal to their audience*
> *Extremes of pain and passion they will never find*
> *In their own lives but through the poems as sense-organs of beasts and men*
> *Are sense-organs of God ....*

Man's mission is to experience for God some of the heights and depths which exist but which God has not experienced himself. Human agony, passion and pain are observed by God and have a cathartic effect upon Him in the same manner that heroic theatrical tragedy affects a human audience.

Man is not the only sense-organ of God, but "one of God's sense-organs". Man's mission is important but not unique. Humans are unusually alert to conceptions of good and evil—not because these notions are real (any more than King Lear's grief would be possible or endurable), but because good and evil are conceptions which God wishes to sound out through the vicarious experiences of man. Jeffers writes that there are other active centers of intense and focused perception in the universe:

> *...and on other globes*
> *Throughout the universe much greater nerve-endings*
> *Enrich the consciousness of the one being*
> *Who is all that exists.*

In comparison to these "greater nerve-endings", man is of little consequence. "The Beginning and the End" provides Jeffers' final assessment of man's ordained mission:

> *This is man's mission:*
> *To find and feel; all animal experience*
> *Is a part of God's life. He would be balanced and neutral*
> *As a rock on the shore, but the red sunset-waves*
> *Of life's passions fling over him. He endures them,*
> *We endure ours.*

The exotic possibilities of animal existence and perception are "part of God's life", a part which man is to endure and experience as a creature of God. Man exists to find and to feel the universe about him, purposes which men are able to fulfill.

"Believe History" takes a sobering look backward at the human past and finds little about which to be gleeful. Incredibly diabolical activities are the part of history of the species which men are apt to neglect. These horrors have accompanied man through time to the "weeping horrors of old age."

BELIEVE HISTORY

I think we are the ape's children, but believe history
We are the Devil's: the fire-deaths, the flaying alive,
The blinding with hot iron, the crucifixions, the castrations, the famous
Murder of a King of England by hot iron forced
Through the anus to burn the bowels, and men outside the ten-foot dungeon-wall
Could hear him howling. Through such violence, such horrors
We have come and survived time.
"It came from the Devil and will go to the Devil,"
The old Norman said.
                    But those were the violences
Of youth. We are not returned to that point.
These are the grim and weeping horrors of old age.

Man's violent present is scarcely an improvement on his ghastly past.

The malicious unpredictability of man is the subject of "To the Story-Tellers". Man does not seem to act in his own best interest; the ridiculous, illogical, bizarre or grotesque are all fully possible with man. The storytellers may write whatever they will of man; it will come to pass.

TO THE STORY-TELLERS

Man, the illogical animal. The others go wrong by anachronistic
Instinct, for the world changes, or mistaken
Observation, but man, his loose moods disjoin; madness is under the skin
To the deep bone. He will be covetous
Beyond use or cause, and then suddenly spendthrift flings all possessions
To all the spoilers. He will suffer in patience
Until his enemy has him by the throat helpless, and go mad with rage
When it least serves. Or he'll murder his love
And feast his foe. Oh—an amazing animal, by education
And instinct: he often destroys himself
For no reason at all, and desperately crawls for life when it stinks.
And only man will deny known truth.
You story-tellers, novelist, poet and playwright, have a free field,
There are no fences, man will do anything.

The human propensity for mischief and evil is worsened by man's perverse denial of "known truth." Jeffers' disappointment—even anger—at man's irrational excesses is at the heart of his uncompromising view of man. Human beings still have not learned or applied the sane and sage advice of the ancient Greeks: Know the Middle Way.

More grim in aspect are the final lines of "Prophets" which intone that the worst of men win wars. Unless a race, group or nation painfully keeps alive the old passions, it is doomed to extinction through warfare with more elemental races and nations. Civilization sublimates, ameliorates, dulls the primal instincts which win wars. The loss of such instincts through civilizing influences ultimately brings that civilization to foreign conquest.

> *We know that as civilization*
> *Advances, so wars increase.*

The prophets forecast the speedy decline of the most civilized of races.

> *You can dance on men's minds, but the deep instincts,*
> *Fear, envy, loyalty, pride of kind and the killer's passion,*
> *   are past your power. They are terribly in earnest,*
> *And the other mere speculation. No wonder they are earnest: for ages*
> *Beyond reckoning those who retain them have killed or*
> *   enslaved those who renounce them. It's a bitter saying that war*
> *Will be won by the worst, what else can I say?—Laugh at that, Puck.*

Jeffers gives no sanction to these vestiges of man's primitive state, but he is forthright in admitting that they are a major factor in the survival of men.

Human life, whatever its circumstances, is thorny and difficult. In his final years Jeffers heard the word "nettlebed" mentioned in conversation by an old friend. That word surfaced in the final lines of his poem "Patronymic" as an apt description of Jeffers' life and especially the last years without his Una who is referred to indirectly in the final lines.

> *... I have twisted and turned on a bed of nettles*
> *All my life long: an apt name for life: nettlebed.*
> *Deep under it swim the dead, down the dark tides and*
> *   bloodshot eras of time, bathed in God's peace.*

One of Jeffers' foremost concerns in his last poems was the placing of man in proper perspective. Such a task could not be accomplished in a polished genteel manner; only the most direct of methods would counterbalance and rectify man's pompous self-image. "On an Anthology of Chinese Poems" expresses regard for the

Chinese painters who were honest in their depiction of man as a minor feature in the spectacular natural landscape.

Beautiful and fantastically
Small farmhouse and ribbon of rice-fields a mile below; and billows of mist
Blow through the gorge. These men were better
Artists than any of ours, and far better observers. They loved landscape
And put man in his place.

"Star-Swirls" is even more blunt.

What a pleasure it is to mix one's mind with geological
Time, or with astronomical relax it.
There is nothing like astronomy to pull the stuff out of man.
His stupid dreams and red-rooster importance: let him count the star-swirls.

Any view of man which ignores the sobering discoveries of astronomy and geology is false.

A somber bit of reality for present-day man are the "torrents of new-born babies"—the population explosion. Man's erstwhile domination of the planet allows him to overpopulate that planet which sustains him. "Passenger Pigeons" compares the great tides of life in nature to those of man. "Birth and Death", laments the passing of individuality and human dignity in an over-populated world.

BIRTH AND DEATH

I am old and in the ordinary course of nature shall die
    soon, but the human race is not old
But rather childish, it is an infant and acts like one.
And now it has captured the keys of the kingdom of un-
    earthly violence. Will it use them? It loves destruction you know.
And the earth is too small to feed us, we must have room.
It seems expedient that not as of old one man, but many
    nations and races die for the people.
Have you noticed meanwhile the population explosion
Of man on earth, the torrents of new-born babies, the
    bursting schools? Astonishing. It saps man's dignity.
We used to be individuals, not populations.
Perhaps we are now preparing for the great slaughter.
    No reason to be alarmed; stone-dead is dead;
Breeding like rabbits we hasten to meet the day.

"Ghost" relates an encounter in the future between Jeffers' spirit and an occupant of Tor House. The ghost, "moping about this place in mad moonlight", is as amazed as ever at humanity's foolhardy self-fixations:

> ..."Who are you? What are you doing
> here?" "Nothing to hurt you," it answers, "I am just looking
> At the walls that I built. I see that you have played hell
> With the trees that I planted." "There has to be room
> for people," he answers. "My God," he says, "That still!"

Most of the hundreds of trees Jeffers planted at Tor House are now cut down.

"Salvage" indicates that the human race is nowhere near nobility. Humanity encroached on many of the things Jeffers held dear: eagles, pumas, privacy; all were eroded by the human presence—"half the glory is gone." Worse still, the masses of humanity interfered with the poet's love and affection for nature. Humanity compared to "a handful of wildflowers" comes off a distinct second.

> I am old, and my wife has died,
> Whose eyes made life. As for me, I have to consider and take thought
> Before I can feel the beautiful secret
> In places and stars and stones. To her it came freely.
> I wish that all human creatures might feel it.
> That would make joy in the world, and make men perhaps
> a little nobler—as a handful of wildflowers,
> Is nobler than the human race.

Jeffers repeats his old hope that all humanity might experience God's beauty, the beauty humanity desperately requires to become whole.

Nor has Robinson Jeffers neglected another theme in *The Beginning and the End*: the definition of the best life for men. "The Silent Shepherds" stands as Jeffers' finest single poem of recommendations for a spiritually healthy life. It records his views on a variety of human and societal fronts. The most ancient of human occupations are also the most highly recommended.

THE SILENT SHEPHERDS

What's the best life for man?
—Never to have been born, sings the choros, and the next best
Is to die young. I saw the Sybil at Cumae
Hung in her cage over the public street—
What do you want, Sybil? I want to die.
Apothanein Thelo. Apothanein Thelo. Apothanein Thelo ...
You have got your wish. But I mean life, not death.
What's the best life for a man? To ride in the wind. To
       ride horses and herd cattle
In solitary places above the ocean on the beautiful moun-
       tain, and come home hungry in the evening
And eat and sleep. He will live in the wild wind and
       quick rain, he will not ruin his eyes with reading,
Nor think too much.
             However, we must have philosophers.
I will have shepherds for my philosophers,
Tall dreary men lying on the hills all night
Watching the stars, let their dogs watch the sheep. And I'll have lunatics
For my poets, strolling from farm to farm, wild liars distorting
The county news into supernaturalism—
For all men to such are devils or gods—and that increases
Man's dignity, man's importance, necessary lies
Best told by fools.

> *I will have no lawyers nor constables*
> *Each man guard his own goods: there will be man-slaughter,*
> *But no more wars, no more mass-sacrifice. Nor I'll have no doctors,*
> *Except old women gathering herbs on the mountain,*
> *Let each have her sack of opium to ease the death-pains.*
>
> *That would be a good world, free and out-doors*
> *But the vast hungry spirit of the time*
> *Cries to his chosen that there is nothing good*
> *Except discovery, experiment and experience and discovery:*
>   *To look truth in the eyes,*
> *To strip truth naked, let our dogs do our living for us*
> *But man discover.*
>   *It is a fine ambition,*
> *But the wrong tools. Science and mathematics*
> *Run parallel to reality, they symbolize it, they squint at it,*
> *They never touch it: consider what an explosion*
> *Would rock the bones of men into little white fragments and unsky the world*
> *If any man should for a moment touch truth.*

This vision Jeffers realizes, is not possible in his own age. He finds it incongruous, though, that an age bent on discovering truth has not the remotest hope of actually doing so—while the real living is done by canines.

If Jeffers recommends the life of a herdsman, he does not—in two of the poems of *The Beginning and the End*—recommend the life of a poet to anyone. "Eager to Be Praised" contains Jeffers' thoughts on the office of poet and the type of life a poet must lead in order to become known. From Vergil to Robert Burns, Jeffers finds a great poet's life is one of sorrows. He cannot understand the young men who visit him eagerly wishing to pursue this decidedly unhealthy occupation.

> *Yet the young men*
> *Still come to me with their books and manuscripts,*
> *Eager to be poets, eager to be praised, eager as Keats.*
> *They are mad I think.*

A poet cannot write truthfully or accurately unless and until he has sacrificed himself to his art, a high price to pay for the hearing he may not receive.

TEAR LIFE TO PIECES

> *Eagle and hawk with their great claws and hooked heads*
> *Tear life to pieces; vulture and raven wait for death to soften it.*
> *The poet cannot feed on this time of the world*
> *Until he has torn it to pieces, and himself also.*

But the two most prominent themes on humanity of *The Beginning and the End* are the relationship of man to nature and the extinction of the human species. "Salvage" expresses the wish that all men might be exposed to nature's beauties since (as noted in "Full Moon") men are—like it or not—still profoundly influenced by nature.

> *You would be amazed what the moon does to us.*
> *Our women come in heat once a month*
> *Following the moon, remembering their outlaw joys in the forest;*
> *Our maniacs lift up their heads and howl*
> *And beat their cell-doors, they cannot sleep at full moon, they are moon-struck.*
> *Nor can the astronomer see his moon-dazzled*
> *Constellations: let him give one night in the month to earth and the moon,*
> *Women and games.*

Modern technologically-oriented man is out of touch with nature; little wonder man himself and his institutions are disjointed and deeply perturbed. "To Kill in War Is Not Murder" castigates some of the "Obedient, intelligent, trained techni- / cians like trained seals" who "know nothing" but are still responsible for the defacing of human dignity and integrity. Jeffers concludes:

> *The beauty of men is dead, or defaced and sarcophagussed*
> *Under vile caricatures; the enormous inhuman*
> *Beauty of things goes on, the beauty of God, the eternal beauty ....*

The God-like beauty of the world will outlive man. It is man's felicity to perceive the beauty while alive; it is also man's destiny to perish. From "How Beautiful It Is":

> *Not we nor our children nor the human race*
> *Are destined to live forever ....*

From "The Beautiful Captive":

> *The troublesome race of man, Oh beautiful planet, is not immortal.*

And the manner of the passing of the human race will be neither poetic nor noble.

END OF THE WORLD

> *When I was young in school in Switzerland, about the time of the Boer War,*
> *We used to take it for known that the human race*
> *Would last the earth out, not dying till the planet died.*
> *I wrote a schoolboy poem*
> *About the last man walking in stoic dignity along the dead shore*
> *Of the last sea, alone, alone, alone, remembering all*
> *His racial past. But now I don't think so. They'll die faceless in flocks,*
> *And the earth flourish long after mankind is out.*

"Passenger Pigeons" concludes with Death turning his "great rolling eyes" to humanity and mockingly agreeing that man will certainly live forever.

"Oh," he said, "surely
You'll live forever"—grinning like a skull, covering his
mouth with his hand—"What could exterminate you?"

To Robinson Jeffers, the end of man is as certain as his own imminent demise.

The Final Years: Man
A Summary

Robinson Jeffers' last four volumes of poetry take a dim view of man. The Second World War was already well under way when *Be Angry at the Sun* was published in 1941. Jeffers, who had previously noted that "men have tough hearts", was confident from the start that America would emerge victorious from the carnage. He was deeply saddened, however, at this prospect since he foresaw the long-term detriments such a victory would bring to a free society. Jeffers' personal pacifism and ideological nonalignment dictated that he strongly advocate in his verse a neutral attitude toward the war. It seemed irrational to him that America should, for the second sorry time, leap into the wars of Europe, but leap she did and Jeffers grieved for the historical error of the decision.

What little confidence Jeffers had left in mankind evaporated with the United States' decision to enter the Second World War. Jeffers, who voted Republican most of his adult life, disliked presenting any of his political views in poetry, but the well-plotted entry of the United States into the war was more than he could tolerate. Several of the poems of *Be Angry at the Sun* and *The Double Axe* are openly critical of the Roosevelt Administration's activities and decisions.

The poems of Jeffers' last years are full of the poet's chief criticism of man, to wit: man is inordinately taken up with self-love. Jeffers' conviction remained adamant that as long as humanity continues to be self-centered, man will never be able to fulfill his real and final destiny here on earth. Many of the poems also reflect Jeffers' conviction that since our present Christian age is slowly suffering from spiritual attrition and accordingly headed downhill, it will only be in a succeeding age that man will find the strength and insight to found a culture based on a more veracious doctrine of man and man's place under the stars. Often Jeffers looks, as it were, over the heads of the present and even over those of the distant future to address the inhabitants of that newer, brighter, more objective age.

The final poems are frequently prophetic. For the immediate future Jeffers foresees the collapse of individual freedom as understood by Western man and as typified by the American experience of that ideal. Under these historically inevitable circumstances, the advice is to turn outward from man to God: "When man stinks, turn to God." Much of the unbridled enthusiasm for man's future found in *Californians* or even in *Roan Stallion, Tamar* has vanished in Jeffers' later years. The view of man in the final poems is not pessimistic, but seeks, in place of human immaturity and solipsism, to provide man with the irrefutable facts about himself and his origin in order to see himself objectively and at last to act intelligently and rationally. To accomplish these ends, Robinson Jeffers—in the best of prophetic tradition—sometimes saw fit to focus on the sordid, cruel, undesirable aspects of human existence which otherwise might be conveniently forgotten.

Clearly Jeffers felt that the complete story of man's past had either not been told or was intentionally neglected. Ultimately, there was more good in presenting a truthful view of humanity than in preserving only the most auspicious of human acts for man's delectation.

Modern science (particularly geology and astronomy) reinforced Jeffers' emphasis on the relative insignificance of man, his planet, and the solar system in the boundless universe of God. These facts available, man had yet to assimilate their true meaning into a corresponding view of himself and his institutions. The last poems expressed only guarded hopes that one distant day man might be able to live in peace with himself and in consonance with his true place in the universe.

Many of the poems of *Hungerfield* and *The Beginning and the End* contemplate the extinction of the human species. Jeffers, himself near death, wrote with ardor of the eventual end of the human race. The poet's neutral stance toward all of God's creation allowed him objectively to see the end of man as a scarcely noteworthy event in the life of the planet. Content with the splendors of the natural world about him and confident that these wonders were greater than man and long would outlast him, Robinson Jeffers was able to commend man to his terminal fate with stoic resignation.

Man was never the primary topic in Robinson Jeffers' poetry. Man is present, it is true, in agony, and a little in glory, but the poet was ever mindful of his true mission: to point the way from—and for—man to God. The poems of Jeffers' final years amplify his ideas on man, ideas which have antecedents in all of his preceding volumes of mature verse. The tone may on occasion be bitter, but the vision is clear and consistent. Jeffers has painstakingly seen to it that the petty balloons of human idealism have all been pricked. The human conceit he cauterized is nothing to the vision he unveiled—the race of man potentially content with its nature and with God's.

Conclusion

One of the qualities of a great poet is great thought. A true poet must think clearly and deeply on the eternally significant and vital issues of the universe. Two of the greatest questions any man can ask and attempt to answer in his lifetime were consistently handled by Robinson Jeffers in his poetry: "Who is God?" and "What is man?"

This consideration has attempted through extensive reference to Jeffers' innermost thoughts as faithfully recorded in his short poems to plot the record of the the poet's wrestling with "these questions; old coins / Rubbed faceless, dateless." Robinson Jeffers' considerations of the primordial human yearning for God and the conjectural provenance of man rank him in the rare company of the great poets.

The God of Robinson Jeffers' poems does not alter appreciably over the years. The painful experiences of Jeffers' time forced him to praise and present his God with consistent clarity and eloquence, his major poetical achievement. The vision of God in Jeffers' early mature works is essentially identical to that in his final poems. Personal chronology did not alter the timeless attributes of his God. Over the years, Jeffers recorded few new concepts of his God; however, he accomplished much which emphasized and elucidated the nature and divine attributes of his deity.

With man, the case is somewhat different. Jeffers' view *of* man did change— slightly. The early Jeffers, imbued with the fresh revelation of his God, moved from a position of eagerly anticipating that some of mankind might finally embrace a rational and natural deity to the stark realization that at present men are not interested in anything outside their own immediate needs and cravings. Accordingly, the poet's view of man, never warm or encomiastic, became colder still and more searchingly realistic. The appalling spectacle of the Second World War only served to vindicate Jeffers' harsh view *of* man, a view which he held staunchly to his death.

On the other hand, Jeffers' vision *for* man, based as it was on the poet's love of his God, did not alter over the decades. He felt from the outset that man, while he had not yet begun to attain his spiritual potential, had a potentially honorable future before him. Even in his own lifetime, Jeffers held that man already possessed the wherewithal (but little of the resolve) to "choose truth" at last. This discrepancy between man's potential and his actual performance deeply grieved and dismayed the poet of Tor House. To the end, however, Robinson Jeffers cherished the long-term hope that man might one day "come of age", that, in the words of an old friend, humanity might "pass through the present crisis, and emerge in a complete renascence of godliness." Jeffers' themes of God and man ultimately are one, for a great poet cannot write of God without including that most alert of God's creations, man.

Robinson Jeffers was raised a protestant Christian; his rearing, though strict, was not conventional. At an early age, he was off on his intellectual own seeking to encounter a more pantheistic God than he had been brought up to worship. The early verse (particularly *Californians* of 1916) is—given familiarity with the mature poetry—a rich vein of Jeffers' views on God and man. Those views remained dormant, however, until an event which we can only surmise took place. That seminal event was what must be termed a mystical encounter with the God he had so diligently sought for years. The time and circumstances of such an experience are matters of conjecture. The event is known only by its results, for the man of middling talent and ponderous designs was suddenly transformed into a poet of titanic genius and positive energy. There is little direct record of that experience in Jeffers' poetry. Perhaps that experience, so dynamic it can be felt towering behind the work just as Una's presence is assuredly but intangibly there in all of Jeffers' poems, was too personal and indescribable to be groped after in a poem—in the same manner Jeffers felt about the divinity of

> *The coast hills at Sovranes Creek*
> . . . . . .
>
> *This place is the noblest thing I have ever seen.*
> *No imaginable*
> *Human presence here could do anything*
> *But dilute the lonely self-watchful passion.*

A place too noble to describe, too divine to trick down into a poem. Was it here that Jeffers encountered his God? Or perhaps more likely the final "conversion" of the poet to his determined pantheistic allegiance came—as Jeffers often prescribed—slowly through silent exposure to the beauties of God's creation.

The searing impact of Jeffers' religious experience provides the core for his poetry. More than any other factor, Robinson Jeffers' theology is central to the understanding of what he actually wrote. His view of the omnipotent, monistic, self-torturing God of fate is the *primum mobile* of his achievement as poet.

Because he is so intensely religious, Jeffers has been intensely misunderstood by his own secular era. The God whose signature is the beauty of things is undeniably present in the natural world of His making, a world which should give man solace and inspiration. But an order of men devotedly in tune with the God of the world is yet to be born.

Jeffers tried steadfastly to avoid the stigma of attempting to pose as a savior of mankind, the last mission he would have undertaken. His theology seeks to uncenter man from himself to enable man to encounter the real God and live a fulfilled life free of man's unique vices: cruelty, filth and superstition. In writing of man, Jeffers' purpose was twofold: to show men of today a way out of themselves and—however haltingly—toward God, and to point the way of the future by disseminating, even in a dying age, the seeds of a holier future. This latter purpose—however visionary—was the real intent of the poet whose spirit continues to proclaim:

> *I admired the beauty*
> *While I was human, now I am part of the beauty.*
> *I wander in the air,*
> *Being mostly gas and water, and flow in the ocean;*
> *Touch you and Asia*
> *At the same moment; have a hand in the sunrises*
> *And the glow of this grass.*
> *I have left the light precipitate of ashes to earth*
> *For a love-token.*

I sadly smiling remember that the flower fades to make fruit, the

fruit rots to make earth.

Out of the mother; and through the spring exultances, ripeness

and decadence; and home to the mother.

—"Shine, Perishing Republic"

Robinson Jeffers, 1937

Bibliography of Works Cited

Significant Works by Robinson Jeffers

Flagons and Apples, The Grafton Publishing Company, Los Angeles, 1912.

Californians, The Macmillan Company, New York, 1916.

Tamar and Other Poems, Peter G. Boyle, New York, 1924.

Roan Stallion, Tamar and Other Poems, Boni and Liveright, New York, 1925.

The Women at Point Sur, Boni and Liveright, New York, 1927.

American Poetry 1927 A Miscellany, Harcourt Brace and Company, 1927.

An Artist, Privately Printed by John S. Mayfield, Austin, Texas, 1928.

Cawdor and Other Poems, Horace Liveright, New York, 1928.

Poems, The Book Club of California, San Francisco, 1928.

Dear Judas and Other Poems, Horace Liveright, New York, 1929.

Descent to the Dead, Random House, New York, 1931.

Thurso's Landing and Other Poems, Liveright, Inc., New York, 1932.

Give Your Heart to the Hawks and Other Poems, Random House, New York, 1933.

Solstice and Other Poems, Random House, New York, 1935.

Roan Stallion, Tamar and Other Poems, (Modern Library Edition),
     Random House, New York, 1935.

Such Counsels You Gave to Me and Other Poems, Random House, New York, 1937.

The Selected Poetry of Robinson Jeffers, Random House, New York, 1938.

Be Angry at the Sun and Other Poems, Random House, New York, 1941.

Medea, Random House, New York, 1946.

The Double Axe and Other Poems, Random House, New York, 1948.

Hungerfield and Other Poems, Random House, New York, 1954.

Themes in My Poems, The Book Club of California, San Francisco, 1956.

The Beginning and the End and Other Poems, Random House, New York, 1963.

Adamic, Louis. *Robinson Jeffers: A Portrait.* Seattle: University of Washington Book Store, 1929.

Adams, Earl *et al.* *Theodore Max Lilienthal.* N.p.: The Roxburghe & Zamorano Clubs, 1972.

Antoninus, Brother, *Robinson Jeffers: Fragments of an Older Fury.* Berkeley: Oyez Press, 1968.

Antoninus, Brother. *The Poet is Dead.* San Francisco: The Auerhahn Press, 1964.

Bennett, Melba Berry. *In Review: Poems.* San Francisco: The Grabhorn Press, 1946.

Bennett, Melba Berry. *Robinson Jeffers and the Sea.* San Francisco: Gelber Lilienthal, Inc., 1936.

Bennett, Melba Berry. *The Stonemason of Tor House: The Life and Work of Robinson Jeffers.* Los Angeles: The Ward Ritchie Press, 1966.

Brophy, Robert J. *Robinson Jeffers: Myth, Ritual, and Symbol in his Narrative Poems.* Cleveland, Ohio: Case Western Reserve University Press, 1973.

Brophy, Robert J. *Robinson Jeffers: Myth, Ritual, and Symbol in his Narrative Poems.* Hamden, Connecticut: Archon Press, 1976. (Reprints the 1973 edition).

Brophy, Robert J. *Robinson Jeffers.* Boise: Western Writers Series, No. 19, 1975.

Brophy, Robert J. (Ed.). "The Robinson Jeffers Newsletter." Los Angeles: Occidental College, 1962 to date.

Brower, David (Ed.). *Not Man Apart.* San Francisco: The Sierra Club, 1965.

Carpenter, Frederick Ives. *Robinson Jeffers.* New York: Twayne Publishers, Inc., 1962.

de Casseres, Benjamin. *Robinson Jeffers: Tragic Terror.* Austin, Texas: Privately printed by John S. Mayfield, 1929.

Cerwin, Herbert. *In Search of Something.* Los Angeles: The Sherbourne Press, 1966.

Chatfield, Hale. "Robinson Jeffers: His Philosophy and His Major Themes" in *The Laurel Review*, Volume 6, Number 2, Fall 1966, Pages 56-71. Buckhannon, West Virginia: West Virginia Wesleyan College.

Clapp, Frederick Mortimer. *Cadenza in C Minor.* New York: The Spiral Press, 1957.

Coffin, Arthur B. *Robinson Jeffers: Poet of Inhumanism.* Wisconsin: The University of Wisconsin Press, 1971.

Dunbar, Maurice. *Fundamentals of Book Collecting.* Los Altos, California: Hermes Publications, 1976.

Everson, William. *Archetype West: The Pacific Coast as a Literary Region.* Berkeley: Oyez, 1976.

Forman, Thomas and Bryan Holme. *Poet's Camera.* New York: American Studio Books, 1946.

Frenz, Horst (Ed.). *American Playwrights on Drama.* New York: Hill and Wang, 1965. (Reprints Robinson Jeffers' explanatory article, "The Tower Beyond Tragedy" which first appeared in *The New York Times*, November 26, 1950).

Gilbert, Rudolph. *Shine, Perishing Republic: Robinson Jeffers and the Tragic Sense in Modern Poetry.* Boston: Bruce Humphries, Inc., 1936.

Greenan, Edith. *Of Una Jeffers.* Los Angeles: The Ward Ritchie Press, 1939.

Gregory, Horace. "Poet Without Critics: A Note about Robinson Jeffers" in *New World Writing*, Seventh Mentor Selection. New York: The New American Library, 1955.

Hart, James D. *My First Publication.* San Francisco: The Book Club of California, 1961.

Hotchkiss, Bill. *Robinson Jeffers: The Sivaistic Vision.* Auburn, California: The Blue Oak Press, 1975.

Jeffers, Robinson. *Brides of the South Wind:* Poems 1917—1922. N.p.: Cayucos Books, 1974. Commentary and Notes by William Everson.

Jeffers, Robinson. *Californians.* N.p.: Cayucos Books, 1971. Introduction by William Everson. (Reprints the 1916 edition).

Jeffers, Robinson. *Cawdor and Medea.* New York: New Directions, 1970. Introduction by William Everson. (Reprints from the 1928 and the 1946 editions, respectively).

Jeffers, Robinson. *Dear Judas and Other Poems.* New York: Norton Publishing Company, 1977. Notes and Afterword by Robert J. Brophy. (Reprints the 1929 edition).

Jeffers, Robinson. *Flagons and Apples.* N.p.: Cayucos Books, 1970. (A facsimile of the 1912 edition).

Jeffers, Robinson. *Granite and Cypress: Rubbings from the Rock.* Santa Cruz: The Lime Kiln Press, 1975. (Special printing by William Everson).

Jeffers, Robinson. *Poetry, Gongorism and a Thousand Years.* Los Angeles: The Ward Ritchie Press, 1949.

Jeffers, Robinson. *The Alpine Christ and Other Poems.* N. p.: Cayucos Books, 1973. Commentary and Notes by William Everson.

Jeffers, Robinson. *The Desert.* Los Angeles: Dawson's Book Shop, 1976.

Jeffers, Robinson. *The Double Axe and Other Poems.* New York: Norton Publishing Company, 1977. Foreward by William Everson; Afterword by Bill Hotchkiss. (Reprints the 1948 edition with the inclusion of Jeffers' original preface and eleven poems not included in the 1948 edition).

Jeffers, Robinson. *The Women at Point Sur.* Auburn, California: The Blue Oak Press, 1975. Afterword by Bill Hotchkiss. (Reprints the 1927 edition).

Jeffers, Robinson. *The Women at Point Sur.* New York: The Norton Publishing Company, 1977. Introduction by Tim Hunt. (Reprints the 1927 edition with reinstatements from the original galleys).

Jeffers, Robinson. *Tragedy Has Obligations.* Santa Cruz: The Lime Kiln Press, 1973. Afterword by William Everson.

Jeffers, Robinson. *Visits to Ireland.* Los Angeles: The Ward Ritchie Press, 1954.

Luhan, Mabel Dodge. *Una and Robin.* Berkeley: Friends of the Bancroft Library, 1976. Edited, with a Foreward by Mark Schorer.

Lyon, Horace. *Jeffers Country: The Seedplots of Robinson Jeffers' Poetry.* San Francisco: Scrimshaw Press, 1971.

Monjian, Mercedes Cunningham. *Robinson Jeffers: A Study in Inhumanism.* Pittsburgh: The University of Pittsburgh Press, 1958.

Nolte, William H. "Robinson Jeffers as Didactic Poet", *The Virginia Quarterly Review,* Volume 42, Number 2, Spring 1966, pages 257—271. Richmond: The University of Virginia.

Nolte, William H. *The Merrill Checklist of Robinson Jeffers.* Columbus: Charles Merrill, 1970.

Powell, Lawrence Clark. *California Classics: The Creative Literature of the Golden State.* Los Angeles: Ward Ritchie Press, 1971.

Powell, Lawrence Clark. *Robinson Jeffers: the Man and his Work.* Pasadena: The San Pasquel Press, 1940.

Powell, Lawrence Clark. "Robinson Jeffers: A Lecture to Professor James L. Wortham's Class in Narrative Poetry". Los Angeles: The Press of the City College of Los Angeles, 1951.

Ridgeway, Ann N. *The Selected Letters of Robinson Jeffers.* Baltimore: The Johns Hopkins Press, 1968.

Rodgers, Covington, and John M. Meador, Jr. *The Robinson Jeffers Collection at the University of Houston.* Houston: Friends of the Library, 1975.

Rutman, Anita, and Lucy Clark. *The Barrett Library Robinson Jeffers.* Charlottesville: University of Virginia Press, 1960.

Shebl, James. *In This Wild Water: The Suppressed [sic] Poems of Robinson Jeffers.* Pasadena: Ward Ritchie Press, 1976.

Squires, James Radcliffe. *The Loyalties of Robinson Jeffers.* Ann Arbor: University of Michigan Press, 1956.

Van Wyck, William. *Robinson Jeffers.* Los Angeles: The Ward Ritchie Press, 1938.

Vardamis, Alex A. *The Critical Reputation of Robinson Jeffers: A Bibliographical Study.* Hamden, Connecticut: The Shoestring Press, 1972.

Walker, Franklin. *The Seacoast of Bohemia: An Account of Early Carmel.* San Francisco: The Book Club of California, 1966.

APPENDIX

Sources of Chapter Titles and Section Headings

Chapter One: The Holy Spirit Beauty (Text, pages 1, 40)

from ''Ode on Human Destinies'', Part VIII, in *Californians* (1916), p. 214 — the final lines of the volume:

I, driven ahead on undiscovered ways
Yet predetermined, do not fail to see,
Over the fog and dust of dream and deed,
The holy spirit, Beauty, beckoning me.

The Early Years: God, ''Pan in the West'' (Text, pages 6, 15)

from *Four Poems and a Fragment*, Copyright edition of 1936:

''Printed for the author and
published January seventh
1936 by Sydney S. Alberts.
This is copy number four.''

''Pan in the West'' (1911) is the second poem in the ''book''.

The Early Years: Man, "What but . . . quotidian Sunday chicken . . ." (Text, pages 43, 48)

from the final section (XX) of "Maldrove" in *Californians* (1916), p. 39 — these lines spoken by the hermit, Peter Graham:

A world at war is well enough — but this,
Rotting in peace — commerce — and for a hope
What but the socialism we're settling to,
Quotidian Sunday chicken, and free love
High over all, the spirit of hugger-mugger,
And cosmopolitan philanthropy
With wide wings waving blessing?

Chapter Two: The Splendor of Inhuman Things (Text, pages 64, 115)

from the final third of "Air-Raid Rehearsals" in *Such Counsels You Gave to Me and Other Poems*, 1937, p. 101:

I wish you could find the secure value,
The all-heal I found when a former time hurt me to the heart,
The splendor of inhuman things: you would not be
    looking at each others' throats with your knives.

The Middle Years: God, "Nobody knows my love the falcon." (Text, pages 65, 112)

from "New Year's Eve" in *Such Counsels You Gave to Me and Other Poems*, 1937, p. 108-9, in which the phrase occurs parenthetically three times as a refrain. The final lines of the poem:

The inhuman nobility of things, the ecstatic beauty,
    the inveterate steadfastness
Uphold the four posts of the bed.
(Nobody knows my love the falcon.)

The Middle Years: Man, "It is time for us. . ." (Text, pages 110, 126)

from "Return" in *Solstice and Other Poems,* 1935, p. 149. The first four lines of the sonnet:

A little too abstract, a little too wise,
It is time for us to kiss the earth again,
It is time to let the leaves rain from the skies,
Let the rich life run to the roots again.

(Tempus est nōbīs vidēlicet)

Chapter Three: All Things Are Full of God (Text, Pages 184, 198)

from the concluding lines of Section II of "Dē Rērum Virtute" in *Hungerfield and Other Poems,* 1954, p. 94. Jeffers concludes this section of the poem by quoting Lucretius:

And the Galaxy, the firewheel
On which we are pinned, the whirlwind of stars in which our sun
    is one dust-grain, one electron, this giant atom of the universe
Is not blind force, but fulfills its life and intends its courses.
    "All things are full of God.
Winter and summer, day and night, war and peace are God."

The Final Years: God, "When man stinks, turn to God." (Text, pages 185, 194)

from "Teheran" in *The Double Axe and Other Poems*, 1948, p. 128. The final lines of
the poem record the grim effects of war and decadent attempts at peace:

Observe also
How rapidly civilization coarsens and decays; its better
    qualities, foresight, humaneness, disinterested
Respect for truth, die first; its worst will be last. — Oh,
    well: the future! When man stinks, turn to God.

The Final Years: Man, "The Last Conservative" (Text, pages lvii, 216).

from the title of a previously unpublished poem in the Tor House collection of Robinson
Jeffers' verse. The poem is also one of Jeffers' last.

INDEX OF POEMS CITED

With Year of First Major Book Appearance (except Juvenilia)
*Indicates complete poem

INDEX

Items italicized are book titles.

A

abalone, 188
A Bibliography of the Works of Robinson Jeffers, 22, 23
abnormal, 232
Adair, 45
Adam, 161
advice, 251
A Further Range, 134
age 247, 257, 262, 267
agony, 249
air-plane, 88, 156
Alberts, S.S., 22, 23
Alison, Ruth, 48, 49
allegiance, 227, 230
Allies, 194
Also Sprach Zarathustra, 192
America, 139, 142, 152, 154, 156, 158, 160, 168, 193, 194, 216, 217, 225, 226, 231, 234, 236, 261, 262
American Indians, see Indian
American Poetry, 1927, A Miscellany, 83, 87, 88, 138
An American Tragedy, 66
ancestors, 46
angels, 222
animals, 145
animosity, 212
"A Note about Places", 32
antitoxin, 90

anxiety, 225
artist, 128, 141
astronomy, 112, 119, 174, 179, 254, 262
atheism, 95
attitude, 229
audience, 217, 249
Avila, brother, 33, 34
axe, 152

B

Bacchanalian, 28
balance of nature, 133
barbarism, 237
Barclay, Rev. Arthur, 175
battle, 217
Be Angry at the Sun and Other Poems, 185, 186, 187, 188, 190, 192, 218, 220, 227, 229, 230, 261
beauty, 40, 89, 105, 138, 148, 152, 159, 175, 179, 196, 199, 204, 206, 209, 233, 239, 240, 241, 242, 255, 258, 259, 266
Bennett, Melba Berry, 8, 200
Bible, 7, 16, 22, 33
Big Sur, 51, 149
biology, 179
biosphere, 55
birds, 145
Birnam, Tom, 165
Bixby Creek, 91
black-out, 193

U

unhappiness, 237
United States, 16, 57, 159, 194, 225, 261
universe, 106, 113, 117, 176, 199, 209, 211,
  249, 262, 264
University of Southern California, 11, 14, 17
Untermeyer, Louis, 83
utopia, 117, 196

V

values, 192
vanity, 131
Varden, Father, 29, 30
Varden, Richard, 29
vellum, 174
Ventana country, 173
Vergil, 257
vice, 164, 267
viciousness, 201
victim, 203, 232
victory, 261
violence, 144, 191, 192, 201, 209, 250
virgin, 29
vision, 257, 264, 265
vulgarity, 204
vulture, 204

W

Walker, Clare, 95
war, 159, 162, 188, 191, 193, 195, 209, 211,
  217, 218, 225, 226, 229, 230, 232, 234, 237,
  240, 245, 251, 261
Washington, D.C., 223

Washington, George, 142
weapons, 247
"Weltanschauung", 95
Westering, 130
White House, 152
Whiteman, Paul, 67
white race, 149
Wolf, 152
Wordsworth, William, 14
world, 130, 132, 144, 151, 161, 163, 198, 200,
  201, 203, 207, 211, 221, 225, 227, 232, 233,
  239, 240, 243, 246, 259, 263
World Fair, 47
World War One, 27, 45, 177, 216
World War Two, 111, 115, 122, 162, 168, 171,
  185, 192, 194, 195, 196, 198, 211, 217, 220,
  222, 229, 230, 234, 236, 261

X

X-ray, 149

Y

Yosemite, 141

My ghost you needn't look for; it is probably

Here, but a dark one, deep in the granite, not dancing on wind

With the mad wings and the day moon.

—"Tor House"

Robinson Jeffers in Doorway of Hawk Tower, Winter 1949

He was
like this mountain coast,
All beautiful, with chances of brutal violence; precipitous, dark-
natured, beautiful; without humor, without ever
A glimmer of gayety; blind gray headland and arid mountain,
and trailing from his shoulders the infinite ocean.

from *Give Your Heart to the Hawks*

This edition of

SHINING CLARITY: GOD AND MAN IN THE WORKS OF ROBINSON JEFFERS

features unpublished photographs of Robinson Jeffers by Horace Lyon and Karl Bissinger. "The Last Conservative" appears herein for the first time. The color reproductions are of an acrylic painting of Tor House by Australian painter , Kenneth Jack, and

of a bronze medal of Robinson Jeffers by Czechoslovakian sculptor, Lumir Šindelář. This first edition consists of nine-hundred copies. An additional one-hundred copies comprise the separate edition. Quintessence Publications, Amador City, Calif- ornia, 1977.